Welcome Holy Spirit

Understanding the Book of Acts

OTHER BOOKS BY THE AUTHOR

Alpha & Omega: The Beginning of the End - An Introduction to the End Times

Rivers of Living Water: The Holy Spirit Today

Leaving the Wilderness Behind: Lessons from the Life of Caleb

Who is Jesus of Nazareth? The Answer Will Change Your Life

At the Door: Key Nations, the Last Days, and the Coming King

Get Smart: Pearls of Wisdom from Proverbs

White Horse Coming: Seven Keys of the Book of Revelation

In the Beginning: An Introduction to the Book of Genesis

The Burdensome Stone: Jerusalem in the Last Days

The Prophet from Babylon: Understanding the Book of Daniel

God's Secret Place: Understanding Psalm 91

The Power of Faith: Understanding the Books of Ruth & Esther

Available at tan.org.au

Welcome Holy Spirit

Understanding the Book of Acts

Kameel Majdali

Teach All Nations Inc.

Melbourne

About the author: Kameel Majdali, PhD, is Director of Teach All Nations. A Bible teacher, author and world trends watcher, he ministers all over the world.

Welcome Holy Spirit: Understanding the Book of Acts

Copyright © 2024 by Kameel Majdali

The author, Kameel Majdali, asserts his rights to ownership of this book.

ISBN: 978-0-6452801-3-5

Teach All Nations Inc.

P.O. Box 493

Mount Waverley, Victoria 3149 AUSTRALIA

Requests for information contact: tan@tan.org.au All rights reserved. No part of this book may be reproduced, stored in a retrieval system or transmitted, in any form or by any means, electronic, mechanical, photocopying or otherwise, without the publisher's prior written consent.

Note: American and Australian words and spelling may be used interchangeably throughout this book.

Unless stated otherwise, all Scripture quotations are taken from the Authorized King James Version of the Bible (KJV). References marked NKJV come from the New King James Version (NKJV), copyright © 1979, 1980, 1982 by Thomas Nelson, Inc. Used by permission. All rights reserved.

Any reference that is numbers only (1:1) is from the **Book of Acts**.

Teach All Nations Inc. is a global Bible teaching ministry with a prophetic edge, based in Melbourne, Australia. For more information about the services and resources of Teach All Nations Inc., contact us at our website: tan.org.au

CONTENTS

Part One: Introduction

Preface 01

Introduction: The Holy Spirit 03

Introduction: The Book of Acts 15

Part Two: Holy Spirit Power in Jerusalem **21**

Chapter One: Waiting for the Holy Spirit 23

Chapter Two: Pentecost – Birthday of the Church 31

Chapter Three: Great Healing – Great Sermon 41

Chapter Four: Facing Opposition 49

Chapter Five: Judgment Within, Trouble Without 57

Chapter Six: Stephen, Service and Strife 67

Chapter Seven: Stephen's Anointed Speech 71

Part Three: Holy Spirit Power in

              Judaea and Samaria **85**

Chapter Eight: Time of Transition 87

Chapter Nine: Saul of Tarsus Repents 97

Chapter Ten: Gentile Pentecost 109

Chapter Eleven: Revival at Antioch	121
Chapter Twelve: Growing Persecution, Growing Church	129

Part Four: Holy Spirit Power to the Ends of the Earth — 137

Chapter Thirteen: From Saul to Paul	139
Chapter Fourteen: Triumph and Trouble	153
Chapter Fifteen: The Council of Jerusalem	161
Chapter Sixteen: The Gate of Europe	171
Chapter Seventeen: The Road to Athens	181
Chapter Eighteen: Revival in Corinth	189
Chapter Nineteen: Ephesus at Last	199
Chapter Twenty: The Long Farewell	207
Chapter Twenty-One: Appointment in Jerusalem	215
Chapter Twenty-Two: Paul's Defense in Jerusalem	225
Chapter Twenty-Three: From Jerusalem to Caesarea	231
Chapter Twenty-Four: Paul's Defense Before Felix	239
Chapter Twenty-Five: 'I Appeal to Caesar'	247
Chapter Twenty-Six: Paul With King Agrippa II	255
Chapter Twenty-Seven: The Stormy Voyage to Rome	263
Chapter Twenty-Eight: Paul in Melita and Rome	271

Appendices   279

Appendix One: A Book of Acts Prayer   281

Appendix Two: An Appeal   283

Appendix Three: Outline of the Book of Acts   289

Dedication

To my eldest grandchild, Jonas. May you be a Book of Acts Christian.

Part One

Introduction

Preface

It was the most unexpected and unlikely way to build a global movement, one that has lasted two thousand years already and turned out to be a grand success story. But how?

After His well-documented resurrection, Jesus Christ gave His eleven surviving apostles the Great Commission (Matthew 28:18–20, Mark 16:15–20; Luke 24:44–49) to evangelise and make disciples of all nations. These men were not at the top of the class in some Jerusalem seminary, nor were they well connected to earthly power and influence. They were humble Galilean fishermen who had few earthly credentials. They were held with disdain by the Jerusalem Jewish elite and ignored by the Gentiles. Yet within a few decades, the movement God started through them spread rapidly across the Roman empire. They were called the men who turned the world upside down (17:6). By the end of the first century AD, the Christian faith had spread so extensively that Rome found it impossible to eradicate it – though it was not for lack of trying.

These Spirit-filled believers, be they Jew or Gentile, were very courageous, always happy, and constantly in trouble.[1] How do we know? We read it all: the promise of the Holy Spirit, the outpouring on the Day of Pentecost, the birth of the church, and constant opposition yet solid growth, all this and more is found in the **Book of Acts**. While God chose to use people to build His kingdom, none of this would have been possible without the blessed Holy Spirit, the third person of the Triune God.

In *Welcome Holy Spirit: Understanding the Book of Acts,* we are going to learn about our collective church history and the indispensable role of the Holy Spirit. If we want to witness the continuation and proliferation of the last days' revival, it is important to know our spiritual heritage.

The church was birthed in power and like a big bang the end of the age will witness a final power surge, too.

Our goal is to give you a readable commentary of the **Book of Acts** while highlighting the person and work of the Holy Spirit. We will see how He worked in Jerusalem first, then in Judaea and Samaria, and finally in the missionary journeys that took the gospel to the uttermost part of the earth. What He did at the beginning of the age He will do even more so at the end.

In these last days, we need and expect a latter-day rain just before the harvest of souls. The **Book of Acts** can give us insight into how this very thing happened at the beginning of the church age. May you have a deeper hunger for God's Word and a greater thirst for the rivers of living water of the Spirit as you read *Welcome Holy Spirit*.

Kameel Majdali

---

[1] Michael Green immortalised these three points in his book, *30 Years That Changed the World: A Fresh Look At the Book of Acts.*

Introduction

The Holy Spirit[2]

Who is the Holy Spirit?

This is both a simple yet multifaceted answer: He – not 'it' – is a glorious divine person; more specifically, the Holy Spirit is the third person of the Triune Godhead. Cults denied the personality of the Holy Spirit as some deny the divinity of Jesus Christ. Let's take a moment to build the case of the personhood of the Spirit, followed by the work of the Spirit.

The Hebrew word for 'Spirit' is *ruach* and the Greek is *pneuma.* These words are often translated as 'wind', 'breath' and 'spirit'. So it is easy to see how some would conclude the Holy Spirit is a thing rather than a person. Nevertheless, we believe the testimony of Scripture is compelling and conclusive: the Holy Spirit is a Person. Here's why.

The Personhood of the Holy Spirit

We know the Spirit is a person because, first of all, personal pronouns are used for Him. For example, look at **John 16:13–14**, emphasis added)**:**

> *Howbeit when **he**, the Spirit of truth, is come, **he** will guide you into all truth: for **he** shall not speak of **himself**; but whatsoever **he** shall hear, that shall **he** speak: and **he** will shew you things to come. **He** shall glorify me: for **he** shall receive of mine, and shall shew it unto you.*

In these two verses, we see that the Holy Spirit has come, guides, hears, speaks, shows things to come, and glorifies Christ, from Whom He will take from Him and declare it to us.

Some may say that things can be labelled 'him' or 'her' without being a person. That's why we go a step further and look for the attributes of

Welcome Holy Spirit

personality. The Holy Spirit has a will (1 Corinthians 12:11). He has emotions: love (Romans 15:30) and can be vexed (Isaiah 63:10) and grieved (Ephesians 4:30). Look at the list of spiritual gifts in **1 Corinthians 12** and you will see that some of them – word of knowledge and wisdom – point to the intellect of the Spirit. He has a mind (Romans 8:27), speaks (John 16:13), and can take the following actions:

- testifies (John 15:26)
- teaches (Luke 12:12; John 14:26);
- guides (John 16:13);
- convicts (John 16:8-10)
- commands (Acts 13:2)
- intercedes (Romans 8:27)
- ordains (Acts 13:2)
- searches (1 Corinthians 2:10)
- decides (1 Corinthians 12:11).

Like any person, the Holy Spirit can react, too. He can be:

- tempted (Acts 5:9)
- lied to (Acts 5:3)
- grieved (Ephesians 4:30)
- vexed (Isaiah 63:10; Genesis 6:3; Ephesians 4:30)
- resisted (Acts 7:51)
- outraged and despised (Hebrews 10:29)
- blasphemed (Mark 3:29, 30).

A non-person could do none of these things.

In summary, we see that the Holy Spirit is an intelligent, decisive and dynamic Person who can convict, guide, teach, intercede, speak, and search. Like human beings, He can be affected by or hurt by lies, grief, insults, and resistance. Unlike human beings, He is not subject to the human limitations of time, space or human strength. He cannot and will not sin. He also can be blasphemed, but despite all that, He is the giver

Introduction: The Holy Spirit

of life and pours out God's love. For all these reasons and more, the Holy Spirit is a person worth knowing.

The Holy Spirit is a *Divine* Person

The historic creeds of Christendom, like the Apostles' Creed, Nicene Creed, and Athanasian Creed, all affirm the divinity of the Holy Spirit. For example, the Nicene Creed wonderfully summarises this doctrine:

> *We believe in the Holy Spirit, the Lord, the giver of life, who proceeds from the Father [and the Son], who with the Father and the Son is worshipped and glorified, who has spoken through the prophets.*

The Athanasian Creed declares with beauty and boldness::

> *So the Father is God, the Son is God, and the Holy Spirit is God.*
> *And yet they are not three Gods, but one God.*
> *So likewise the Father is Lord, the Son Lord, and the Holy Spirit Lord.*
> *And yet not three Lords, but one Lord.*
> *But the whole three Persons are coeternal together, and coequal: so that in all things, as is aforesaid, the Unity in Trinity and the Trinity in Unity is to be worshipped.*
> *He, therefore, that will be saved must thus think of the Trinity.*

The Holy Spirit's divinity was affirmed in the tragic incident of Ananias and Sapphira, where Peter accused the former of lying to the Holy Spirit because Satan had filled his heart. The conclusion: '*Thou hast not lied unto men, but unto God* (**Acts 5:4**).

When it comes to the attributes of God, the Holy Spirit ticks every box.

God is omnipresent (present everywhere): **Psalm 139:7** (NKJV). declares: '*Where can I go from Your Spirit? Or where can I flee from Your presence?*' So no matter where you go – heaven, hell, here, there, mountains, valleys, the centre of the earth or out on parts of the ocean – God the Holy Spirit can be found. Since it is futile to run from Him, wisdom decrees that we should embrace Him.

God is omniscient (all-knowing): We learn from **John 16:13**: *'Howbeit when he, the Spirit of truth, is come, he will guide you into all truth'* (emphasis mine). God is God because He knows everything. He knew and understood the world even before He created it. Meticulous in both care and detail, God numbers the very hairs on our heads and is mindful of every sparrow that falls from the sky.[3] God's all-knowing power is known as 'omniscience'. Does this apply to the Holy Spirit? Scripture tells us that the Spirit searches all things[4] and teaches all things.[5] Yes, the Holy Spirit is omniscient because He is God.

God is omnipotent (all-powerful): The Holy Spirit is God in this earthly realm. Jesus told His disciples that they would 'receive power' when the Holy Spirit came upon them.[6] Micah triumphantly proclaimed that he was full of power by the Spirit of the Lord.[7] The Apostle Paul acknowledged that his ability to 'fully preach' the gospel of Christ came through mighty signs and wonders by the power of the Spirit of God.[8] The Holy Spirit's power helped to confirm the divine Sonship of Jesus through the resurrection of the dead.[9]

God is eternal (past, present and endless future): He knows no beginning and no end. He was before time, and He will long outlast it. The Holy Spirit is called 'eternal' in **Hebrews 9:14**. As the third member of the Holy Trinity, He is not a created being but has always existed, like the Father and the Son.

God is holy (morally, ethically and spiritually outstanding, blameless, unblemished): As God is holy,[10] so is the Spirit.[11] That is why He is called the *Holy* Spirit.

God has foreknowledge (totally aware of persons, things and events before they were born or happened). God knows things ahead of time. This is called foreknowledge. As God has foreknowledge,[12] the Holy

Introduction: The Holy Spirit

Spirit also demonstrated this trait when He showed King David the betrayal of Jesus one thousand years before Judas Iscariot was born (cf. Psalm 41:9; Acts 1:16).

God is love: This is the greatest trait of all. God is love,[13] and so is the Holy Spirit.[14] This divine love is wonderful and multifaceted.

Like God, the Holy Spirit was involved in the creation,[15] prophecy,[16] intercession[17] and inspiration of Scripture.[18]

Biblical Symbols of the Holy Spirit

The ever-presence of the powerful, all-knowing yet invisible God the Holy Spirit is difficult for the unregenerate mind to imagine. Therefore, God wisely employs visible symbols as a way to convey spiritual truth about the nature of the Holy Spirit. Symbols are powerful pictures of an intangible that is all too real. A gold ring is not a marriage but symbolises wedding bonds. A flag is not a nation but can motivate people to weep and fight for the nation it represents. We have seven symbols from the Bible to convey the Holy Spirit's person and power.

Water: Water represents power, purity, cleansing and fluidity. Water is vital for life itself. The Holy Spirit as the 'water of life' brings a fresh, real experience.[19]

Wind: Wind, like the Spirit, symbolically represents invisible but real power. The Spirit's origin and destination are unknown to the natural man, and He shows us a different and higher way than the carnal path. It is the wind that came rushing through the house on the Day of Pentecost. Jesus alluded to the wind as a means of understanding the new birth.[20]

Fire: Not unlike the 'wind', fire represents an intense, powerful, purifying, purging and unpredictable force. It has become a popular symbol for revival and even of God Himself.[21]

Welcome Holy Spirit

Dove: The dove is an ideal symbol of the Holy Spirit, representing grace, gentleness, peace, beauty and courage, without a hint of guile.[22]

Wine: This can be a controversial symbol because of the pitfalls of alcohol. The Bible appears to allow moderate wine usage but with restrictions: no drunkenness, no partaking if it will offend another person and if a person takes a Nazarite vow. Yet Melchizedek greeted Abraham after the battle of the kings with oil and wine, Christ celebrated the Passover and last supper with wine, and His first recorded miracle was changing the water into wine. For our purposes, wine as a symbol of the Holy Spirit represents abundance and joy as well as the first fruits.[23]

Oil: It is pure, clean, refreshing, nourishing, aromatic and flavourful. Furthermore, it is a potent and universal symbol of the anointing of the Holy Spirit.[24]

Dew: In an arid region like the Holy Land, dew is a life-giver and lifesaver. Like the dew, the Holy Spirit quickens, restores, and refreshes.[25]

The Work of the Holy Spirit

The works of the LORD are great, sought out of all them that have pleasure therein. His work is honourable and glorious: and his righteousness endureth for ever.
– Psalm 111:2–3

No question about it: God's work is great, wonderful and everlasting. Everything He does is honourable and glorious. For this, we owe Him endless praise. Having established the personhood and divinity of the Holy Spirit, we should examine his works. The Bible college class that focuses on the Holy Spirit is called 'Pneumatology'. The amplified definition is 'the study of the honourable and glorious person and work of the Holy Spirit.' The **Book of Acts** is a great place to start such a study.

Since the Holy Spirit is mentioned throughout the entire expanse of the Bible, from **Genesis 1** to **Revelation 22**, we need to package the study of His works into two categories, especially from a New Testament

Introduction: The Holy Spirit

context. Therefore, we propose to look at what is called 'the two-fold work of the Holy Spirit today'. He causes people to be:

1) born of the Spirit
2) baptised in the Spirit.

First Work: Born of the Spirit

Entering into an eternal relationship with the living God requires being born of the Spirit. It is a simple idea, refreshingly devoid of human effort, religious works and clever ideas. Well-meaning as these things may be, they are simply insufficient to bring about eternal salvation and abundant living.

God's solution to the great human challenge is breathtakingly simple: basically, the Holy Spirit causes our human spirit to be 'reborn', so that we experience what is known as 'the new birth', being 'born again', 'saved', 'born of the Spirit', 'born of God', 'regeneration' and becoming a 'redeemed believer'. To be a believer means that we totally believe and completely trust Jesus Christ to be our source of life and for our eternal salvation. All that we need to be or do, now or in the future, can be found in Him.

Christ atoned for our sins by dying on the cross, being buried and rising from the dead on the third day. This is a summary of the gospel and the good news (1 Corinthians 15:3–5). This is the solution to our problem of sin and death. Yet, before we are ready to receive the solution, we have to recognise that we have a problem in the first place.

That's where the Holy Spirit comes in. He brings conviction of sin, righteousness and judgement through the written word (e.g. John 16:8–11) and His superintending power, showing us that we are not righteous: **Romans 3:23** declares *'For all have sinned, and come short of the glory of God'* and **Romans 6:23** states that *'the wages of sin is death'*. Now that we have God's perspective on the matter, how do we escape from eternity's death row? Through *'the gift of God is eternal life through Jesus Christ our Lord* (ibid)'.

Welcome Holy Spirit

On our part, we cannot earn this great salvation – it is a priceless gift – so we simply receive it by faith. But first, we need to repent, a prerequisite for salvation. **Acts 20:21** and **Hebrews 6:1** speak of repentance and faith.

In its simple form, repentance means to change your mind, attitude and actions; having gone in the wrong direction, you now turn around and go in God's direction. Jesus says twice in **Luke 13** (vs. 3, 5) that without repentance we perish. Thus, repentance towards God and faith in Christ's gospel are the steps to being born again.

Regarding faith, it is like a multi-faceted diamond. It means to believe, receive, confess, commit, trust and obey. Once repentance and faith are exercised, the new birth is activated by the Holy Spirit; hence, we are 'born of the Spirit'.

The new birth delivers many benefits. Here are a few:

- the gift of eternal life (John 3:16)
- becoming a new creation (2 Corinthians 5:17)
- adopted into God's family (Romans 8:16-17)
- Christ living in us (Galatians 2:20)
- consecrated and transformed (Romans 12:2)
- our sins forgiven (Luke 24:47)
- led by the Spirit (Romans 8:13–14)
- delivered from the sin-dominated self-life.[26]

If you agree the new birth is from God, but you can't honestly say that you have been born again or have the assurance of salvation, then go to the back of this book to *Appendix Two: An Appeal*, and pray with conviction the prayer that is written.

At the new birth, we are baptised by the Spirit into the Body of Christ (1 Corinthians 12:13), meaning we become part of the universal church, the body of believers from the Day of Pentecost to the second coming of

Introduction: The Holy Spirit

Jesus. We are also made to drink of one Spirit. It is this 'drink' that leads us to the next work.

Second Work: Baptised in the Spirit

Like the work called 'born of the Spirit', 'baptised in the Spirit' deserves a lot of coverage. This is but a simple summary. The baptism in the Holy Spirit was promised in all four gospels by John the Baptist.[27] In **Acts 1**, Jesus also said on the eve of His ascension that they would be baptised in the Spirit not many days from then (vs. 4-5).

First, the word 'baptised' comes from the Greek word βαπτίζω, *baptizo*, meaning to 'dip, plunge, immerse, and submerge.'[28] So this means that the believer is dipped, plunged, immersed and submerged in the Holy Spirit.

An amplified description of the Holy Spirit Baptism is that the Holy Spirit comes down, upon, in and through a believer to fill, anoint, embolden and empower for Christian service. Another way to explain it is that the Holy Spirit takes full control.

The Bible describes this experience with various phrases:

- The promise of the Father (Luke 24:49; Acts 1:4)
- Endued with power from on high (Luke 24:49)
- Baptised with the Holy Spirit (Acts 1:5)
- Filled with the Holy Spirit (Acts 2:4)
- The gift of the Holy Spirit (Acts 2:38)
- The Holy Spirit fell on all of them (Acts 10:44)
- Poured out the gift of the Holy Spirit (Acts 10:45)
- Received the Holy Spirit (Acts 19:2)
- He will baptise you with the Holy Spirit and fire (Luke 3:16ff).

Essentially, the Baptism in the Spirit is both an immersion from the outside and a filling up inside. The individual is continuously surrounded, enveloped and immersed by the presence of the Spirit and can, at any time, open up wide and receive a massive infilling as well. Born of the Spirit leads to salvation; baptised in the Spirit means empowered to be an emboldened global prophetic witness for Christ (see Acts 1:8). The power of the Spirit also aids you in living a fruitful, fulfilled God-honouring life, giving you access to the fruit of the Spirit (Galatians 5:22–23) and gifts of the Spirit (1 Corinthians 12).

Contrast between water baptism and Holy Spirit baptism		
Aspect	Water Baptism	Spirit Baptism
Source	From below	From above
Visibility	Visible	Invisible
Duration	One time	For all time
Purpose	Obedience	Power
Baptizer	Human	Divine
Result	Outward immersion	Inward-filling

There is so much more that can be shared because, with God the Holy Spirit, there is always more.[29] Our study of the **Book of Acts** will show us even more than we can imagine.

Introduction: The Holy Spirit

[2] Much of the material in this chapter is derived from the book, *Rivers of Living Water: the Holy Spirit Today*, by Kameel Majdali, Melbourne: Teach All Nations 2010, 2013.

[3] Matthew 10:29–31.

[4] 1 Corinthians 2:10.

[5] John 14:26.

[6] Acts 1:8.

[7] Micah 3:8.

[8] Romans 15:19.

[9] Romans 1:4.

[10] Leviticus 11:44; 1 Peter 1:16.

[11] Ephesians 4:30.

[12] Acts 2:23; 1 Peter 1:2.

[13] 1 John 4:8.

[14] Romans 5:5, 15:30; Galatians 5:22.

[15] Job 33:4; Genesis 1:2; Psalm 104:30.

[16] 2 Samuel 23:1–3.

[17] Romans 8:26–27.

[18] 2 Peter 1:21; 2 Timothy 3:16.

[19] Water as a symbol of the Spirit: Isaiah 12:1–6, 44:3–4; Ezekiel 36:25–27; Joel 2:23–29; John 4:14; 7:37–39.

[20] Wind as a symbol of the Spirit: Genesis 2:7; Ezekiel 37:1–14; John 3:7, 20:21–23; Acts 2:1–2.

Welcome Holy Spirit

[21] Fire as a symbol of the Holy Spirit: 1 Kings 18:38; Isaiah 4:4, 6:5–8; Malachi 3:2–3; Matthew 3:11–12; Hebrews 12:28–29.

[22] Dove as a symbol of the Holy Spirit: Genesis 8:8–12; Matthew 3:16, 10:16; Luke 3:22; Galatian 5:22–23.

[23] Wine as a symbol of the Spirit: Genesis 14:18; Leviticus 23:13; Psalm 105:15.

[24] Oil as a symbol of the Holy Spirit: Psalm 23:5, 92:10; Isaiah 61:1; Luke 4:18; Acts 10:38; Hebrews 1:8–9; 1 John 2:27.

[25] Dew as a symbol of the Holy Spirit: Deuteronomy 32:1–2; Psalm 133:1–3; Hosea 14:4–6.

[26] Romans 6:6–7, 11–14, 18, 22.

[27] Matthew 3:10; Mark 1:8; Luke 3:16; John 1:33 (where John points out that Christ is the Baptiser in the Holy Spirit).

[28] G907 - baptizō - Strong's Greek Lexicon (kjv). Blue Letter Bible. Accessed 2 May, 2024. https://www.blueletterbible.org/lexicon/g907/kjv/tr/0-1/

[29] If you want further information about the Holy Spirit, we refer you to the book, *Rivers of Living Water: The Holy Spirit Today*, from Teach All Nations.

Introduction

The Book of Acts

Name

The New Testament Greek name for Acts is *praxeis*. While we call it 'Acts of the Apostles', only three major apostles are prominently mentioned: Peter (chapters 1–12), Philip (8) and Paul (chapters 13–28).

Author

Luke, the beloved physician, is the universally agreed author, both of the Gospel of Luke and Acts of the Apostles. His writings are lengthy, and it is arguable that word for word, verse for verse, he wrote more of the New Testament than the apostle Paul.

Portrait of Christ in Acts

Therefore let all the house of Israel know assuredly, that God hath made that same Jesus, whom ye have crucified, both Lord and Christ — **Acts 2:36**

Jesus Christ is the resurrected, ascended Saviour, Lord and Christ. He is also known as:

- the Holy One and Just (3:14)
- the Prince of Life (3:15)
- Thy holy child Jesus (4:27)
- a Prince and a Saviour (5:31)
- Lord of all (10:36)
- Light of the Gentiles (13:47).

Welcome Holy Spirit

Purpose

The Gospel of Luke tells the story of Jesus' words and deeds. Acts is the 'second chapter' of this great story, which has no end. It is the bridge between the gospel narrative and the epistles.

Theme

The birth and growth of the Christian church by the power of the Holy Spirit.

Timing

We don't have an exact date of composition. The narrative ends abruptly with Paul under house arrest in Rome. So, it may have been written before the year 62 AD.

Background

Acts starts in the first part of the first century AD. Ancient Israel was under Roman occupation. The Israelites had some degree of religious and political autonomy, but they were expected to pay their taxes and keep the peace (Pax Romana).

Religious scene: Judaism of Christ's day was divided into various sects. The Sadducees were the aristocrats and priestly class. The Pharisees were the mainstream observant Jews whose teachings were the closest to Jesus Himself (Matthew 23:1–3). The Herodians were the party that aligned themselves with the Roman puppet government of the Herodian dynasty. The Zealots were the nationalist party that was fiercely anti-Rome; some may have resorted to violence and been considered 'terrorists' in their day.[30] The Essenes, a pious group, withdrew from the Jerusalem scene altogether because they felt even the religious establishment was corrupt. They are believed to be the sect that wrote the Dead Sea scrolls at Qumran.

Introduction: The Book of Acts

To this mix would soon be added a new sect, the Nazarenes, those Jews who accepted Jesus of Nazareth as the long-awaited Jewish Messiah. After the destruction of Jerusalem and the temple by Rome in AD 70, only two of these sects survived: the Pharisees became what we call post-Biblical Rabbinic Judaism and the Nazarenes became known as the Christian Church.

Political scene: The Roman Empire was one of the greatest in history, and was in some aspects noble. They provided infrastructure through roads, giving ease to travel throughout the empire. Other infrastructure includes aqueducts, bridges and seaways. They guaranteed justice and some vestige of the 'rule of law' (something that did not operate in the trial of Jesus, however). Religious tolerance was normally part of the Roman scene, and the Jewish religion was considered a 'legal religion' (*religio licita*). However, the emerging Christian faith would be subject to periodic persecution because its Roman status was *religio illicita*.

Cultural scene: Hellenism was the order of the day. Alexander the Great's vision for the entire civilised world was to think, act and speak Greek. This vision made great inroads, and ancient Israel was greatly affected by Hellenism. The Old Testament was translated from Hebrew to Greek in a legendary translation called the Septuagint (abbreviated as LXX, the Roman numeral for 'seventy'), because the traditional account is that seventy rabbis took seventy days to make the Septuagint). This translation caused a revolution: for the first time in history, the Word of God was available in the *lingua franca* (international language). This prepared the Gentiles to receive the gospel three centuries later, as recorded in the **Book of Acts**. The New Testament was written in *koine* Greek, the lingua franca of antiquity. Hellenism helped to develop concepts of philosophy, theology, analytical thinking and the best – and worst – of human beings, known as humanism. (There is a Christian version of humanism, as well as a secular one.)

The book begins with the resurrected Christ giving His last command to His disciples before the ascension. The command: you will be my global, prophetic witnesses to the ends of the earth; however, don't leave Jerusalem until you receive power from on high.

Ten days later on the Day of Pentecost, the Christian Church was born thanks to a dynamic partnership of the Holy Spirit with the surviving apostles of Jesus. The transformation was stunning: the same disciples who had fled in great fear from the Garden of Gethsemane less than two months before were now fearless in proclaiming Christ to the Pentecost day crowds. On the Church's birthday, three thousand people were added to the church in one day.

With this Holy Spirit momentum, the infant church grew exponentially. Such success came at a price: envy and persecution from the religious leadership who did not believe. Yet the persecution helped to facilitate, not inhibit, the growth of the church: it got the salt out of the shaker. From Peter, the leader of the Jerusalem church, to Paul, the apostle of the Gentiles, we see the gospel spreading throughout the Middle East, Asia Minor and Europe, all the way to Rome.

The **Book of Acts** is indispensable to our understanding of how the church came into being and grew supernaturally thanks to the superintending power of the Holy Spirit.

Luke's care for detail is meticulous: he records dozens of speeches, people by name, and over seventy geographical locations. By these features and more, he demonstrates that the **Book of Acts** is based on historical fact, not fantasy.

Key verses

But ye shall receive power, after that the Holy Ghost is come upon you: and ye shall be witnesses unto me both in Jerusalem, and in all Judaea, and in Samaria, and unto the uttermost part of the earth.
— *Acts 1:8*

Introduction: The Book of Acts

And they continued stedfastly in the apostles' doctrine and fellowship, and in breaking of bread, and in prayers. 43 And fear came upon every soul: and many wonders and signs were done by the apostles. 44 And all that believed were together, and had all things common; 45And sold their possessions and goods, and parted them to all men, as every man had need. 46 And they, continuing daily with one accord in the temple, and breaking bread from house to house, did eat their meat with gladness and singleness of heart, 47Praising God, and having favour with all the people. And the Lord added to the church daily such as should be saved.
— *Acts 2:42-47*

Key subjects

1) Birth of the Church (2:1–47)
2) Life of Stephen, the first Christian martyr (6–8)
3) Repentance and salvation of Saul of Tarsus (9:1–19)
4) The door to the Gentiles opened (9:32–12:25)
5) Paul the Apostle to the Gentiles (13:1–21:17)
6) Paul the Prisoner (21:18–28:31).

Key Words

(used dozens of times in Acts)

Jew(-ess, -s), Spirit, Holy Ghost, Gentiles, nations, Word (of God), Name (of Jesus, Lord), pray (-ed,-er, -er, -ing, -s).

---

[30] https://www.gotquestions.org/Zealots-Bible.html

Part Two

Holy Spirit Power

in Jerusalem

CHAPTER ONE

Waiting for the Holy Spirit

Who: Christ and the apostles

What: Commanded to wait for the Spirit

When: Forty days after the resurrection

Where: Jerusalem, Mount of Olives and the Upper Room

Why: To build God's kingdom

How: By the power of the Holy Spirit

> *And, being assembled together with them, (Jesus) commanded them that they should not depart from Jerusalem, but wait for the promise of the Father, which, saith he, ye have heard of me. For John truly baptized with water; but ye shall be baptized with the Holy Ghost not many days hence.*
> — *Acts 1:4–5.*

Promise of the Spirit (1:1–5)

He must have been a very special man, of whom we know nothing except his name and blessing. His name: Theophilus, 'friend of God'. The blessing: he was the initial recipient of the Gospel of Luke and the Book of Acts (1:1). With a remarkable eye for historical detail, Luke's gospel seeks to demonstrate *'all that Jesus began both to do and teach'* (1:1). This is a common-sense order: we need to be 'doers' of the Word before we are 'teachers'.

Jesus continued to 'do' and 'teach' until the very day of His ascension to heaven (1:2), approximately forty days after the resurrection. Prior to His ascension, Jesus gave a command to the apostles *'Whom he had chosen'* (1:2). Remember that apostles are sent out by God and are divinely selected, not self-appointed. This is especially true of the greatest apostle of them all – Paul – who, though not numbered with the original Twelve, is certainly the key apostle in the **Book of Acts.**

During the forty post-resurrection days, Jesus did more than just give commands. He provided *'many infallible proofs'* that he had truly risen from the dead (1:3). The Greek word here is *tekmērion*, meaning 'proof and/or indubitable evidence'.[31] The resurrection of Jesus is not fantasy, fiction or a fairy tale; it is a verifiable fact witnessed by many credible witnesses over forty days. They believed this event so passionately that they risked, or gave, their lives for its veracity.

While He made these post-resurrection appearances, Jesus spoke of the kingdom of God, which is another tell-tale sign of His true identity. Of all the commands He gave his apostles, the most pertinent was to stay put in Jerusalem until they received 'the promise of the Father' (1:4). He had already given them the Great Commission: to preach the gospel to all nations (Mark 16:15–18) and disciple (teach) all nations (Matthew 28:18–20). How could eleven surviving apostles – Galilean fishermen, devoid of all the trappings of influence, connections and power – achieve this daunting task? By being baptised with the Holy Spirit (1:5). According to Jesus, they would not have to wait long for His appearance.

The Ascension of Christ (1:6–11)

So, Christ's last command – wait for the Holy Spirit and then fulfil the Great Commission – was meant to be the apostles' first priority. However, they had other things on their minds. As pious Jews, they were

One: Waiting For The Holy Spirit

keenly aware of the promise of God to King David to have an everlasting covenant, an everlasting throne, and not be occupied by a foreign power anymore. Their burning question, *'Lord, wilt thou at this time restore again the kingdom to Israel?'* (1:6) may not mean much to modern Christians but it was of the utmost importance to Jesus' Jewish disciples. They knew that one thousand years before, God had promised David an everlasting throne that would rule the world from Jerusalem. We call this the Davidic covenant (2 Samuel 7; 1 Chronicles 17). Jesus was the chosen 'Son of David' to sit on his throne. Would He be doing so at this time? Would He put an end to the hated Roman occupation?

Jesus does not give a direct answer to this question. While some think He was rebuking His disciples for even asking, that is not the case. The issue is not if the kingdom is coming; the issue is there is a vital job to do in the meantime. Therefore, the timing of the kingdom's coming is not the priority at this time. Make no mistake: God's kingdom is the highest priority, but it was not the time for its visible earthly manifestation.

Again, what were the disciples to do? They were to wait for the Holy Spirit to come upon them. We have several descriptions of this, including 'promise of the Father' and 'baptised with the Holy Spirit,' but it all leads to the same thing: the disciples would be immersed and filled with the Holy Spirit. Once poured out, they would be empowered to be global prophetic witnesses, first of all in Jerusalem, then in neighbouring Judaea and Samaria and finally to the ends of the earth (1:8). Left to our own resources, the weight of the commission would be crushing. Yet, by partnering with God the Holy Spirit, it can and will be fulfilled.

After commissioning them to build His church by the power of the Spirit, Jesus was ready to go to heaven. After speaking these timeless words, He was taken up and a cloud received Him. Of course, the apostles were perplexed – one moment they saw Him, and the next moment He was gone. But immediately they discovered they were not alone. Two men in dazzling white apparel stood by them and asked, 'Why do you keep looking up into heaven?'

Welcome Holy Spirit

Then they made a major announcement: the same Jesus which has been taken up from you into heaven will return in the same manner as you have seen Him go up to heaven (1:11). An important point: Jesus is returning to this planet the same way He departed – spectacularly, supernaturally, for every eye to see. If you hear of Christ returning quietly through some back door, then it's the wrong Jesus

Waiting on God (1:12–26)

It must have felt like they were forsaken a second time. The first time was the arrest and crucifixion of Jesus. Now He was taken from them again at the ascension and only the Heavenly Father could say when He would return. The disciples still had his commands and promises which had lately been given, but there was nothing else to do but return to Jerusalem from the nearby Mount of Olives and wait for the Spirit. They assembled in an upper room, including the disciples of Jesus, the faithful women, Mary the mother of Jesus and his brothers. 'These all continued with one accord in prayer and supplication' (1:14). In other words, they 'waited on God'.

In our busy world, few people 'wait on the Lord', but we all should. **Psalm 62:5** says, '*My soul, wait thou only upon God; for my expectation is from him*'. Everything in life that you need, want and ever hoped for can be found in God, and God alone. Waiting on God is part of our daily quiet time or devotional time with God. The benefits it bestows are enormous: direction, provision, promotion and power in prayer.

> *For since the beginning of the world men have not heard, nor perceived by the ear, neither hath the eye seen, O God, beside thee, what he hath prepared for him that waiteth for him.*
> *– Isaiah 64:4*

The very best this world has to offer is like lightweight sawdust compared to the gold bullion bar of glory waiting for you in God.

So, what do you do while waiting? Prayer and supplication is a good place to start, along with Bible reading and devotion, praise and

One: Waiting For The Holy Spirit

worship, silent meditation and, if healthy and led by the Spirit, fasting with prayer. There are times we 'passively' wait on God, meaning after we have done everything possible, we wait in faith and get on with life. There is also 'active' waiting, where there is diligent seeking of God with prayer, praise and fasting. Remember this: those who wait upon the LORD will not fail to get to the next level.

> *But they that wait upon the LORD shall renew their strength; they shall mount up with wings as eagles; they shall run, and not be weary; and they shall walk, and not faint.*
> *– Isaiah 40:31*

The apostles will have the greatest promotion of all when the Holy Spirit comes upon them in the very next chapter.

Peter's good idea: The whole idea of waiting on God is so that we will be told the will of God. There are 'good ideas' and there are 'God ideas', and it's the latter that works. What we are about to see here is that it is possible to wait on God and still get a man-made, home-cooked, good idea instead. When on the Mount of Transfiguration, Peter had a 'good idea': let's make three tabernacles for Moses, Elijah and Jesus (Luke 9:33). God was not buying it. Instead, He had a much better idea: *'This is my beloved Son: hear him'* (Luke 9:35).

Here in Acts, Peter had another 'good idea'. So he gets up to speak with the one hundred and twenty disciples that were assembled. Like Jesus, Peter talked about the need to have the Scriptures fulfilled. He acknowledged that the Holy Spirit spoke through David and what was recorded became recognised as 'Scripture'. He pointed out that Judas was the guide to those who arrested Jesus. **Psalm 41:9** was probably in mind: *'Yea, mine own familiar friend, in whom I trusted, which did eat of my bread, hath lifted up his heel against me.'*

Peter acknowledged that despite his serious character flaw and unforgivable crime, Judas had been chosen by Jesus as one of the twelve and *'was numbered with us'*. He obtained *'part of this ministry'* (1:17). The implication is that he had had a seat at the table, a seat that was now empty. Peter wanted it filled.

The sin of betraying Jesus reaped a huge judgement. **Mark 14:21** says, *'The Son of man indeed goeth, as it is written of him: but woe to that man by whom the Son of man is betrayed! Good were it for that man if he had never been born'*. Leave it to your imagination what happened to Judas. Peter gave an interesting description: Judas' money, the thirty pieces of silver, was used to purchase the potter's field which was used to bury foreigners. He fell headlong, burst asunder, and his bowels gushed out (1:18). In **Matthew 27:5**, it says he cast the money of betrayal into the temple and hung himself. A contradiction? No: he hung himself, the rope broke and the rest is obvious. Judas died a terrible death, and his eternal destination was even worse.

The money Judas obtained by betraying Jesus was used to purchase Aceldama, the field of blood (1:19), which became a cemetery for foreigners. It happened that visitors to Jerusalem, including pilgrims, would get sick and die. Since they had no family burial plot, they were taken to a place like Aceldama. The most likely location was the Valley of Hinnom, on the west side of Jerusalem. This hideous place was used as the municipal rubbish tip (garbage dump), a place of human sacrifice (called 'Tophet' in Jeremiah) and to bury foreigners. That's why the Valley of Hinnom has become the prototype of hell itself, *'where their worm dieth not, and the fire is not quenched'* (Mark 9:44–48). Ironically, the Valley of Hinnom, also known as Gehenna, is next door to Mount Zion, the dwelling place of God – they're next-door neighbours.

Peter quotes **Psalm 69:25** – *'Let their habitation be desolate; and let none dwell in their tents'* (1:20) – and **Psalm 109:8** – *'Let his days be few, and let another take his office'*. Peter has a high view of Scripture and has no hesitation in invoking it since it has inherent authority. This is all good. However, when it comes to the will of God, you still need to be led by the Holy Spirit, Who inspired the Scripture in the first place. It is both working with the Spirit and Scripture that you 'get it right' regarding God's will. The Word alone is not enough. Remember the saying of Jesus

One: Waiting For The Holy Spirit

in **Matthew 22:29** that the Sadducees were in error because they did not know the Scriptures nor the power of God. That power comes from the Holy Spirit (Acts 1:8). Word and Spirit mixed together lead you to God's will and the ability to fulfil it.

A twelfth apostle: After building the case that Judas forsook his apostolic call through apostasy and suicide; his office was now vacant, Peter went further and said Judas' seat must be filled. In short, Peter wanted to appoint the twelfth apostle. He said that Number Twelve must have accompanied them from the baptism of John to the ascension (1:21-22). Furthermore, he must be a witness of the resurrection or encountering the risen Christ. Interesting criteria but who decided: Peter or God?

The meeting proceeded: there were two men named, Joseph Justus known as Barsabbas and Matthias (1:23), of whom we know nothing more. The apostles prayed and cast lots. Casting lots was also done in the Old Testament; for example, Aaron cast lots for the goat and scapegoat (Leviticus 16:8), Joshua cast lots (Joshua 18:6) and Saul did the same (I Samuel 14:42). Of course, soldiers cast lots for the garment of Jesus (Matthew 27:35; Mark 15:24; Luke 23:34; John 19:24), fulfilling prophecy (Psalm 22:18). The lot fell on Matthias and he was pronounced the twelfth apostle (1:26).

God's will or an act of presumption?: Peter eagerly wanted to fill Judas' vacancy. He quoted Scripture, prayed and cast lots. Remember that apostles are God-chosen, not man-chosen (1:2). Was Peter doing God's will? Please consider that Jesus gave His apostles a clear commandment to wait for the outpouring of the Holy Spirit on them. Nowhere does He tell them to appoint another apostle. While it is possible that while 'waiting on God', the Spirit gave a command to fill Judas' vacancy, a command unrecorded in Scripture. Yet it is equally possible that Peter, impetuous as he often was before he was under the baptism and control of the Holy Spirit, got impatient about 'waiting for God' in prayer and decided to take action – a 'good idea' rather than a 'God-idea'. Prayer and quoting Scripture, wonderful as they are, must be

Welcome Holy Spirit

accompanied by the leading of the Holy Spirit. Otherwise, we risk being in error. We never hear of Matthias again. And the apostle whom no man appointed turned the world upside down (17:6) and dominated the **Book of Acts**. His name is Paul.

---

[31] G5039 - tekmērion - Strong's Greek Lexicon (KJV). Blue Letter Bible. Accessed 30 Mar, 2017. https://www.blueletterbible.org//lang/lexicon/lexicon.cfm?Strongs=G5039andt=KJV

CHAPTER TWO

Pentecost – Birthday of the Church

Who: The Holy Spirit and the apostles

What: The apostles are filled with the Spirit

When: Ten days after the ascension of Christ

Where: Jerusalem

Why: To start the Christian Church

How: By the power of the Holy Spirit

> *And they were all filled with the Holy Ghost, and began to speak with other tongues, as the Spirit gave them utterance.*
> *— Acts 2:4*

The Holy Spirit's Coming (2:1–13)

Without exaggeration, it was the day that changed the world. Two major things happened. The first was the long-awaited, promise of the Father, the outpouring of the Holy Spirit, had come. The second thing was that the followers of Jesus became a publicly recognised body of believers, born of the Spirit and now baptised by the Spirit. Before the day was finished, three thousand souls were added to the one hundred and twenty disciples who had met earlier that morning. At first, they were known as a minor sect of Judaism but eventually came into their own identity as the Christian church. That day was called Pentecost: the birthday of the Church.

Welcome Holy Spirit

Pentecost, known in Hebrew as *Shavuot* (feast of weeks), is one of the three pilgrimage feasts where Israelites were to *'appear before the Lord'*. The other two are Passover (*Pesach*) and Tabernacles (*Succot*).

The chapter begins with the one hundred and twenty disciples meeting in the upper room where they were in *'one accord'* (2:1). Around nine o'clock in the morning, there came a powerful sound of a rushing, mighty wind and the entire house was filled with its presence (2:2). And there was more: in addition to feeling the windy presence, they saw divided fiery tongues appear which sat on each of them (2:3). John the Baptist spoke of the Coming One Who would baptise in the Spirit and fire (Matthew 3:11; Luke 3:16). The tongues of fire is at least part of that fulfilment.

Then comes **Acts 2:4**: this verse spawned the century-long Pentecostal revival, just as **Habakkuk 2:4** did for the Protestant Reformation. It says they were all filled with the Spirit, which is exactly what God wanted. It also linked speaking in tongues, which means speaking in unknown languages of angels and men, to the baptism in the Spirit. This is known as 'glossolalia' and is a God-given sign that the Spirit has filled an individual. It is a valid port of entry into the Spirit-filled life. The disciples who were filled that day had transformed lives and revolutionary ministries.

A note of explanation: when speaking about the Holy Spirit, we are referring to God Himself and all our human attempts to explain His work have their limitations. Jesus promised a *'baptism with the Spirit'* (1:5) and here they were *'filled with'* the Spirit. Are these the same thing or are they distinct? We already learned that the word 'baptised' (Greek: *baptizō*)[32] means 'to dip repeatedly, to immerse, to submerge and to overwhelm'. Let's consider it a permanent immersion, unlike water baptism which is quick and temporal. To be 'filled' (Greek: *pimplēmi*) means exactly that – to be filled with the Holy Spirit (Luke 1:15, 41, 67; Acts 4:8, 31, 9:17, 13:9). The Spirit baptism is an outward immersion and an inward filling. The more a person opens up and drinks from the Spirit

Two: Pentecost - Birthday of the Church

– the rivers of living water (John 7:37-39) – the more he or she will be filled.

While a point of contention in the past, the early Pentecostal revivalists of Azusa Street in Los Angeles (in 1906) and elsewhere, believed that speaking in tongues was the initial physical evidence that a person had been filled with the Spirit. It was this precise belief that lit the fire of revival in the first place. Not only was it the accepted sign among the Jewish believers at Pentecost (Acts 2:4) but also with the Gentiles at Cornelius' house in Caesarea (Acts 10:44–46). Paul knew the twelve disciples at Ephesus were filled with the Spirit because they spoke in tongues and prophesied (Acts 19:7). The Samaritan revival (Acts 8) and Saul of Tarsus coming to faith in Jesus (Acts 9) do not explicitly mention tongues, but in Paul's case, he spoke in the heavenly language more than anyone (1 Corinthians 14:18).

Speaking in tongues is not baptism in the Spirit. It is not a requirement for salvation. Indeed, it and the Spirit baptism are gifts to the believer as salvation is a gift to the sinner. Tongues are a physical sign of a dynamic invisible spiritual reality; remember, it is the Spirit who gives the utterance. The words are His while the voice is the believer's. It also serves other functions: as a prayer and praise language (1 Corinthians 14:15), an edification language (Jude 20), a spiritual warfare language (Ephesians 6:18) and brings rest and refreshing to our spirits (Isaiah 28:11–12).

Jesus taught that out of the abundance of the heart, the mouth speaks (Matthew 13:34). If the heart is full of evil, it will speak wicked things. If it is filled with the Holy Spirit, out of the mouth will come the language of the Spirit. The good news is that when you appreciate and use the gift God has given, He will give you more.

Since the Pentecostal revival commenced in 1901, it has spanned the globe and claims the allegiance of almost one in ten people worldwide. This could only be possible by a move of the Holy Spirit. We believe God wants another billion souls added to His kingdom in the next decade; again, what is impossible for man is gloriously possible with God.

What happened in the upper room did not stay there; a multitude came together and were confounded. This is because a large contingent of Diaspora Jews[33] were in Jerusalem celebrating the Feast of Pentecost. Pilgrims came from Parthia, Media, Elam, Mesopotamia, Judaea, Cappadocia, Pontus, Asia, Phrygia, Pamphylia, Egypt, Libya, Rome, Crete and Arabia - in essence, they represented the Middle East, Asia Minor, North Africa and the Imperial City itself (2:9–11). They heard these uneducated Galileans speaking in their native languages (2:5–6) about the wonderful works of God (2:11). How could they do this? Were they drinking too much new wine (2:13)? It was only nine o'clock in the morning.

A Preacher Named Peter (2:14–41)

Peter was Jesus' most loyal and outspoken follower. Confessing Jesus as Messiah, Son of the living God at Caesarea Philippi (Matthew 16:16) while denying Him at the Sanhedrin, standing nearby while He was transfigured in glory or fleeing in terror when He was arrested at Gethsemane, this apostle entered into a process of radical transformation, starting here and continuing to chapters 9 and 10. The man who denied Christ in front of a few would boldly proclaim Him as Lord and Christ in front of thousands. And this was all within less than eight weeks. The Holy Spirit made this possible

Without notes or trappings of authority, Peter stood up with the eleven, lifted his voice and invited the Judean and Diaspora Jews to hear his message (2:14). He began by debunking the notion that the newly Spirit-filled disciples had drunk too much wine (after all, it was only 9 am) with the phrase 'this is that' (2:16). The 'this' was the amazing phenomenon of Galileans speaking in world languages. 'That' is they were fulfilling Biblical prophecy, specifically **Joel 2:28–32**.

Two: Pentecost - Birthday of the Church

In **Joel 2**, it was prophecy delivered; in **Acts 2:17**, it was prophecy fulfilled. God promises to pour out His spirit on all flesh in the last days. Note that this is not just 'Jewish flesh', as in **Acts 2,** but 'all flesh'. This was being fulfilled in the 'latter rain', Pentecostal revival, which began in 1901 and has swept the globe to become 'the surpassing phenomena of 20th century Christianity' according to *Life* magazine and 'the third force of Christendom' according to Fredrick Bruner.[34] Today the banner of Pentecostal/Charismatic/Third Wave is estimated to encompass seven hundred and fifty million people, eighty per cent in the non-Western world. This is that.

When the Holy Spirit is universally poured out, sons and daughters, men and women will prophesy (2:18). In addition, young men shall see visions while old men shall dream dreams (2:17). On male and female servants God will pour out his Spirit in those days and they shall prophesy. This wholesale distribution of the prophetic gift is made possible because born-again believers are called to be Spirit-filled. When the Holy Spirit is in a person, they will prophesy, just like in the days of old. So instead of the prophetic gift being for a chosen few, it is now liberally distributed to the true Church at large.

On the 'Day of the Lord', God will show wonders in the heavens above and signs on the earth below, including blood, fire and vapour of smoke. It will be very dramatic, perhaps even frightening (2:19–20). In addition, the sun will be darkened (a blackout) and the moon will turn to blood (a blood moon) before the Day.

While none of the spectacular heavenly signs occurred on Pentecost Day, the outpouring of the Spirit, fulfilment of prophecy, the speaking of tongues and the salvation of many souls did happen all at once. Whoever – male, female, young, old, Jew or Gentile – calls on the Name of the Lord will be saved and that's the greatest miracle of all (2:21).

Now to the main subject: Jesus of Nazareth. Few people knew Him better than Peter. Now he will present Him to the world, starting with the 'men of Israel', local and Diaspora (2:22).

Welcome Holy Spirit

Jesus, this controversial, itinerant preacher from Nazareth, though rejected by mere men, had the grand approval of God Himself. How do we know? He did miracles, wonders and signs through Him, a fact that was well-known since much of His ministry was witnessed by the general public. Yet despite doing so much good and being favoured by God, their 'wicked hands' had crucified and slain Him. This had happened through the 'determinate counsel' and 'foreknowledge' of God. This means that God knew about their evil plans even before they did them (2:23). It also was His 'determinate counsel' because this horrible betrayal and crime would result in the redemption of the world. God is sovereign and He allows the wrath of man to work for His glory.

Peter continued his first post-Pentecost sermon. Jesus' crucifixion and death were allowed by God for redemptive purposes. But the story does not stop there. God raised Him from the dead. He was set free from the agony of death since death could not keep a permanent hold on Him. If it is hard to 'keep a good man down', it is impossible to keep the 'God-man dead' (2:24). Jesus, the Prince of Life, was raised from the dead. Without this resurrection, the Christian Church would never have been born (read 1 Corinthians 15, the 'resurrection chapter'). The new birth would not have been possible (1 Peter 1:3) without it.

The blessed resurrection of Jesus fulfilled the prophecy. Peter quoted **Psalm 16:8–11**, where a thousand years before Christ, the Holy Spirit inspired David to write that the physical body will live in hope. Then he prophetically affirms that God will not abandon him in the grave or let His holy one see decay/corruption (2:27). While David may be referring to the end-time resurrection, Peter used this verse to speak of Christ's resurrection since He did not remain in the grave or have bodily decay (2:24). This applies to Jesus completely.

Though not formally trained in ministry, Peter attended the best Bible college of all: Mary's (of Bethany) University at the feet of Jesus (Luke 10:38-42). He was adept with the written word because he walked with Christ, the Living Word. This is evident by his generous use of Scripture throughout this impromptu sermon.

Two: Pentecost - Birthday of the Church

Then he got to the point: the prophecy of **Psalm 16** was not about David; it was about the 'Son of David', Jesus. David was the prophet (2:30) who entered into a covenant with God. Expressed simply, a covenant is a binding agreement between God and man. God had sworn with an oath that David's biological son would be the Messiah/Christ to succeed him on the throne. This is why the only crime the Romans could condemn Jesus for was sedition, being a rival monarch to Caesar. That's why above His cross was the signage that told of His 'crime': the 'King of the Jews'. It was prophesied that he would die and be buried, but it also was foretold that He would rise again, not seeing death's decay or corruption. We are witnesses of this truth (2:31–32).

Where is Jesus today? He is exalted and seated at the right hand of God (2:33). He received the 'promise of the Father', namely the Holy Spirit, Who has been poured out on the disciples, as you can see and hear. On earth, Jesus received power from on high and now from heaven He pours out the same power to all who believe.

Peter quoted (in 2:34–35) **Psalm 110:1**, one of the great Messianic prophecies. It speaks of the Lord, namely God the Father, speaking to the Lord, Christ the Son, to sit at His right hand until all enemies become a footstool for his feet. David referred to Messiah, who happens to be His Son, as his Lord as well. Messiah is the Son of David and the Son of God simultaneously (see Luke 1:32).

Finally came the call to action. Peter told the multitudes it was time for all of Israel – at home and abroad – to know this fact: God had taken the crucified Jesus and made Him Lord and Christ (2:36). Thanks to the power of the Holy Spirit, the words of Peter sunk deep down in the hearts of the listeners. They were pricked in their heart (2:37) and responded, *'What shall we do?'* This is a vital point in any person's life, where conviction of sin leads a person to repentance and faith, which brings the new birth. They were being set up for a powerful mass conversion experience.

Welcome Holy Spirit

When a person feels convicted of their sins and ready to take action, what is the answer? Repent and be baptised in the name of Jesus Christ (as a sign that you have repented and your sins forgiven and remitted). Once this happens, you will receive the same gift of the Holy Spirit (2:38) as the apostles did, without the ten-day wait. In verse 38, water baptism precedes Holy Spirit baptism but that order is not absolute; for example, Cornelius in **Acts 10** was baptised in the Spirit before he was baptised in water (Acts 10:47).

Peter affirmed that the promise of the Father, the gift of the Spirit, is for everyone: for you (current generation), your children (next generation), and for all who are far off (third and subsequent generations), as many as the LORD our God shall call (2:39). That means the promise extends to us today and has been validated by the on-going Pentecostal revival which began in 1901.

The sermon was not finished. Peter continued to exhort the Pentecost Day crowd with many words, including *'save yourself from this corrupt generation'* (2:40). It is like a warning siren telling people to flee from soon-coming danger. Salvation implies withdrawing from the corruption of our culture (Luke 9:41, 11:29, 17:25; Philippians 2:15).

The sermon and exhortation of Peter, anointed by the Holy Spirit, had the desired effect. People went from conviction of sin to gladly receiving the word. The latter phrase means they heard and chose to obey what God's word says. The text says that three thousand were baptised and added unto them (2:41). This is an impressive first day for the Christian Church, birthed in the power of the Holy Spirit. It is assumed that these people had repented before and they probably made a confession of faith, even though the text does not say so explicitly.

> LESSON FOR LIFE: The birth of the Christian church did not begin with a committee meeting nor military conquest but from a dynamic outpouring of the Holy Spirit

Two: Pentecost - Birthday of the Church

Church Life (2:42–47)

Four activities are listed here as part of church life. The 'apostles' doctrine' is the teaching of the apostles, which they derived from the Saviour. For us, this is the same as solid Bible study. The Greek word *didache*[35] is where we get the word for 'doctrine'. 'Fellowship' comes from *koinonia*,[36] deep caring and sharing, not merely a cup of tea and a biscuit after a church service. 'Breaking of bread' can either be a fellowship meal or holy communion. Prayers are self-explanatory (2:42).

Church life today includes:

1) fellowship and gathering of faithful believers in Christ
2) praise and worship to God
3) giving witness to Christ
4) baptism in water and the Spirit
5) spiritual gifts, including healing and casting out devils (Romans 12:6–8)
6) teaching and preaching of God's Word
7) the five-fold gifts of Ephesians 4:11–12 equipping the saints for ministry
8) prayer and fasting to be encouraged (Acts 1:14; 6:4; 12:5; 13:2, 9)
9) supporting mission outreach (2:39; 13:2–4).

The Holy Spirit gave the touch of the supernatural to the apostolic ministry. People were in awe of what they witnessed (2:43).

There was a true sense of community in the infant church. The Jerusalem church brought all believers together and they had all things in common They sold their assets and the proceeds were distributed to every person who had a need (2:45). Unlike secular leftist ideologies, which are atheistic, deceitful and coercive, this was done voluntarily, in truth, love, and the fear of God. The early church was Jewish and Jerusalem-based, with great unity. The text says they continued daily in one accord. This was at the Jerusalem temple and they had meals in private homes with gladness and singleness of heart (2:46).

Everything else mentioned earlier contributed to the saving of souls daily (2:47). That includes the fact that the early church was praising God. Their exemplary, Godly and supernatural lifestyle made them a powerful witness to the larger community. It would lead to 'divine appointments' and strategic miracles, as we are about to discover.

---

[32] G907 - baptizō - Strong's Greek Lexicon (kjv). Blue Letter Bible. Accessed 3 Mar, 2023. https://www.blueletterbible.org/lexicon/g907/kjv/tr/0-1/

[33] The term 'Diaspora' refers to the dispersion of the Jews from beyond the borders of Israel; it commenced in the eighth century BC (from Israel) and sixth century BC (from Judah). It is now the term used of Jewish people who do not live in Israel.

[34] Kameel Majdali, *Rivers of Living Water: The Holy Spirit Today*, Melbourne: 2013, p. 17.

[35] 'Doctrine' "Acts 2 (KJV) - And they continued stedfastly in." Blue Letter Bible. Accessed 6 Jun, 2024. https://www.blueletterbible.org/kjv/act/2/42/t_conc_1020042

[36] Ibid.

CHAPTER THREE

Great Healing – Great Sermon

Who: Peter and John

What: Healed the lame man and gave a sermon

When: The ninth hour (3 pm)

Where: At the Gate Beautiful at the Temple

Why: To build God's kingdom

How: The faith in the Name of Jesus Christ and the power of the Holy Spirit

Repent ye therefore, and be converted, that your sins may be blotted out, when the times of refreshing shall come from the presence of the Lord; 20. And he shall send Jesus Christ, which before was preached unto you: 21. Whom the heaven must receive until the times of restitution of all things, which God hath spoken by the mouth of all his holy prophets since the world began.
— *Acts 3:19–21*

A Strategic Miracle (3:1–11)

Now that the infant Christian Church had welcomed the Holy Spirit, a great spiritual dynamic had been introduced. In the days of Jesus, He was the main preacher and miracle worker. With the Spirit now present on earth, Jesus' role was multiplied among His servants. There would be more miracles, more anointed preaching, more church growth and more persecution.

Welcome Holy Spirit

Jesus died on the cross, being the perfect sacrifice for sin. After His death, the veil of the temple was torn asunder from top to bottom. Like an Israelite tears his garment as a sign of mourning, so God the Father tore this veil in response to the death of His Son. This barrier between a holy God and sinful humanity had been split in two so that we all can have access to the throne of grace (Hebrews 4:16).

The apostles of Christ still went to the temple to pray; after all, it was meant to be the house of prayer for all nations (Isaiah 56:7; Matthew 11:17). Animal sacrifices were still being offered in this temple, but whether the early (Judaeo-) Christians participated in the sacrificial system is unclear. In 70 AD, the Romans would come and destroy the temple, thus causing the now-defunct animal sacrifices to cease.

In Acts 3, Peter and John went to the temple to pray around 3 pm (3:1). At the Gate Beautiful, a man born lame was taken there to beg for his living (3:2). It was probably the only occupation he ever knew. He saw Peter and John walk by and reached out his hand, asking for alms (3:3). The two apostles took a long, strong look at the beggar and commanded him to look at them. He was to give them full attention (3:4). Even so, though he obeyed their command, the beggar had misplaced expectations that he would receive alms (3:5).

God had better things in store for him. All the money in the world could not buy for him what he was about to receive. Peter made the following famous pronouncement: *'Silver and gold have I none; but such as I have give I thee; In the name of Jesus Christ of Nazareth rise up and walk'* (3:6). What we have in Christ is more powerful, costly and wonderful than any amount of money or store of material blessings. Faith and anointing of the Holy Spirit were more than enough to cause this lifelong lame man to receive total healing. Who needs alms when they can receive the ability to walk and work?

Confession activates faith. After confessing the Name of Jesus, Peter took the lame man by the hand and lifted him up (3:7). As he stood, his feet and ankle bones were strengthened, and he was able to walk.

Three: Great Healing - Great Sermon

Yet the man did more than just walk. He was so excited at this unexpected, welcome yet overwhelming healing that he did more – he walked, leapt and praised God (3:8). As a healed and liberated man, he went with the apostles into the temple precincts. Imagine – until his healing, the lame man had been physically near God's house yet was far from Him. Responding to the Name of Jesus brought him within the sacred precincts to worship his Healer and Saviour.

This was not just any miracle: it was a strategic one. Healing this man at the temple area was a public act with many witnesses that could not be refuted. All the people saw the former beggar fully mobile (3:9). The public heard the commotion and saw the lame man holding onto Peter and John and were full of wonder and amazement (3:10–11). They became an attentive audience. Thus, this miracle led to Peter's second recorded post-Pentecost sermon. It would be powerful and prophetic, as any Spirit-anointed sermon should be.

Peter's Sermon (3:12–26)

Peter seized the moment. Led by the Holy Spirit, he addressed the temple crowd as the 'men of Israel' and asked them why they were astonished or looked at the apostles as if their own power had healed this man (3:12). No, this miracle was one hundred per cent from God.

The apostle referred to the Lord as the God of the patriarchs, Abraham, Isaac and Jacob, and to Jesus as God's Son. Yes, it is the same Jesus whom they delivered up and denied in the presence of the Roman governor, Pontius Pilate, who wanted to release Him. Yes, this same despised man was now being glorified by this miracle of healing (3:13). Peter's point was not to bring condemnation but to spawn Holy Spirit conviction, which leads to repentance and faith in the gospel.

Again, Peter did not hesitate to further remind the people of their collective guilt. He rightly accused them of rejecting God's Messiah while demanding the release of Barabbas, a convicted seditionist and murderer. Imagine the irony: these people were standing in the holy temple, doing their religious duty, yet when it came to the crunch, they would prefer a terrorist and murderer instead of the Holy and Just One (3:14).

Peter pointed out that they had witnessed a mighty miracle of healing. Yet the apostles of Christ had witnessed an even greater miracle than that: the Prince of Life, whom we all had collectively killed, God raised from the dead (3:15).

Source of healing: This is a point that is as valid today as it was to the early church. The lame man, and indeed, all people, was healed 'in the name of Jesus' (3:6) and by 'faith in the name of Jesus.' This powerful Name brought healing, strength and perfect wholeness (3:16). All power in heaven and earth belongs to Him (Matthew 28:18). At the mention of His Name, every knee shall bow and every tongue shall confess (Philippians 2:10–11).

After chiding the crowd for their complicity in the death of Jesus, Peter sounded a note of conciliation. He said their sin was done in ignorance and so was the sin of the Israelite rulers (3:17). Nevertheless, sin is sin, and it has to be dealt with if we are going to be reconciled with God and spend eternity with Him.

Prophecy fulfilled: Then the apostle showed that the evil actions against Jesus were a fulfilment of prophecy. God showed ahead of time through the holy prophets that Christ would suffer. This was not a plan that went awry. By the foreknowledge of God, Christ's suffering and death atoned for our sins and His resurrection brought our justification. All these things were fulfilled by the passion of Christ (3:18).

Now that the people were convicted of their sin, having seen the powerful healing, what should they do? Repent – change your mind, attitude and actions. Instead of going in the wrong direction, turn around one hundred and eighty degrees and go in the right direction. Peter exhorted the people to be converted so that by saving faith, their sins would be blotted out. When this happened, times of refreshing

Three: Great Healing - Great Sermon

would breeze through from the presence of the Lord (3:19). The Holy Spirit, of course, is the source of refreshing: the hot, dry, irritating east wind is transformed into the cool, refreshing moist wind of the north (Song of Solomon 4:16).

Prophecy is wonderful in its own right, but it has an ultimate goal: it is the testimony of Jesus Christ (Revelation 19:10). The pinnacle of it all is the return of Christ to Earth, not again as the Lamb of God who takes away the sins of the world but as a Warrior, Judge and King. Peter says with total confidence that God was again sending Jesus back to this planet. This is the same Jesus Who ministered in Galilee and Judea before His crucifixion (3:20).

Then, we are given an important milepost along the way that points to the times of seasons of Christ's return. Jesus will remain in heaven until the times of restitution of all things. The Greek word for restitution, *apokatastasis*, used only once in the New Testament, means 'restoration', and 'reconstitution, the perfect condition before the fall of man and a true theocracy'.[37] It can mean restoring something to its original condition or to its rightful owner. This time of restitution was spoken by the mouth of all the holy prophets since the world began (3:21).

What things will be restored before Christ's return? They are mentioned by the holy prophets. We have many prophecies in Scripture, up to thirty-three per cent of the whole. They are not merely confined to the major and minor prophets of the Old Testament; they are found in Genesis, the rest of the Torah, the Psalms and Revelation. Indeed, they are woven within the very fabric of Scripture.

To know what is being restored is a lifetime of Bible study. But in short, things to watch for include the 'restoration' of the move of the Holy Spirit found in the modern-day Pentecostal revival (Acts 2:17), the 'restoration' of national Israel and the ingathering of the exiles (Amos 9:14–15) and the international obsession over Jerusalem (Zechariah 12, 14).

Moses and the prophets: Peter continued and concluded his sermon by referring to Moses, who predicted a coming prophet in **Deuteronomy 18:18–19**. In what ways did Jesus emulate Moses and fulfil this prophecy?

- Both were meek yet immensely powerful
- Both initiated covenants: Mosaic and New
- Both had the Spirit's anointing
- As Moses led his people out of the bondage of Egypt, Christ led His people from the desert of sin and death
- Moses pointed out the sacrifice of the lamb for a sin offering; Christ was the lamb of God who took away the sin of the world.

Whatever these two men spoke, the people need to hear (3:22). Christ, the prophet like Moses, speaks words of life to the world. Refusal to heed these words means the rebel will be cut off from the people (3:23). All the prophets, from Samuel and onwards, all who have spoken, proclaimed about these matters (3:24). Why Samuel? He was the greatest prophet in Israel since the time of Moses; he was also Israel's last judge. Elkanah and Hannah had to tarry a long time for the birth of Samuel, but he was worth the wait (3:24)

Remarkably, Peter referred to the men of Israel as 'children of the prophets'. Israel had a biological link to Abraham and the prophets, seeing they were of the same people group. In addition, they were the heirs of all the theocratic covenants which were given in the Old Testament. This included the Abrahamic covenant (Genesis 12, 15, 17), where God promised the patriarch the land of Canaan, innumerable seed (descendants) and through him and his seed a universal blessing. Peter then quoted **Genesis 12:3**, the famous verse where God promises to bless those who bless Abraham and his seed, yet curse him that curses Abraham. Through Abraham's offspring, particularly Jesus, all the people of the earth will be blessed (3:25).

Finally, on the note of blessing, Israel is first in line to receive it. The phrase often used is 'to the Jew first' (Romans 1:16, 2:10) and then the

Three: Great Healing - Great Sermon

Gentiles. Now that Messiah had been raised from the dead, God sent Christ, the seed of Abraham (Galatians 3:16), to bless Jews and Gentiles by turning (repentance) everyone from his sins (3:26).

Peter's sermon was rich and effective. Many came to Christ that day, just like they did on the Day of Pentecost. Yet when God is at work, the devil will also work. Great receptivity to the gospel is accompanied by great resistance and outright persecution. This all will be made manifest in the very next chapter.

---

[37] G605 - apokatastasis - Strong's Greek Lexicon (kjv). Blue Letter Bible. Accessed 26 Mar, 2024. https://www.blueletterbible.org/lexicon/g605/kjv/tr/0-1/

CHAPTER FOUR

Facing Opposition

Who: Jerusalem religious leaders and the apostles

What: Persecution of the apostles

When: After the lame man was healed

Where: Jerusalem

Why: To stop the spread of the Gospel

How: Threats and intimidation

> *And when they had prayed, the place was shaken where they were assembled together; and they were all filled with the Holy Ghost, and they spake the word of God with boldness.*
> — *Acts 4:31*

Peter and John Before the Sanhedrin (4:1–22)

Up to this point, there was no denying that the Holy Spirit, poured out on the Day of Pentecost, was clearly working in the lives of the apostles. Supernatural signs were in abundance and the early church was growing quickly. However, as God was working mightily by His Spirit, the devil was also working hard to hinder and harass the work of the church.

This opposition began with Jewish priests, the captain of the temple and the priestly aristocracy called the Sadducees (4:1). The latter did not believe in angels, spirits or the resurrection from the dead; however, the Pharisees did (23:8). Jesus' teaching was closest to the Pharisees, and it is

Welcome Holy Spirit

His church, and the Pharisees, that survived the Roman destruction of the temple and Jerusalem in AD 70 and has continued until this day.

The Jerusalem Jewish leadership was 'grieved' that the apostles were teaching the people the doctrine of Christ. The Sadducees were particularly upset with the teaching of the resurrection in general, and of Jesus in particular (4:2). If the doctrine of the resurrection were true, their belief system and power base could collapse.

Their response? Since it was evening, they arrested Peter and John and kept them in custody for the night until they decided what to do with them (4:3). This did nothing to dampen the growth of the church, which, at this point numbered five thousand men (4:4).

The next morning there was a convocation of the 'who's who' of the Jewish religious leadership: the rulers, elders and scribes joined by Annas the high priest, Caiaphas, John, Alexander and relatives of the high priest. It was like the Sanhedrin that Jesus faced during His passion. Their purpose was to decide the fate of the apostles (4:5–6).

The Jewish leadership put the apostles in the middle of the council. Then they asked, *'By what power, or by what name, have ye done this?'* (4:7). Jesus was asked the same thing: by what authority do you do these things? His inquisitors weren't prepared to be honest with Him, hence, He would not give them an answer (Matthew 21:23-27). They were no different to the ones we see now.

In this intimidating environment, what was most apparent was Peter's utter fearlessness. The man who had denied Christ three times was now as bold as a lion (Proverbs 28:1). In a room full of important and menacing people, he did not flinch. The secret? Peter was filled with the Holy Spirit (4:8). This is the same Spirit who filled him in **Acts 2:4** and again in **4:31**. We can – we must – be filled again and again.

Peter rightly assumed he and John were being questioned about the good deed done to the lame man, who was now completely healed. The apostle wanted it to be very clear that the reason the man was healed

Four: Facing Opposition

was because of the Name of Jesus Christ of Nazareth. This is the same Jesus Whom the council had crucified yet God raised Him from the dead. The purpose of reciting this fact was not condemnation but to spawn conviction of sin and repentance (4:8–10).

As should be the case with all Spirit-filled Christian workers, Peter quoted Scripture from memory. He started with **Psalm 118:22**: *'This is the stone which was set at nought of you builders, which is become the head of the corner'* (4:11). Other references are **Isaiah 28:16, Zechariah 10:4, Matthew 21:42, Ephesians 2:20** and **1 Peter 2:7**. What was rejected of men was embraced and celebrated by God.

After quoting the psalms, Peter was inspired by the Spirit to add a classic of his own. This verse is worth memorising for there is salvation in His name; indeed, salvation is found through no one else. *'For there is none other name under heaven given among men, whereby we must be saved'* (4:12).

We learn in **Exodus 6:3** and elsewhere that God has a Name: YHWH. We call this the 'Tetragrammaton'. It is God's wonderful but unpronounceable Name. The reason is that through the centuries, Israel concealed the vowels of the Tetragrammaton so we cannot pronounce God's name and inadvertently use it in vain. The good news for us is that God has given us a most wonderful, pronounceable name – the name of Jesus – where there is salvation and healing for all. It is the mention of His Name which caused the council to tremble.

The council was greatly perplexed. They could not reconcile the authority and boldness of Peter and John with the fact that they had no 'formal training'. It says they were unlearned and ignorant men (4:13) but, again, this does not mean they lacked intelligence; it is just that they had not studied in an approved, accredited institution. Yet, they confounded the council with their word and deeds. Then they remembered that these two men had been with Jesus. Even though the Nazarene was no longer physically present on earth, the council would have even more of a challenge suppressing His doctrine now than when He had walked among them.

There was another problem: they could not deny or explain away this miracle of healing. Having been positioned at the temple gate for a long time, the healed man was known to everyone, and his miracle was undeniable (4:14). The credibility of this miracle was that the lame beggar was over forty years old and known to the people at the time of his healing. There was no mistake about it: this man had been touched by the power of God (4:22).

Excusing the apostles, the healed man and their company from the room, the council deliberated on what to do (4:15). The topic: how can we stop this teaching and the invocation of the Name of Jesus (4:17)? Once the apostles returned to the council chamber, they were commanded neither to speak nor teach in the Name of Jesus (4:18). This was problematic: if they could not speak in His Name, there would be no power or authority to do anything.

When faced with bullying, the Holy Spirit filled the apostles with courage and boldness. Peter made the statement that the council could judge whether it was right for the apostles to obey their prohibition more than God's command. The obvious answer was, 'No, it is not right' (4:19). However, Peter also implied that their command was in contravention of God's. Bullies will take full advantage if you cower in the corner in fear; they are set back by a confident reply. The reality was that Peter and John could not stop talking about the things they had seen and heard, even if they had wanted to. God's work in their lives was too powerful to suppress (4:20).

Of course, the council would not admit it, but the boldness of the apostles caught them off-guard. It also helped put them in their place. Even so, apostolic boldness did not stop the council's threats, but it softened them. They let the apostles go because they found no way that they could punish them (4:21). After all, the regular people held the 'balance of power'. They were so impressed with the miracle at the Gate

Four: Facing Opposition

Beautiful that they glorified God. To touch the apostles severely could have brought anger and retribution from the people

Time to Pray (4:24–31)

After being let go, the apostles went to their colleagues and gave a full report of what had been said to them by the priests and elders (4:23). One could feel discouraged by being rejected by one's religious leaders and fellow countrymen.

In addition to courage, the other way to respond to bullying is fervent prayer. To 'lift up your voice' means you lift up your countenance and lips to God with a whole heart. They began their prayer by addressing 'the right God', acknowledged as Creator, who made the heaven, earth, sea and all that is in them (4:24). It is always good to praise and bless God before we start asking Him to meet our needs. This is known as supplication.

Power in prayer includes praying Biblically, in the Spirit and in a God-pleasing manner. When inspired, we should make Bible-based declarations. Here the apostles quoted the beginning of the great Messianic psalm, **Psalm 2**. They acknowledged that it was God Himself who spoke through the mouth of David. The psalm begins with the question *'Why did the heathen rage, and the people imagine vain things?'* (4:25, cf. Psalm 2:1). Interesting that they applied this verse regarding 'heathen' and 'the people' to their Jewish leaders since the leadership had behaved exactly like the groups mentioned – irrational, envious and intimidating. Remember that envy or 'tall poppy syndrome' is a real motivator to oppose the people of God, along with being stirred up by spiritual principalities and powers.

The prayer continued (in 4:26) by quoting **Psalm 2:2**. It was not just regular people who were stirred up; it was their kings and leaders who conspired together against the Lord and his Christ (meaning, His anointed one). In this case, it was Herod, Pontius Pilate, the Gentiles and the people of Israel who had collaborated against Him. Jew, Gentile, king, subject, all groups were represented by this grand conspiracy; no one was excluded (4:27). Their plot was doomed to failure very quickly. Whenever you fight God, you lose!

Yes, the Gentiles and Jews conspired together against the Lord's Anointed but paradoxically they also fulfilled prophecy and God's greater will. In the verse, it says, *'For to do whatsoever thy hand and thy counsel determined before to be done'* (4:28). God foreknew and foreordained all that transpired. That is, Christ was destined to suffer, die, be buried and rise from the dead so that repentance and remission of sins could be preached in His Name. As Joseph told his brother, what they meant for evil, God used it for good (Genesis 50:20).

In power prayer, after they praised God and confessed His Word, the time came to supplicate, meaning, 'to give your petition'. They asked God to behold the threats against them (something He had already done) and that his apostles would be able to preach the Word with all boldness (4:29). Note they were not asking for some self-centred prayer; they were asking for something to help them complete the ministry. Like Solomon's request for wisdom, ask for the things important to God and He will give you the things important to you.

A great boost to boldness comes from God's supernatural intervention. With this in mind, the apostles prayed that the Lord would confirm His word by stretching forth His hand to heal the sick (4:30), with many signs and wonders to be done in the presence of the LORD. Miracles and preaching belong together (3:1-10; 4:8–22, 29–33; 5:12–16; 6:7–8).

What was the result of this apostolic prayer? The meeting place was shaken, they were all filled with the Holy Spirit and spoke the Word of God with boldness (4:31). So, again, we have another 'filling' of the Spirit (2:4) which came as a result of prayer, especially corporate prayer by anointed apostles. Come to the river, drink of the river and keep drinking. That's the secret of being continuously filled with the Spirit (Ephesians 5:18).

Four: Facing Opposition

To be Spirit-filled is what enables you to be bold and a vessel for the miraculous. Words such as 'filled', 'clothed' and 'empowered' describe how the Holy Spirit empowers people for service (2:4; 4:8, 31; 9:17; 13:9, 52). It's the perfect antidote to spiritual opposition. A person who is bold and fearless is virtually unstoppable, as we see with the apostles and especially note with Paul. They preached the Word of God with boldness and no doubt signs and wonders followed. When you consider it, having the priceless infilling of the Spirit is of far greater worth than any worldly achievement, recognition, or possession.

Life in the Early Church (4:32–37)

For a moment, we move from persecution and opposition to life in the early church. The body of believers was called *'the multitude of them'* because they were growing by the day (4:32). They were of *'one heart and of one soul'* speaking of their perfect love and unity. They were not possessive of their possessions. They had all things in common. They put God first and loved their neighbours as themselves. **Psalm 133** speaks about unity bringing the anointing.

The apostles were anointed with great power with *'signs and wonders'*. This fortified their testimony so they could bear witness to the resurrection of the Lord Jesus. The verse adds that *'great grace was upon them all'* (4:33). When you are well-endowed with God's amazing grace, you have everything that you need.

The fellowship of the saints included watching after each other's welfare, spiritually and materially. Rather than the grand welfare state of today, the early church looked after its own like one big happy family. Nobody lacked in the necessities of life. Those who had substance, like lands and houses, sold their assets and brought to the apostles the equity that was sold. By giving their proceeds at the apostles' feet, it showed immense respect and trust to the men who had given up everything. They served as a sterling example for all to see. Everyone was cared for and no one lacked. Unlike the coerciveness of communism, which disdains private property, family and faith, the believers did this voluntarily. Their love for God and people transcended their love of material possessions (4:34–35).

Barnabas introduced (4:36–37): His name was 'Joses' or 'Joseph' and he was of the tribe of Levi, from the island of Cyprus. The apostles gave him the surname 'Barnabas', meaning 'son of consolation or encouragement'. He lived up to this name. Every church could use a dozen, if not a hundred, people like Barnabas. He sold his land, brought the money and gave it to the apostles. From this point, Barnabas was being prepared by God for some significant ministry in Antioch and on the first missionary journey with Paul. He gave up his material substance and ended up with a consequential ministry and a great heavenly reward.

Unfortunately, not everyone who gave was blessed like Barnabas. If you approach a Spirit-anointed servant of God with the wrong motives or crafty deceit, the outcome could be deadly, as we are about to see.

CHAPTER FIVE

Judgment Within, Trouble Without

Who: Apostles, Jewish leaders, Ananias, Sapphira

What: Lies within, persecution without

When: Very early years of the Church

Where: Jerusalem

Why: Church is growing

How: By the power of the Holy Spirit

> *And we are his witnesses of these things; and so is also the Holy Ghost, whom God hath given to them that obey him.*
> — *Acts 5:32*

Acts 5, forty-two verses long, has an interesting emphasis: judgement within the church, trouble outside (predominantly with the Jewish religious elite) and God's hand of blessing and empowerment on His dedicated apostles. The judgment and trouble do not hinder the work of God; these things cause them to be *'more than conquerors'* (Romans 8:37).

Judgment in the Church (5:1–11)

One of the fundamental doctrines of the Christian Church has to do with the *'resurrection of the dead'* followed by the *'final judgment'* (Hebrews 6:2). With sobering clarity, **Revelation 20:11–15** speaks of where the dead gather around the great white throne, the Book of Life is opened and the dead are judged according to their works. **Matthew 10:28** gives us an early warning service on this very issue.

This is what makes the gospel of Christ so wonderful. The free gift is that Christ took our place on death row, uploaded our sins onto His cross, and downloaded His righteousness in our hearts. We cannot earn this gift – it is too priceless – but we can receive it by faith.

Scripture teaches that there is a judgment of believers called the *'judgment seat of Christ'* (Romans 14:10; 2 Corinthians 5:10). It is not about the salvation of the soul but the works of the body. One author called it 'God's big thank you' for all the kingdom work we have done in this life. Yet, it is a judgment, and everyone's work will be tried by fire. Silver and gold works will be refined and wood, hay and stubble work will be burned. Fortunately, the believer is still saved because, as we learned, it is a free gift.

This fifth chapter of Acts begins with a localised individual judgment of a married couple who liquidated their assets but did so with the wrong motive. It cost them their lives. They were Ananias and his wife, Sapphira. Like others at the end of chapter four, they sold a possession but conspired to keep back part of the price while laying the remainder at the apostles' feet (5:1–2). In other words, they were being deceitful under the pretext of generosity.

The Holy Spirit was involved here, and He alerted the apostle Peter through the spiritual gift called 'word of knowledge' that Ananias had kept back part of the money. He asked Ananias a pointed question: why did Satan fill your heart to lie to the Holy Spirit (5:3)? These are very strong words. Lying to the church and its leadership is the same as lying to the Holy Spirit.

The questioning continued. Peter then asked the obvious: before it was sold, didn't it belong to you? After you sold it, wasn't the money at your disposal? The obvious answer was 'Yes'. The selling of the possession and giving of money was voluntary, but the actions must be

Five: Judgment Within, Trouble Without

with integrity. So why did he and Sapphira do it? Answer: praise of people and love of money. He was being a hypocrite, putting on a misleading appearance that did not correspond to reality. Lying to the Holy Spirit is lying to God (5:4).

Then something immediately happened that shook the entire church to the core. After Ananias heard these words of Peter, he dropped dead on the spot. Those who saw it had *'great fear'* (5:5). Understandably, this seems like a severe price, especially when we consider that some in the church have done much worse. Yet the early church was blessed with great grace and power; therefore, *'to whom much is given, much is required'* (Luke 12:48). If this doesn't inspire the 'fear of the Lord', nothing will.

In true Jewish fashion, when it came to death, everything was done quickly. Young men came and *'wound him up'*, meaning they wrapped him in a burial shroud and carried him out for a prompt burial (5:6).

Sapphira was not present and was unaware of what had happened to her husband and that she was now a widow. Three hours later, she was about to find out when she came to the room, and it would be shocking (5:7).

Upon arrival, Peter inquired if she had sold the land for a certain amount. Without hesitation, she repeated the lie of her husband Ananias: 'Yes, we sold it for that amount' (5:8). She was a willing co-conspirator and would end up paying the ultimate price.

Peter pronounced a great judgment on Sapphira. Her sin? She had agreed with her husband to tempt the Spirit of the Lord (5:9). Note the reference is not just to God in general but to the Holy Spirit in particular, since He is the member of the Godhead who is represented here on earth.

To 'tempt' the Spirit of God means to lie to or put to the test. Israel in the wilderness did this to the Lord ten times (Numbers 14:22) and the result was that they were stranded there for forty years. Israel's tempting God was mentioned as one of their top five wilderness sins in **1**

Welcome Holy Spirit

Corinthians 10:9[38] and the result was that they were bitten by snakes. When God shows His faithfulness, respond with gratitude, not griping.

Sapphira was then given the bad news: her husband was dead, the feet of those who buried him were at the door and they were now ready to carry her out. Immediately upon hearing these words, Sapphira fell down and died (5:10). The couple who lied together died together. The young men came, checked her vital signs and confirmed that she was dead. So, she, too, had her body immediately wrapped in a shroud and was buried next to her husband.

How did the church respond to this stunning drama? They experienced 'great fear'. So did everyone who heard these tidings. What are we to make of it? Ananias and Sapphira were judged for their deceitfulness, greed and hypocrisy. God is long-suffering and kind, but there comes a time when enough is enough. Tempting God, lying to God and whingeing to God, are key ways to get stranded 'in the wilderness', and, if not repented of, the wilderness becomes the graveyard. All these things that happened are examples and are written in the Scripture as a warning for us, heirs of the Lord and the age-old promises (1 Corinthians 10:11).

Many Signs and Wonders (5:12–16)

After the deaths of Ananias and Sapphira, it appears that there was an even greater outbreak of signs and wonders. These were very public manifestations since they happened on Solomon's porch, which was the precincts of Herod's temple. The apostles and people were *'all with one accord'*, thus highlighting their unity and effectiveness (5:12).

It says that no one dared to join the disciples (at least in the public temple area). The reason for this is not stated but presumably because the multitude sensed the growing opposition of the religious leaders and did not want to be ostracised. As it says in **John 12:43**, *'For they loved the praise of men more than the praise of God'*. Still, they were highly regarded among the people (5:13). The text says that believers were *'added to the*

Five: Judgment Within, Trouble Without

Lord' and speaks of 'multitudes' of men and women (5:14). Whenever the Holy Spirit is allowed to move without being quenched (1 Thessalonians 5:19), there will be church growth.

One way the Holy Spirit powerfully moves and helps 'build the house of the Lord' is through gifts of healing (1 Corinthians 12:9). The people brought the sick into the streets, laying them on beds and couches. The goal was to at least have Peter's shadow cast upon them as he passed by (5:15). Is there any power in Peter's shadow? In Peter himself? No, none at all. However, Peter's shadow, one's handkerchief or the 'laying on of hands' provide a point of contact whereby faith is released. It is our faith in the Name of Jesus (3:6, 16) that makes us every bit whole. The physical things are just objects to which we can direct our faith.

The apostles were getting the same response to their ministry that Jesus had with His – without advertising, people were coming from near and far to receive healing. Multitudes came from the regional areas to Jerusalem, bringing the sick and those vexed by evil spirits. Everyone was healed (5:16). The major difference was that Jesus did much of His ministry along the shores of the Sea of Galilee whereas the apostles were Jerusalem-based. Remember that Jerusalem, unlike Galilee, gave a mixed response to the miraculous: some believed while others did not.

More Success, More Trouble (5:17–28)

Whenever God moves by His Spirit, the devil will react. He can use all kinds of people, including the religious, to oppose God's work. The high priest and the sect of the Sadducees heard of these things – the signs and wonders – and *'were filled with indignation'* (5:17). Again, this is the vice of envy (tall poppy syndrome) rearing its ugly head. **Galatians 4:29** says, *'But as then he that was born after the flesh persecuted him that was born after the Spirit, even so it is now.'* Being religious does not deliver you from the flesh – it accentuates the flesh. The result is that it resists and opposes a move of the Holy Spirit often more than regular worldly sinners.

Welcome Holy Spirit

Persecution of the apostles culminated with the high priest and Sadducees arresting Peter and other apostles (5:18). They were put in a common prison, presumably, that which housed real *bona fide* criminals. After a few hours in the hold, late at night, God's angel came to the prison, opened the doors and brought the apostles out (5:19). It is possible that fervent prayer was offered on their behalf when news came that they had been unjustly arrested. Not everyone is released. In Paul's case, he was imprisoned several times and ultimately died while incarcerated. Yet in his last epistle, he triumphantly proclaimed in **2 Timothy 2:9**: *'Wherein I suffer trouble, as an evil doer, even unto bonds; but the word of God is not bound.'* The same is true of the Holy Spirit; He cannot be bound, either, and where He dwells, there is liberty (2 Corinthians 3:17).

The religious establishment intended to prevent the apostles from preaching the message of Christ. However, the angel of the Lord countered this by telling them to go back into the very public area of the temple and speak to the people *'all the words of this life'* (5:20). The new birth offers new life in Christ. Tell the world! When they heard these words of the angel, the apostles returned to the temple *early* and began to teach as if nothing ever happened. Notice that despite the intimidation of the religious establishment, the apostles were not afraid to do what God had commanded them (5:21).

While they spoke, the high priest and Sadducees called the council and senate together and ordered the apostles to be brought from the prison. To the shock and dismay of the council, the officers went to their cell but could not find them (5:22). The dumbfounded officers reported that the prison was safely shut and secured, and keepers were standing at the doors. Yet, when the doors were opened, no one could be found within (5:23).

When the high priest, captain of the temple and chief priests heard this incredible story, they were greatly puzzled and wondered what would come next (5:24). Someone finally discovered the whereabouts of the apostles. They came running to the high priest and said that the men

Five: Judgment Within, Trouble Without

who were put in prison were teaching the people in the temple precincts (5:25).

The captain of the officers, who were only doing their job, went to the temple area to get the apostles. They did not use force for fear of upsetting the people and risking getting stoned. Note that the apostles were cooperative and did not resist (5:26), even in the face of this harassment. God's servants are not rebels.

The 'council' was most likely the Sanhedrin, the similar body that Jesus and Stephen faced. The apostles stood before this group and were going to be interrogated (5:27). The high priest himself said that they were told not to teach in 'this name' (apparently, he did not even want to utter the name 'Jesus' or 'Yeshua'). Instead of obeying the council, the apostles filled Jerusalem with their doctrine. Then, in an interesting twist, the high priest said that the apostles were intent on making them guilty of shedding this Man's blood (5:28). The more Jesus was magnified, the more condemned the council were, since they had rejected Him and lobbied Pilate for His crucifixion.

Fearless in the Face of Fury (5:29–32)

How would the apostles respond to this menacing group of powerful people? With the same spirit of boldness that accompanies those who are filled with the Spirit (4:31). The apostles' answer, given by Peter the spokesman, is one we should all share: *'We ought to obey God rather than men'* (5:29). This alone is a good description of the 'fear of the Lord'.

This injunction stands true in all ages, though it is less needed when you have stable democratic governance with the rule of law, balance of powers, separation of powers, public accountability, freedom of conscience, speech, religion, respect for basic human rights and so on. But what about increased, anti-Christian authoritarianism that has been regular throughout church history? When we are told not to preach, pray, and/or meet together? We have to wisely balance the exhortation of **Romans 13:1** to be subject to the higher powers (governmental) with obedience to God (5:29). We are to be law-abiding, peace-loving citizens, but not at any cost. A simple rule of thumb is whenever the higher powers demand action that contradicts clear commands, God's will must come first. There may be a furious reaction, but the boldness, grace and peace of God will be on the believer and God will deliver. This empowerment and boldness come from the Holy Spirit.

After declaring that God's will must come first, Peter began to explain that the God of their fathers raised up Jesus from the dead. His name is shared freely, Whom they, the council, slew and hanged on a tree (5:30). In **Deuteronomy 21:23**, those who hung on a tree were cursed by God. Jesus took our curse to His cross so that the blessings of God would be ours. This verse in Deuteronomy must have been in the minds of the council. Yes, it appeared that Peter wanted to make the religious authorities guilty of the blood of Jesus; however, the ultimate goal was conviction, not condemnation.

Peter continued his speech. God not only raised Jesus from the dead, but He also exalted Him at His right hand to be a Prince and Saviour (5:31). Israel had the opportunity of repentance from dead works and the forgiveness of sins. In a region where pride and honour are everything, and shame must be avoided like death, this must have inflamed the religious hierarchy. After all, the very One they rejected is now being proclaimed as the Son of David, Son of God, and Messiah. How could they have gotten it so wrong?

Peter concluded that their proclamation of Messiah was not a fairy tale. It was based on fact and by credible eyewitnesses. This included the words and work of Messiah and His resurrection from the dead. Not only the apostles but also the Holy Spirit was a witness. He is given to all people who obey God and His gospel (5:32). The obedience of 5:29 brings many benefits, including the baptism and fullness of the Holy Spirit.

Five: Judgment Within, Trouble Without

A Wise Speech (5:33–42)

The council did not feel the conviction of sin at all; indeed, they were livid (5:33) and conspired how to slay the apostles. They had already killed one Righteous Man, so their seared consciences would not flinch from killing some more. However, the apostles' time had not yet come, and God provided another form of deliverance from a most unlikely source.

Gamaliel, a Pharisee and doctor of the law, a highly respected member of the council and probable mentor of Saul of Tarsus, wanted to speak and asked that the council put the apostles outside for a short while (5:34). God would use him to calm the raging storm within the council chambers.

The first thing wise Gamaliel said was that the 'men of Israel' needed to be very careful what they did with the apostles (5:35). He began by using the example of one man named Theudas, who thought he was a 'somebody' and drew a following of four hundred men. Once he was slain, all who followed him were scattered and his movement came to nothing (5:36). The next example was Judas of Galilee, an insurrectionist. During *'the days of the taxing'*, emotions and nationalism were sky-high, and Judas had taken advantage of the discontent to gather a large following. Yet he also had been killed, his followers dispersed and his movement abruptly ended (5:37).

Gamaliel's advice was starkly simple: let these men alone. If what they are doing is man-made, it will come to naught, just like the previous two examples (5:38). Then came an equally stark warning. If these men were doing the work of God, they could not stop it. If they tried, they would be fighting God Himself (5:39). Of interest is that Gamaliel implied the possibility that the apostles' work was God's work.

Amazingly, this respected man with God's help persuaded the council. This is the line of least resistance. So, they called for the apostles, scourged them, demanded they should not speak in Jesus' Name and let them go (5:40). How did the apostles respond to this injustice? Not the way most people would expect. They left the presence of the council, rejoicing that they were counted worthy to suffer shame for Jesus' Name (5:41). Only the new birth and Holy Spirit filling could make such an attitude possible.

Did they obey the council's command? Far from being dissuaded, the apostles were emboldened by the council's action and worked harder than ever. Daily in the temple and from house to house, they did not cease to teach and preach Jesus Christ (5:42). Despite the opposition, God grew His church by its spiritually empowered leadership and the gates of hell were powerless to stop them. As church history reveals, even the Roman Empire itself could not stop the church.

In the next chapter, we will discover how a growing church, filled with the Holy Spirit, would care for its own.

---

[38] The other wilderness sins included lust, idolatry, fornication and murmuring.

CHAPTER SIX

Stephen, Service and Strife

Who: Stephen

What: Practical service

When: 'Now in those days:' The very early years of the Church

Where: Jerusalem

Why: Church was growing

How: By the Spirit, wisdom, and faith

> *Wherefore, brethren, look ye out among you seven men of honest report, full of the Holy Ghost and wisdom, whom we may appoint over this business. But we will give ourselves continually to prayer, and to the ministry of the word.*
> — *Acts 6:3–4*

The early church faced several big challenges, as we already noted, but a lack of growth was not one of them. This is not surprising because the Lord was building His house (Psalm 127:1) by the Holy Spirit. Whatever God builds is made to last. In those early days of the church, the number of disciples multiplied. Great growth can bring problems, known as 'growing pains'.

One of those problems had to do with practical ministry and care. The church cared for both body and soul; thus, there was a communal feeding program, in this case among the widows. There were murmurings from the Hellenistic (Greek-speaking) Jewish widows because they were being neglected in the daily ministration in favour of the Hebrew-speaking widows (6:1). Jerusalem's elitism and favouritism of local Hebraic Jews at the expense of Diaspora Jews was a festering problem.

This situation was so strife-filled that it demanded the involvement of 'the twelve', namely the apostles who convened a meeting. They started with a commonsense premise: it was not good for the church leaders to leave ministering the word of God or the gospel to wait on tables, yet by implication, somebody was needed for this task (6:2).

Wanted: Spirit-filled Waiters (6:1–7)

If you owned a restaurant and advertised a position for a waiter, what qualifications would they need? Presentable, clean, good people skills, a customer service attitude, good hygiene, honesty, character reference and work ethic. Concerning the early church, the criteria were practical and spiritual. First of all, they wanted to choose men. Amazingly, they did not insist on 'women in the kitchen' – they wanted men to serve these widows. Yet not any type of man would do. They had to:

- bear an honest report
- be full of the Holy Spirit
- be full of wisdom.

It was these criteria that guided their decision of whom to choose (6:3)

Once the men were chosen, the apostles could return to their primary task: prayer and the ministry of the Word (6:4). There is no greater honour than this. To 'give attention' comes from the Greek *proskartereo* means 'to be steadfastly attentive unto, to give unremitting care to a thing; to persevere and not to faint'.[39]

So who were these anointed deacons/waiters? They were Stephen (a man full of faith and the Holy Spirit), Philip, Prochorus, Nicanor, Timon, Parmesan and Nicolas (a proselyte from Antioch) (6:5).

Now that they were chosen, they had to be publicly anointed. The seven men were brought to the apostles. Prayer and the laying on of

Six: Stephen, Service and Strife

hands were offered, even for this seemingly simple task of waiting on tables (6:6). Yet, everything we do for God, including waiting on tables, is a spiritual vocation and requires a spiritual application. When we welcome the Holy Spirit in all aspects of life, expect to be anointed in all you do.

The ministry of the church was to the 'whole person' (namely, feeding destitute widows as well as prayer and the ministry of the Word). In addition, there was the wise delegation of responsibility to Godly men. What was the result? The Word of God increased; the number of disciples in Jerusalem multiplied greatly. Of interest is that in the early years of the church, something else wonderful happened: *'a great company of the priests were obedient to the faith'* (6:7). Before Judaism predominantly hardened to the gospel, it should be noted that some, perhaps many, in the religious establishment, became followers of Jesus. May the Lord return us to such an outcome in our day (Romans 11:26).

From Meals to Miracles to Trouble (6:8–15)

Stephen appeared to be the head deacon, full of faith and power. The result is that he did great wonders and miracles among the people (6:8). Such ministerial success will not be without problems. As in the ministry of Jesus, Whose miraculous signs and wonders drew envy and resentment from the religious elite, the same would happen to Stephen.

The inevitable envy and resentment boiled over in the Synagogue of the Libertines. Other quarrellers included the Cyrenians, Alexandrians (North Africa), Cilicians and Asia (Turkey). All these ganged up on Stephen, not to debate theology but to give him strife (6:9).

Though this group attacked Stephen, they were powerless to overcome him through rhetoric alone (6:10). He demonstrated wisdom and was Spirit-anointed. These 'religious elite' resorted to 'dirty tricks', by commissioning deceitful people to offer trumped-up charges against Stephen. He was accused of blasphemy against Moses and God (6:11). Note that opponents of the gospel in Jesus' time did the same thing to

Welcome Holy Spirit

Him as was now happening to Stephen. **Matthew 10:24** says that *'The disciple is not above his master, nor the servant above his lord.'*

The deceivers stirred up the people, elders and scribes against Stephen. They caught him and took him to the council (6:12), the Sanhedrin, the same group that illegally tried Jesus in a late-night closed trial. Stephen, the servant, would have a parallel experience of persecution and suffering, just like the Master

Like in the trial of Jesus, they installed false witnesses who made the ridiculous claim that Stephen did not cease to speak blasphemous words against the 'holy place' and 'the law' (6:13). Of course, the fact that Stephen's emphasis was on Jesus and the gospel instead of the holy place and the law would give superficial credence to their spurious claim.

The false witnesses said that Stephen preached the predicted destruction of the temple by Jesus of Nazareth. He would also *'change the customs which Moses delivered us'* (6:14). There is some truth to their statements, but the devil is a master of mixing truth with falsehood to make it all sound right.

In light of the false and ludicrous claims levelled against him, those present were curious about Stephen's reaction. For someone accused of such heinous actions, Stephen did not look like a criminal at all. There was a purity and innocence about him; his appearance was as one without a speck of guile or corruption. As the council looked steadfastly at him, he had the appearance of an angel (6:15). This was the anointing of the Holy Spirit upon his life.

In our next chapter, we will witness Stephen's lengthy speech and utter fearlessness. What happened in his sham trial left an imprint on the world to this very day.

---

[39] G4342 - proskartereō - Strong's Greek Lexicon (kjv). Blue Letter Bible. Accessed 29 Mar, 2024. https://www.blueletterbible.org/lexicon/g4342/kjv/tr/0-1/

CHAPTER SEVEN
Stephen's Anointed Speech

Who: Stephen and the Sanhedrin

What: Defending himself and indicting his adversaries

When: Early days after his arrest

Where: Jerusalem

Why: Responding to opposition

How: By the Spirit

> *But he, being full of the Holy Ghost, looked up stedfastly into heaven, and saw the glory of God, and Jesus standing on the right hand of God.*
> — *Acts 7:55*

One of the transformational things we see in the Spirit-filled believer is supernatural courage in the face of brutal adversity. We observed it in Peter, we will see it with Stephen and especially in Paul. When they are on trial, with temporal authorities wielding the upper hand, they don't even flinch. Instead of being on the defensive, we will see them extemporaneously bringing forth the gospel. Their utter boldness put their accusers on trial instead.

After listening to their false accusations of himself, Stephen was permitted to speak. Unlike the trial of Jesus where the Lord refused to speak, Stephen was more than willing to do so (7:1–2). However, he does not seek to refute the charges or defend himself. Instead, he gives a speech about the history of Israel. The council listened in intense silence.

Starting with Abraham (7:2–7)

The council was reminded that while Abraham still lived in Mesopotamia, before he moved to Charran (Haran in south central Turkey), the God of glory appeared to him (7:2). The message of God to Abraham was simple: *'Get thee out of thy country'* (7:3). In other words, separate and leave your loved ones and come to the land which I will show you. According to **Hebrews 11:8**, when God called Abraham, he obeyed and left, even though he did not know where he was going. Abraham was guided by faith and faith demands obedience to the clear commands of God.

In faithfulness to God, Abraham came out of the land of the Chaldeans. En route to Canaan, he dwelt in Charran (also known as 'Haran'). It was a boomerang-shaped route: from Ur of the Chaldees to Canaan was due west; however, Abraham followed the Fertile Crescent. He went north-west from Ur to Haran and eventually would go south-west to Canaan. The move from Charran happened after his father Terah was dead. His heathen father would not be with him in the land of faith (7:4).

Though the Abrahamic covenant promised land, posterity and universal blessing, Abraham owned no land in Canaan and for the longest time, his wife was barren. He moved to Canaan in faith, but he had to wait for the promises to come (7:5). God did not leave Abraham in the dark. He told him that his seed, when it eventually came, would leave Canaan and dwell in a strange land, in bondage and evil, for four hundred years (7:6). The nation that enslaved the Hebrews, namely Egypt, would be judged. After that, Abraham's seed would come out and serve God in the land of promise (7:7).

Seven: Stephen's Anointed Speech

From Abraham to Joseph (7:8–16)

First things first: to join in this strategic covenantal family arrangement, Abraham and his household were given the covenant of circumcision (Genesis 17, Acts 7:8). Of interest is that the patriarch and his household, which consisted of at least three hundred men, were circumcised on the very day God commanded Abraham. Imagine the logistics of it all. Abraham's prompt obedience is why he is called God's friend. Jesus says that you are His friend if you do whatever He commands you (John 15:14). And that includes an impromptu circumcision ceremony.

Fast-forward to the time of Jacob, grandson of Abraham. His many sons were known as patriarchs, the fathers of the twelve tribes of Israel. Yet their chosen status before God did not stop them from being all too human. They were envious of their younger brother Joseph and the favouritism that their father Jacob had showered on him. Their envy caused them to do a very evil thing: they sold their brother as a slave and he was taken to Egypt (7:9). The silver lining is that God was with him.

Though it took years, Joseph received divine favour and wisdom (7:10). While his earthly father's favour got Joseph into trouble, divine favour delivered him from all evil. Because of this heavenly grace, Pharaoh, king of Egypt, made Joseph the governor over Egypt and all his house. While Joseph waited for his time to come, Genesis says, 'The Lord was with Joseph' (Genesis 39:2, 21).

Joseph came into a position of supreme leadership not a moment too soon. As predicted by two pharaonic dreams, a famine came over Egypt and Canaan for seven years, with great affliction. The patriarchs had no sustenance or food (7:11) and without taking action, they would have starved. During this distressing situation, Jacob heard there was corn in Egypt (7:12). He sent his sons to go and get some.

During their second visit to Egypt, the governor of the land, their brother Joseph, made himself known to his brethren (7:13). After they recovered from the shock, embarrassment and conviction for the evil they had done to him years before, the patriarchs were introduced to

Pharaoh. The king gave them a gracious invitation to go, fetch their father Jacob, and all their family members and come make their home in Egypt. Since there were yet another five years of famine, they made the move. Seventy-five members of the extended chosen family came to Egypt (7:14).

Nonchalantly, and with little detail, the Bible mentions that the patriarchs, who were called to inherit Canaan, lived their last years, died and were buried in the land of Egypt (7:15). **Exodus 1:6** says, *'And Joseph died* (in Egypt)*, and all his brethren, and all that generation'*. By faith, the seed of Abraham would return to Canaan – and it did.

Though Jacob and all his sons died in Egypt, the Bible records that two of them – Jacob and Joseph – were interred in Canaan, the land of promise (7:16). We know that Abraham purchased land for burial in Hebron (Genesis 23) and Jacob did the same thing in the Shechem area (Genesis 33:19). What is not so clear is why Abraham is mentioned as the purchaser rather than Jacob. Of course, it is not uncommon to ascribe to the prime patriarch actions that are fulfilled by the descendants. The main point is that at the very least, the two patriarchs, Jacob and Joseph, returned to the promised land, even though it was in death.

Moses (7:17–22)

While God understands timelessness, He also has a keen sense of timing. There is a time and season for everything. It is important that the mature, discerning individual senses when the seasons are changing and moves accordingly (7:17). This was especially true when the time came for God to fulfil His promises. In this case, the four hundred years of Egyptian sojourn was coming to an end. *'The time of the promise drew nigh, which God had sworn to Abraham'* (7:17).

During these four centuries, Israel grew from a family of seventy-five, which had come out of Canaan with Jacob, to six hundred thousand men of military age, not counting women and children. This could be upwards of two million plus. *'The people grew and multiplied in Egypt'* (7:17), which is why God sent them there in the first place. Unlike little

Seven: Stephen's Anointed Speech

crowded Canaan, with seven nations vying for turf, Egypt was well-watered by the Nile River and spacious, giving the children of Israel ample room to grow. Had the pharaoh not been so vehemently oppressive, the Israelites may have been tempted to remain in Egypt. Yet his well-documented hostility and hardness of heart were an incentive to leave for the land God promised them.

One way of discerning the changing of the seasons is when the once-friendly locals become unfriendly. In this simple verse, a pharaoh arose at the end of the sojourn period *'which knew not Joseph'* (7:18). This means that he ignored or overlooked the goodness of God through Joseph and the protection it afforded his people. Therefore, this ungrateful monarch would oppress Israel more than most.

This horrible pharaoh dealt harshly with the children of Israel and ill-treated the fathers. He even decreed that male babies be cast out into the Nile so that they would not live (7:19). During this troublesome time of male infant genocide, Moses was born. The mercy of God was upon him. He was fair to look upon (7:20) and neither his mother nor the pharaoh's daughter could kill him. Defying the king's decree, they kept Moses safe for three months. After this period finished, when they could hide Moses no more, they put him safely in an 'ark-like' basket by the reeds in the Nile River. Pharaoh's daughter discovered him, felt mercy over the weeping babe and adopted him as her son (7:21).

Like Daniel in Babylon, Moses was well-educated in all the wisdom of the Egyptians as well as in royal issues. Since the hand of God was upon him, he became mighty in words and actions (7:22). Yet despite living the privileged life of an Egyptian prince, Moses did not forget his roots or people. At the age of forty years old, he decided to visit the children of Israel (7:23).

Moses' False Start (7:23–29)

What was it like for Moses to connect with his people after his extended time at the Egyptian court? The encounter would affect him for decades.

The visit got off to a bad start. He saw one of the Israelites being oppressed by an Egyptian. Moses stuck his neck out to defend the Israelite man. In so doing, he killed the Egyptian (7:24). He viewed his actions as self-defence on behalf of his people.

Moses wrongly assumed that the Israelites would understand and appreciate that he was raised up to save them from the oppressor (7:25). It was God protecting them by his own hand. However, *'they understood not'* and this would cause complications. Exodus says that the Egyptian was buried in the sand to cover up the deed (Exodus 2:12). Moses did not want this thing to be known. His next Hebrew encounter would not be much better.

The following day Moses found two Israelites fighting among themselves. In this case, because they were all brethren, he tried to mediate among them. 'You are brothers,' Moses chimed, 'So why do you want to wrong each other?' Again, he thought his good intentions would be received with gratitude. Again, they were not (7:26).

The man 'in the wrong' greatly resented Moses' intervention (7:27). He thrust him away and then taunted, 'Who made you a ruler and judge over us?' Though Moses had lived the high life at the Egyptian court, he had no sway over his enslaved people. Hebrews are not impressed with high-ups and celebrities, and this is one example (see Galatians 2:6).

Then the man of Israel asked another taunting question: Since I am not listening to you, will you kill me, just like you did to the Egyptian yesterday (7:28)? Moses realised that despite his efforts to cover up the slaying, everyone knew what he had done. He wisely decided to escape from the land and go to Midian until everyone's tempers had cooled. Pharaoh heard about Moses' deed and sought to slay him (Exodus 2:15). Yet Moses knew how to run fast.

Moses: Prophet and Lawgiver (7:30–44)

All it took was one sentence from the cheeky Israelite and Moses went from court dweller to fugitive. Had he not, surely the pharaoh would

Seven: Stephen's Anointed Speech

have executed him. So, he travelled eastward across the Sinai to the land of Midian, dwelt there for forty years and married Zipporah who bore him two sons (7:29).

While Mount Sinai in south central Sinai Peninsula is what comes to mind, tradition only identified it as the place two thousand years after the time of Moses. Another possibility is that Mount Sinai is actually in Midian. Jabal al Lawz in North Western Saudi Arabia is the prime candidate. After all, Paul says that Mount Sinai is in Arabia (Galatians 4:25), which is close to where Moses lived for forty years. In any case, his encounter at the holy mount changed the world.

After forty years in Midian, when Moses was eighty, the angel of the Lord appeared to him in a flame of fire in a bush (7:30). Rather than being intimidated by this awesome, spectacular and terrifying site, Moses drew near. More overwhelming than what he saw was what he heard. God spoke to him from the bush (7:31).

It was time to reveal God's identity. God spoke to Moses as the God of his fathers – namely, the patriarchs: *'I am the God of thy fathers, the God of Abraham, and the God of Isaac, and the God of Jacob'* (7:32). God is not ashamed to call Himself their God because they were men of faith and obedience. When Moses heard God's voice, he trembled and did not dare look anymore at the bush.

God told Moses to remove his shoes because he stood on holy ground (7:33). In Asia and other parts of the world, people take off their shoes before entering the home. The ostensible reason is for sanitation and respect. However, it may also symbolically represent the separation of the home's sanctity from the dirt and corruption of the outside world, which is found on the shoes.

Twice God says, *'I have seen'* (7:34), which implies an emphasis on the fact that He is not far away in heaven and uninvolved. Instead, God is passionately interactive in the affairs of His people. God saw the affliction of the Israelites in Egypt, heard their groaning and came down to earth to deliver them. God invited Moses to come so he could be sent back to Egypt for the greatest mission of his life. God's method was not a method but a man.

At this point, the Lord did something wonderful: he honoured and promoted His servant, Moses. The same Moses whom the Israelites rejected, saying, 'who made you our ruler and judge', God made a ruler and deliverer through the angel who appeared in the bush (7:35).

Indeed, Moses fulfilled his call and was faithful in all his house (Hebrews 3:2). He brought Israel out of Egypt in the power of God, after he had demonstrated signs and wonders in three places: Egypt, the Red Sea and the wilderness over forty years.

> LESSON FOR LIFE: Great people can and do experience rejection, even from their own, only to have God vindicate and promote them in due time.

In Stephen's spirited self-defence, he alluded to a famous prophecy regarding Moses and 'the coming prophet'. Predicted in **Deuteronomy 18:15** and **18** and reiterated in **Acts 3:22–23**, Moses predicted a future prophet like himself coming from the ranks of his brethren. Israel shall listen to him (7:37) and there are dire consequences for ignoring his voice. By implication, Stephen affirmed that Jesus of Nazareth was a prophet like Moses, just as He is a priest like Melchizedek and a king like David.

Moses' greatest honour was not as the miracle-working deliverer, but as the man who handled the life-giving Word of God from Mount Sinai and passed it on to people (7:38). The term 'church in the wilderness' does not refer to a normal Christian church; it comes from the Greek word *ekklesia*, meaning Israelite assembly or congregation. Yet this word *ekklesia* is what is meant by the words 'church', 'assembly' and 'congregation'.[40]

Seven: Stephen's Anointed Speech

Sadly, but without surprise, the 'fathers' or Israelites who came out of Egypt did not obey the oracles (7:39). That's why the tablets of stone, written by the finger of God and containing the Ten Commandments, were broken by Moses. Thus, they thrust Moses from them and in their hearts, they turned back to Egypt, altogether forgetting the bondage and repression there.

Their rejection of Moses and the Law culminated in demanding Aaron to make visible, tangible gods to go before them. Then they claimed that Moses, who was on Mount Sinai for forty days, had gone missing in action (7:40). Failure to wait for God and His message can have dire consequences since the gods Israel desired were of their own making.

So, in the days that Moses was doing holy business on the mountaintop, the carnal Israelites below made a golden calf. This is bald-faced idolatry. They offered sacrifice to the idol. They were having an orgy of celebration with this calf as the centrepiece, rejoicing in what their hands have made (7:41). The 'golden calf' syndrome would be repeated centuries later when Jeroboam I, the first monarch of the Northern Kingdom of Israel, made two of them and set up sanctuaries in Bethel and Dan (1 Kings 12:29). This sin of the golden calves would be the undoing of the Northern Kingdom.

> LESSON FOR LIFE: While the carnal are in party mode like chickens in the barnyard, those who wait on God soar like eagles in the sky.

'God gave them up (7:42). God is amazingly, even legendarily, patient. Yet there comes a point when He has had enough. Idolatry and the worship of false gods are highly offensive to the Lord; this is known as an abomination. Scriptures give ample testimony to this so that there is no excuse.

Despite His great love, mercy and kindness, the Israelites persisted in the worship of heathen gods (7:42). So, God turned and gave them up

(Psalm 81:12; Ezekiel 20:25, 39; Romans 1:24; 2 Thessalonians 2:11) so they could worship the host of heaven (Deuteronomy 4:19; 17:3; 2 Kings 17:16, 21:3; Jeremiah 19:13). Quoting **Amos 5:25–26**, Stephen said, *'O ye house of Israel, have ye offered to me slain beasts and sacrifices by the space of forty years in the wilderness?'* (7:42).

It gets worse. After Amos' quote, Israel was accused of worshipping in the tabernacle of Moloch the star of the false god Remphan, which are figures that were made by human hands. As a result of this wilful and idiotic idolatry, God threatened to deport them far beyond Damascus. Indeed, they would dwell in Babylon and beyond (7:43).

Israel's apostasy was even more outlandish because they had a *'tabernacle of witness in the wilderness'* (7:44). Unlike the man-made religions, this came about because God had appointed Moses. He was to make a tent of meeting *'according to the fashion that he had seen'*. Unlike the heathen and their false worship, Israel had experienced the real thing – true worship of the living God – and yet they still succumbed to the ways of their godless neighbours.

Joshua, David and Solomon (7:45–50)

This divinely designed tent of meeting was portable. The generation who came after the Exodus generation, the ones born in the wilderness, brought the tabernacle with them when they crossed into Canaan and conquered the Gentiles (7:45). In the KJV, the name 'Jesus' is written, though this means 'Joshua, the son of Nun.' Why 'Jesus?' His Hebrew name is *Yeshua*, which is the diminutive of *Yehoshua*, which is Joshua. The names Joshua and Jesus are both translated as 'saviour'. In this regard, Jesus and Joshua are synonymous. God drove out the Gentiles/Canaanites before the face of Joshua's Israelite army. This continued to the days of David.

David had found favour with God and wanted to *'find a tabernacle for the God of Jacob'* (7:46). More precisely, David wanted to build God a permanent dwelling place rather than retain a portable tent.

Seven: Stephen's Anointed Speech

As Scripture teaches, God did not want David to build a temple because his hands were stained with too much blood through warfare. That task would be left to his son and successor, Solomon (7:47), whose Hebrew name *Shlomo* is derived from the word *shalom*, meaning 'peace.'

Stephen's Stinging Indictment (7:51-53)

Though Solomon succeeded in building God a temple, the fact is that God does not dwell in man-made edifices (7:48). He is so big. This was affirmed by the very prophets themselves. Stephen was seeking to address the issue of blasphemy and speaking against the temple, for which he was being tried. It was not that Stephen was 'anti-temple' so 'let's destroy it', but that the God of Israel, the God of the universe, is just too big to fit into this planet, let alone in a temple made with human hands.

To support the teaching of the 'big God' versus a man-made temple, Stephen quotes **Isaiah 66:1**: Heaven is God's throne and the earth His mere footstool. What does it mean for the house you have built God? Where does it stand in such a scenario? Where can He get away and relax or where can people relax in His presence? God's true house is already built and God is the One who built it, not Solomon nor Herod (7:49–50).

Just as Jesus gave a scorching assessment of His opponents days before His arrest (Matthew 23), so Stephen finally launched his indictment: his hypocritical accusers were 'stiff-necked', and though circumcised outwardly, they were uncircumcised inwardly in their hearts and ears. They *always* resisted the Holy Spirit (7:51). They were following in the footsteps of their wayward fathers.

The fathers of Stephen's accusers persecuted the prophets. The question is, was there any prophet that backslidden Israel did *not* persecute (7:52)? If that was not all, they had slain those who showed the coming of the Just One. And, to cap it off, this Sanhedrin had betrayed and murdered the Just One Himself, namely Jesus of Nazareth. This echoed Peter's words in **3:14–15**: *'But ye denied the Holy One and the Just, and desired a murderer to be granted unto you; And killed the Prince of life, whom God hath raised from the dead; whereof we are witnesses.'*

Stephen continued. You received the Law of God by the hand of the angels but you have not and still don't keep it (7:53). These are fighting words and will be the beginning of the end. When Peter spoke strongly in **Acts 3**, he was not murdered (though attempts were made on his life). In Stephen's case, the end of his speech sealed his fate. Under the Roman occupation, the Sanhedrin had no legal right to execute anyone. This is why the condemned Jesus was handed over to the Roman procurator Pontius Pilate for execution. Here they would take matters into their own hands.

Jesus Stands Up for Stephen (7:54–60)

In the natural, things looked very grim. The Sanhedrin was about to mete out 'mob justice'. In a matter of moments, Stephen would become the first recorded Christian martyr – the first of many. He was following in the footsteps of the Master. Remarkably, he conveyed no worry, fear or fretting. We'll get insight into why in a moment.

This is not a happy section. A Godly man was unjustly accused and about to be viciously murdered by, of all things, a religious tribunal. A very tragic incident indeed. Yet, two things should be borne in mind. Since this is part of God's inspired Word, by divine design, why is it part of Scripture? First, note how his opponents react. Is this religiosity gone viral? Second, notice how he responded to his enemies. Third, see how he handled the prospect of death and even his reaction while dying. Finally, remember that since it is part of God's Word, how did this incident help advance the cause of Christ?

After Stephen called them *'stiff-necked'*, *'uncircumcised in heart and ears'*, the children of those who murdered the prophets and the Just One, they were *'cut to the heart'* (7:54). They lost all sense of reason and self-control. They gnashed their teeth as a sign of their intense anger and

Seven: Stephen's Anointed Speech

displeasure. They had gone from being a respectable-looking gathering to a rioting, uncontrollable, 'foaming at the mouth', murderous mob.

While they were experiencing tormenting unrest and uncontrolled fury, Stephen was enjoying glory. He was *'full of the Holy Ghost'* (7:55) as he looked steadfastly into heaven.

Listen to what he saw: the glory of God and Jesus standing at the right hand of God (7:55). Upward of seventeen times in Scripture, it talks about the Chosen One sitting at the right hand of God. Here, however, Jesus is standing instead of sitting. Why is He standing? While the text does not give the reason, we can surmise.

On Graduation Day at the university, the Chancellor sits on the platform. While the Master's degree graduates file past to receive their certificates, the Chancellor remains seated. Yet when it comes time to give out the doctoral certificates, the Chancellor suddenly stands up. Why? This is viewed as an act of honour and respect to those who have joined the 'scholar's club' and can now be called 'Doctor.'

Likewise, Jesus was probably so moved by Stephen's actions and words that He stood up to receive him into glory. The anointing of Stephen's life was obvious: He had an authority that commanded hushed silence from his listeners; his knowledge of God's Word was excellent and put to good use; His boldness and fearlessness were a marvel to behold. Now the anointing of the Spirit was leading Stephen to the Anointed One Himself.

Stephen did not keep this vision to himself. He told the mob that he saw the open heaven and the Son of Man standing at God's right hand (7:56). While to the redeemed, this is the aroma of life, to the impenitent, it is the smell of death (2 Corinthians 2:16).

This unhinged mob could not handle any more glory. Their safe space has truly been invaded, rocked and broken. Life would never be the same again. So as not to hear any more from Stephen, they cried with a loud voice, stopped their ears and ran out to him with one accord (7:57).

Welcome Holy Spirit

They cast Stephen out of the city and stoned him (7:58). They laid their garments at the feet of a young man named Saul who approved of his death. He may have heard Stephen's anointed speech and the good seed of God's gospel was planted in his heart.

As he was being stoned to death, Stephen called upon God in prayer, *'Lord Jesus, receive my spirit.'* Then he kneeled down, cried out in a loud voice so others could hear and prayed a magnanimous one-liner: *'Lord, lay not this sin to their charge'* (7:59–60). After this prayer, *'he fell asleep'.* His body slept but his spirit – filled with the Holy Spirit – went immediately to God. Both of these realities were reflected in his prayers. There are no recorded words of pain, anguish or fear. The Holy Spirit's power gave Stephen the words to speak and the boldness to deliver them.

Psalm 73:24 says, *'Thou shalt guide me with thy counsel, and afterward receive me to glory.'* The Spirit prepared Stephen to look forward and upward, and he was prepared to meet the Master, Who stood up in his honour to receive him. God the Spirit passed on Stephen to God the Son.

> LESSON FOR LIFE: The illegal, unjust stoning of saintly Stephen had two major benefits: Saul got the gospel and Stephen the glory.

---

[40] https://biblehub.com/greek/1577.htmekklesia. Accessed 30 March 2024.

Part Three

Holy Spirit Power

in Judaea and Samaria

CHAPTER EIGHT

Time of Transition

Who: Philip and the Apostles.

What: Preaches in Judaea and Samaria

When: After the death of Stephen

Where: Jerusalem, Judaea and Samaria

Why: To build God's kingdom

How: By the power of the Holy Spirit

> *Then laid they their hands on them, and they received the Holy Ghost.*
> *— Acts 8:17*

The Gospel Spreads (8:1–8)

Transitions – they may not be expected or easy, but they are most necessary to be promoted to the next level. Christ gave a clear commission to preach the gospel to the whole world, starting at Jerusalem. Yet, from chapters two to seven, the church appears to have been 'Jerusalem-bound'. No mission or evangelistic outreaches have been recorded up to now. The salt remained in the shaker.

Yet with the martyrdom of Stephen, a transition was forced upon the homebody church. As Stephen transitioned from earth to heaven, from Spirit anointed to the presence of Jesus, the church, too, would experience a transition. It was time to go from Jerusalem to all of Judaea and Samaria, from the Jews to the Samaritans, and eventually the Gentiles. All were called to repent and believe the gospel of Christ.

Until Stephen, being a Christian in Jerusalem was to earn the esteem of the normal people but contempt of the religious establishment elite. Now the pressure increased and it could cost you your life. Yet it was this pressure from persecution that would facilitate the transition out of Jerusalem and into the nations of the world.

Acts 8 begins with a simple statement: *'And Saul was consenting unto his death'* (8:1). Saul of Tarsus witnessed the mob execution of Stephen. He was more than just an attendant in the open-air cloakroom. Saul consented to his death and perhaps was radicalised by it. Though he did not cast a stone, Saul was complicit in this great sin. As we learn more about this young Pharisee, he will become the bully, abuser and even murderer of members of the early church. He could rightly be called the 'persecutor.' Yet it is equally possible that Saul was also moved by the grace and glory that appeared on Stephen and this planted the seed of repentance and faith in Messiah that he would experience in the very next chapter.

Once the Jewish officials made their move against Stephen and silenced his voice, the ripples spread to the entire Jerusalem-based church. A great persecution broke out against it and the disciples scattered throughout Judaea and Samaria, except for the apostles (8:1).

Devout men paid respect to Stephen by fetching his corpse and bringing it to his burial (which happens soon after death, usually on the same day). As they did so, in true Middle Eastern fashion, they made loud and great lamentation over him (8:2).

Duly emboldened by the slaying of Stephen which he personally witnessed, Saul the cloak-keeper became Saul the religious persecutor. He decided to devote his energies to causing havoc in the church. He entered people's homes, dragged out men and women and threw them into prison (8:3). This is probably why others fled Jerusalem and were

Eight: Time of Transition

scattered everywhere. An energetic Saul would be running after them, all the way to Damascus in the north.

The silver lining in all this heartbreak and dispersal was, as the church spread out of Jerusalem, the church shared the Word of God everywhere (8:4). Of course, they were meant to be doing this from Day One (1:8), but for unexplained reasons, the Jerusalem church, salt of the earth, failed to spread. Now the saltshaker was turned upside down, given a mighty shake and the 'salt of the gospel' spread throughout Judaea, Samaria and the uttermost part of the earth. It took persecution to get their feet on the gospel road.

The apostle Philip went to Samaria to preach Christ (8:5). For pious Jews, this was a no-go zone, but for Christ and the apostles, it was a ripening field (see John 4). 'Samaria' was most likely the city of Sebastia, built by Herod the Great in the 1st century BC. It was constructed on the ruins of the city of Samaria, which had served as the capital of the Northern Kingdom of Israel until 722 BC. This was when the Assyrians deported the ten tribes of Israel (2 Kings 17).

People paid careful attention to what Philip preached; the main reason was that they heard and saw the miracles that he did. These included the casting out of unclean spirits from many people, who shrieked with a loud voice. Those who had palsies and lameness were also healed. No wonder they were so attentive. The result of the ministry of Philip was that there was great joy in that city (8:6–8).

Samaritan Pentecost and Simon the Sorcerer (8:9–24)

Though very much a minor character in Acts, Simon the sorcerer gets a bright spotlight. He practised his sorcery in the city of Samaria. The text says that he 'bewitched'. This means that through magic, he could cast a spell and gain control over another person. It could also mean to enchant and delight an individual. Because of his sorcery, he gave the impression that he was a great man (8:9) with great power. His business also made him very wealthy.

Welcome Holy Spirit

Everyone, great and small, listened to Simon intently and believed that he had great power from God (8:10). Of course, this was not the case at all, but when Philip arrived in Samaria, they would see even greater and more impressive power encounters than anything Simon could cook up.

Simon was highly regarded among the local people in Samaria because he had bewitched them with sorceries for a long time. It appears that this was a long-lasting communal spell (8:11).

Despite this spiritual challenge, Philip the evangelist showed up in Samaria. He powerfully preached about the kingdom of God and the name of Jesus Christ. Backed up by signs and wonders, the Samaritans, male and female, submitted to water baptism (8:12).

Remember that water baptism is a command from the Lord. It is a public testimony that you are identifying with Christ's death, resurrection and Lordship. It is also the official beginning of your life of discipleship. Baptism represents a clean break from one's old life and ways. **Galatians 3:27** states *'For as many of you as have been baptized into Christ have put on Christ'*. If you are a genuine believer but have not yet been water baptised by full immersion, make plans to do so soon. In the **Book of Acts**, people were baptised on the same day as they repented.

Surprise, surprise: Simon the sorcerer himself believed also and was baptised (8:13). He was no 'small fish'. His submission to the gospel may very well have stoked the fires of revival – if the gospel was good enough for Simon, it would be good enough for everyone. Perhaps this is why Luke, led by the Holy Spirit, gives so much attention to this one man.

Simon continued to follow the ministry of Philip and was most impressed with the miracles and signs that were done. When the Jerusalem-based apostles heard that Samaria said yes to the word of God, they sent Peter and John (8:14). While this statement almost comes across as a 'matter of fact', it is very revolutionary. These kosher Jews,

Eight: Time of Transition

who had never been inside a Gentile or Samaritan house, were going to break a long-term cultural taboo by visiting the very region that had been long rejected by their fellow countrymen. Yet the Saviour also had no phobia about Samaria or Samaritans either (Luke 9:51–56, 10:25–37, 17:11–19; John 4:4–9). In **John 4** and **Acts 8**, the Samaritans were much more responsive to the gospel than the Judeans and especially the Jerusalemites. The same receptivity applied to the Gentiles.

> LESSON FOR LIFE: In a spiritually charged world, remember that the power of God via the Holy Spirit will overcome all other sources of power.

Why did Peter and John come from Jerusalem to visit the newly-born Samaritan church? Their purpose was to pray for them to receive the Holy Spirit (8:15). They had already received Jesus as Saviour and Lord; now, the same Spirit baptism the apostles received in **Acts 2** was to be bestowed on Samaritans in **Acts 8**.

Here's a note of clarification: Luke explains that the Holy Spirit had not yet fallen on any of them. The only baptism they had received thus far was baptism in water in the name of the Lord Jesus (8:16). Though there is disagreement between evangelicals and Pentecostals, there is evidence that the Spirit baptism is a separate and subsequent experience to the new birth. Evangelicals generally believe that you are baptised in the Spirit the moment you repent. While you can receive your fullness of the Spirit very quickly after repentance, even within moments, it is still a separate and subsequent event.

The apostles laid hands on the Samaritan believers, and they received the Holy Spirit. 'Laying on of hands' is one of the foundational doctrines of the Christian faith (Hebrews 6:1). Paul longed to get to Rome so he could impart to them some spiritual gift (Romans 1:11) for the purpose of establishment. Such impartation is possible through the laying on of hands, which, when done by Peter and John, resulted in the Samaritans receiving the Holy Spirit (8:17). What God did for them long ago, He will do for you today.

'When Simon saw…' (8:18). This simple statement says a lot. The sorcerer who had made so much money and gained so much 'respect' by doing magic tricks was impressed by what he 'saw' at the laying on of hands. While the text does not say precisely what he saw, chances are it included 'speaking in tongues'. Simon, a rich man, then offered money to the apostles so he could have this same ability to impart the Holy Spirit through the laying on of hands (8:18–19). Just name the price, he said. Simon was setting himself up for a mighty rebuke.

Peter snapped. Let your money perish with you – a very strong statement. It is as if he was saying 'Drop dead' or 'To hell with you, and may your money follow suit'. Anointed people can be frighteningly furious when they are angry (see David in **1 Samuel 25** in the story of Nabal and Abigail; he was dangerously mad). The main point is that the gift of God is too priceless to be purchased with money (8:20).

The rebuke by Peter continued. He declared that Simon had no connection with the ministry of the apostles because his heart was not right before God (8:21).

One of the wonderful things about the Lord is that He does not merely highlight problems – He also offers solutions. Simon needed one very quickly. So, what could he do about his misguided offer? Repent (8:22). He had done it already when he had received Jesus as Saviour and Lord. Now he had to do it again because his heart was not right before God. His repentance was for this wicked notion, and his prayer to God was that his evil thoughts might be forgiven.

One more thing: Peter offered a statement of discernment. While carnal people look at outward appearances, spiritually mature people, like the Lord Himself, look at the heart (1 Samuel 16:7). Peter was getting very good at ministry in the Holy Spirit. He told Simon that he perceived he was in the gall of bitterness and bond of iniquity (8:23). The latter is

Eight: Time of Transition

easy to understand because of his vocation; the former might not have been so obvious on the surface.

What was Simon's response to Peter's rebuke? He took the message seriously and asked for prayer that *'none of these things which ye have spoken come upon me'* (8:24). Though the text does not state the result, it appears that Simon listened to the words of Peter to repent the second time, as he listened to the words of Philip the evangelist to repent the first time. There is always hope for people who listen to the word of the Lord and resolve to change.

> LESSON FOR LIFE: People may and do get seduced by outward appearances, but God and His servants must always focus on the heart.

A Strategic Conversion (8:25–40)

The preaching of the gospel is like scattering seeds. As we learn from the Parable of the Sower, the seed of God's Word is always good, but the ground may vary: some shallow, some rocky, some strewn with thorns, and some as fertile, tilled and ready to grow. The evangelist, Philip, scattered the good seed of the gospel in Samaria – normally off-limits for pious Jews – and soon he will be deployed to the south on the road from Jerusalem to Gaza.

Before returning to Jerusalem, the apostles:

- testified and preached the word of the Lord
- preached the gospel in many villages of Samaria (8:25).

This was a revival and the Lord used the most unlikely vessels, namely Jews, to reach a people that they normally abhorred – the Samaritans. Whether they realised it or not, the current transition was a fulfilment of Christ's commission to be His witnesses in Jerusalem, all Judaea and Samaria. Soon they would be out of the Israelite gate and headed to the uttermost parts of the earth with the glorious gospel of Christ.

Welcome Holy Spirit

Philip was a man on the go. The angel of the Lord sent him on a very strategic mission: He would minister to Africa without stepping foot on the continent. It was time to go south towards the road to Gaza, which was desert (8:26).

Philip, the man of God, obeyed the Lord immediately. '*And he arose and went*' (8:27). As he travelled, he met a man of great authority in the court of Candace, queen of the Ethiopians. He was a eunuch and in charge of her treasury. This man was uniquely placed to influence a famous monarch and her nation. His purpose was to worship at Jerusalem (8:27). Was he an Ethiopian Jew? A proselyte? A God-fearer? We don't know. He appeared to have finished his Jerusalem journey and was returning to Ethiopia. As he returned to his chariot, he took time to read Isaiah the prophet (8:28). He was probably reading from a scroll. So, it is possible that an assistant was doing the driving while he read.

The Holy Spirit spoke to Philip to go near and join himself with the chariot (8:29). Yes, the Person of the Holy Spirit speaks to us. Being Spirit-led is not just an optional extra; it is part and parcel of a God-pleasing, Bible-based, Spirit-filled Christian life. Philip's experience of hearing from the Holy Spirit should be normal for all true believers.

Philip ran towards the chariot and was probably amazed that he heard the Ethiopian reading aloud from **Isaiah 53**. Though they were perfect strangers, Philip, full of boldness from the Holy Spirit, asked the question, '*Do you understand what you are reading* (8:30)?'

The Ethiopian honestly answered that the only way he could understand this inspired passage was if someone guided him. He perceived that Philip could fulfil that role and beckoned to him to come up into the chariot, sit with him (8:31) and explain the passage.

> LESSON FOR LIFE: The Holy Spirit is willing to guide you and even give you the right words to speak at the right time to get the right results.

Eight: Time of Transition

Isaiah 53 is the famous chapter called the 'Suffering Servant' (8:32–33). From a New Testament and Christian viewpoint, it is clear that this passage is talking about the passion of Christ.

Isaiah's prophecy had the attention of the Ethiopian eunuch. He wanted to know if Isaiah was writing about himself or another man (8:34). A good question, and a key to understanding the true nature of Messiah, the coming King. The Holy Spirit couldn't have given a better set-up and opportunity for Philip to preach the gospel to this strategic man at the heart of the Ethiopian court. Starting from this passage, Philip preached Jesus the Messiah (8:35).

The gospel message is Christo-centric: the person and work of Christ. Note that in the New Testament, there are frequent references to Old Testament passages that were fulfilled in Jesus. Remember, the Old Testament was the Bible that Christ, the apostles and the early church read. We owe it to ourselves to learn and appreciate the Old Testament, too.

As they travelled, they came to a place where there was water. Remember, they were on the road to Gaza, which was desert. Finding water was a blessing and a sign of divine provision. The eunuch commented on the availability of water and wanted to know the requirements of baptism (8:36).

Philip replied that if the eunuch believed with all his heart, he was ready to be baptised. His reply was a confession of faith: *'I believe that Jesus Christ is the Son of God'* (8:37). Confession activates faith (Romans 10:9–10).

As soon as Philip heard this confession of faith, he commanded that the chariot stand still. They both went 'down' into the water and Philip baptised the eunuch (8:38). Please note here that the implication is that the eunuch was immersed in the water, not merely sprinkled. As we already learned, the word *baptizo* means 'dip, immerse, submerge, wash'.[41] This can only happen where there is sufficient water. If baptism was merely by sprinkling, then why did John the Baptist go to the Jordan River and baptise people there? He could have easily done it anywhere with a bottle of water. This meaning and mode of water baptism have been a contentious issue in the church for centuries. Again, it is best to go to the text and let it speak for itself while having a charitable attitude towards believers who may hold a different position.

The fellowship between Philip and the Ethiopian eunuch was short-lived. No sooner had they come out of the water than the Holy Spirit caught Philip and carried him away (not unlike Elijah). Though surprised, the eunuch went back to Ethiopia rejoicing (8:39).

Philip ended up in Azotus (8:40), which is Ashdod, a coastal city and seaport in the south of Israel. It was one of the five Philistine cities, along with Ekron, Gath, Gaza and Ashkelon. Philip travelled north on the coastal sector of the Afro-Eurasian highway from Azotus to Joppa and then to Caesarea, where he made his home (21:8). In the next chapter, we will witness an even more strategic salvation.

> LESSON FOR LIFE: The eunuch went back to Ethiopia and his land eventually became a Christian nation. Investing in ministry to a strategic person can help spread the gospel more quickly.

---

[41] G907 - baptizō - Strong's Greek Lexicon (kjv). Blue Letter Bible. Accessed 14 Nov, 2023. https://www.blueletterbible.org/lexicon/g907/kjv/tr/0-1/

CHAPTER NINE
Saul of Tarsus Repents

Who: Saul and Peter

What: Saul repents, Peter helps Lydda and Sharon to repent

When: Early years after the death of Stephen

Where: Damascus, Jerusalem, Lydda and Joppa

Why: To build God's kingdom

How: By the power of the Holy Spirit

> *And Ananias went his way, and entered into the house; and putting his hands on him said, Brother Saul, the Lord, even Jesus, that appeared unto thee in the way as thou camest, hath sent me, that thou mightest receive thy sight, and be filled with the Holy Ghost* — **Acts 9:17**

> *But all that heard him were amazed, and said; Is not this he that destroyed them which called on this name in Jerusalem, and came hither for that intent, that he might bring them bound unto the chief priests? 22. But Saul increased the more in strength, and confounded the Jews which dwelt at Damascus, proving that this is very Christ*
> — **Acts 9:21-22**

If we understand the salvation of the Ethiopian eunuch was timely and strategic, leading to the Christianisation of an entire nation, what are we to make of the events of this chapter and the transformation of Saul of Tarsus?[42] Was this strategic?

Short answer: Yes. He went from being a furious and relentless adversary of the early church to its greatest advocate. His legacy is still paying rich dividends daily two millennia later. This includes the Christianisation of a continent and being the human author of half of the New Testament.

The strategic event of this chapter does raise some important questions. Did Saul of Tarsus experience a conversion or did he just repent? Did he become a Christian or was he still Jewish? Did he change his religion after **Acts 9**? How did he view his meeting and reconciling with the Messiah? These questions are not just academic: they go to the heart of the Abrahamic covenant, the call of Israel, the plan of salvation, the nature of the church and the 'peoplehood of God'.

While we don't have the space to go into great depth about these questions, we take a position, here and now, that Saul did not 'convert' and become a 'Christian'. This term only appears three times in the New Testament, and its first appearance is in **Acts 11:26**.[43] He continued to be from the stock of Israel, the tribe of Benjamin, a Hebrew of the Hebrews and a card-carrying Pharisee (Acts 23:6; Philippians 3:5). He did not cease to be a Jew and become a Gentile. Yet he also appeared willing to turn his back on everything, including his identity and heritage, if he could take hold of Christ and be found in Him (Philippians 3:7–8). Furthermore, his calling to evangelise the Gentile world, while remaining a Jew, represented the reconciliation of both people into 'one new man' with the wall of separation torn down in Christ (Ephesians 2:15).

The Road to Repentance (9:1–9)

While the church was growing, Saul was fuming. As an eyewitness to the martyrdom of Stephen, he became a radicalised zealot. Saul was so full of religious hatred that he couldn't even breathe without threatening

Nine: Saul of Tarsus Repents

the disciples of the Lord with slaughter. Determined to destroy the early church, Saul went to the high priest (9:1) to aid him in his menacing mission.

What did Saul want from the high priest? Letters to the synagogues of Damascus. If there were any believers in Messiah, known as 'this way', whether they were male or female, young or old, he would have priestly authority to arrest them and bring them to Jerusalem (9:2). This was serious: believing in the Messiahship of Jesus of Nazareth was worth imprisonment and even death in the eyes of the religious elite. But why the surprise? They had murdered Jesus and Stephen in that same religious spirit and believed they were doing God's service.

The distance from Jerusalem to Damascus is two hundred and eighteen kilometres (one hundred and thirty-six miles). Unlike today, the road between Syria and Israel was open. As Saul approached the city, a bright light from heaven shone around him (9:3).

He fell off his donkey due to the brightness of the light. As he did, a voice asked him, *'Saul, Saul, why are you persecuting Me'* (9:4, NKJV). This would have been a most unsettling experience.

The voice behind the bright light was about to identify Himself. Saul got to the point: *'Who are you, Lord?'* *'I am Jesus, Whom you are persecuting'* (9:5, NKJV) was the reply. To persecute believers, who are the body of Christ, is the same as persecuting the Lord Himself and the punishment is great, if not repented of before.

The Lord uses the phrase that it is hard for Paul to kick against the pricks (or goads). A goad is pointed metal on the end of a stick. It helps goad the ox to keep going forward. To resist the goad is useless and will incur more injury. By resisting the gospel and fighting the church, Saul was attracting more injury to himself. Resistance was in vain.

Saul asked a leading question in light of meeting Christ: *'What do you want me to do?* (9:5, NKJV)' The reply: Arise, go into the city and receive further instructions (9:6).

Welcome Holy Spirit

What was the response of Saul's companions to this celestial experience? They were terrified and speechless (9:7); they heard a voice but saw no one.

When Paul got up from the ground, he was temporarily blind. So, his companions led him into the city by hand (9:8). In **John 9:39**, we read, *'And Jesus said, "For judgment I am come into this world, that they which see not might see; and that they which see might be made blind."'* Here is a perfect example: while Saul could *see*, he was *blind* to Christ and the gospel and still steeped in sin. Then, when *blinded* by the bright heavenly light of Christ, Saul could *see* Jesus and the truth and was *blinded* to the sins of the world.

Damascus is the world's oldest continually occupied city. It is wonderfully located on two rivers and is a beautiful metropolis and oasis in the desert. However, Saul would not be doing sightseeing in Damascus since he couldn't see at all. At the house, he was three days without his sight. He could not (or would not) eat or drink (9:9). This would give him sufficient time to process the fact that God had called him to repentance.

> LESSON FOR LIFE: The first step on Saul's road to global impact and historic significance was the needful act of repentance. The rest is history.

A Man Named Ananias (9:10–18)

Divine appearances are a great blessing but also entail great responsibility; they can also be unnerving to the beholder. Saul received an appearance that resulted in his world-changing apostolic call. Here, Ananias, a local believer in Damascus, would meet with Jesus and appropriately respond, *'Behold, here I am'* (9:10). That's how we should all answer when God calls.

The Lord's instructions were clear and concise: arise, go to Straight Street, ask for the house of Judas. Inside is Saul of Tarsus who is praying

Nine: Saul of Tarsus Repents

(9:11). Saul has seen you in a vision coming in and putting his hands on his eyes so that he might regain his sight (9:12).

Understandably, Saul of Tarsus had a bad reputation among Messiah's followers, so it is not surprising that Ananias would hesitate. He told the Lord that he heard many things about this (evil) man, who had been the direct source of much suffering to the saints in Jerusalem (9:13). Ananias was well aware of why Saul had come to Damascus: he had the authority to bind all who call on Christ's name (9:14). The implication: how shall we go and bless such a man as this?

The Lord was firm: Ananias, go your way and do as I say. Saul of Tarsus is a chosen vessel of mine. He will bear my name before the Gentiles, kings and the children of Israel (9:15). On top of his ministry call, I will show him how great things he must suffer for My Name's sake (9:16). In one sense, Saul was such a tough man that he had to soften through the 'marinade of suffering'. Another thing is that he caused so much suffering to the church that he would reap what he sowed for the glory of God and the expansion of His kingdom.

> LESSON FOR LIFE: The repentance and call of Saul of Tarsus is one of the great mysteries of Scripture: how a full-time enemy of the early church became its greatest asset and promoter.

Ananias wisely obeyed the command of the Lord, went to Judas' house at Straight Street and met with Saul. His simple message: Brother Saul, the Lord Jesus who appeared to you has sent me. The purpose is so you can see again and be filled with the Holy Spirit (9:17).

No sooner had Ananias uttered the words than scales fell off Saul's eyes and he received his sight. Immediately, he rose up and was baptised (9:18). No time was wasted in fulfilling this fundamental and initial command of the Lord after repentance and faith.

Welcome Holy Spirit

From Damascus to Jerusalem (9:19–31)

After Paul broke his fast and ate, he was strengthened. Then he stayed with the disciples in Damascus (9:19) and was given a crash course on Christian discipleship. Did he also receive the baptism in the Holy Spirit? The text does not directly confirm but the following account of Paul's bold ministerial activism leaves no doubt. The Spirit baptism, along with water baptism, was so normal in the early church that it probably did not seem necessary to mention it on every occasion.

His life-changing encounter with Jesus on the Damascus road and the miraculous healing of his sight transferred his anti-Christian zealotry into zeal for the gospel. Saul boldly went to the synagogues of Damascus to proclaim Jesus as the Son of God (9:20).

Everyone who heard Paul preach was stunned. Wasn't this the same man who tried to destroy believers in Jerusalem who called on this Name? Didn't he come to Damascus to bring the local believers in chains back to Jerusalem and the high priest (9:21)? Saul's reputation had certainly preceded him.

Despite the puzzlement, Saul increased in strength and energy and confounded the local Jewish community in Damascus. He set out to prove that the Jesus he once despised was truly the Messiah, Son of David (9:22). *'A wise man is strong; yea, a man of knowledge increaseth strength'*, as it says in **Proverbs 24:5**. Saul of Tarsus made the wisest decision of his life to say 'Yes' to Jesus the Messiah and he became strong to the point of being unstoppable.

> LESSON FOR LIFE: Baptism in the Spirit gives boldness and strength to do the work of the ministry, short-, medium- and long-term.

Saul of Tarsus' message was irrefutable when it came to preaching Jesus and laying out the case of His 'Messiahship'. He was pungent and persistent in his mission. This was all too much for the local Jews in

Nine: Saul of Tarsus Repents

Damascus, especially since he was a radically different man from the one they had expected. So, they took counsel on how and when to kill him (9:23). They mistakenly reasoned that if you kill the messenger, you silence the message. No way. Besides, their blindness was of such a nature that they had not considered the consequences of killing an innocent man (Exodus 20:13).

Fortunately, Saul was informed of their plot to murder him. They stood positioned by the gates of Damascus day and night so that as soon as he walked through, they would kill him (9:24). Yet, like the Master Himself (Luke 4:30; John 8:59, 10:39), Saul had a 'Houdini-like escape', because his 'time had not yet come'. God had history-making work for him to do and premature death could delay it. So, the disciples took him in the night-time and let him down the wall in a basket (9:25). Paul writes about this very incident in **2 Corinthians 11:32–33**: *'In Damascus the governor under Aretas the king kept the city of the Damascenes with a garrison, desirous to apprehend me: And through a window in a basket was I let down by the wall, and escaped his hands.'* Aretas is probably the one whose burial monument (tomb), known popularly as the iconic Treasury, is at Petra in Jordan, which is recognised worldwide.

Once he arrived in Jerusalem, Saul tried to join himself with the disciples. They could not believe that this enemy of the church had now become one of them (9:26). Jerusalem was the same, but Paul was not. He had been transformed by repentance of sin, faith in Messiah and infilling of the Holy Spirit. They would soon see this for themselves.

Joses, known as Barnabas, meaning 'son of encouragement', would be a great blessing to Saul and John Mark. He advocated for Saul among the leaders of the Jerusalem church. He affirmed that Saul saw Jesus on the Damascus road, received a word from Him and then preached boldly in His Name in Damascus (9:27). Thanks to Barnabas' intervention, Saul of Tarsus was brought into fellowship with the church at Jerusalem. He freely went in and out and did his ministry (9:28).

Welcome Holy Spirit

Now that Saul had been received by the Jerusalem church, he boldly pursued his preaching and apologetic ministry. Yet his hands-on, upfront, 'in your face' approach would stir up more trouble in Jerusalem than it did in Damascus. He got into disputes with the Grecians or Hellenists, who loved to philosophise and debate. However, these Jerusalem Hellenists (Greek-speaking Jews) were threatened and intolerant. They discussed ways in which they could slay Saul (9:29).

When the early church in Jerusalem heard that Saul was under threat, they decided that the safest course of action was to get him out of the city (9:30). After all, Jerusalem was known for killing prophets, the Messiah Himself and a saint called Stephen. The Holy City could be simultaneously hot-tempered and stone-hearted. So, Saul was quickly sent to the port of Caesarea on the Mediterranean coast where the Roman governor resided, and then he sailed to his home city of Tarsus.

Chances are Saul remained in obscurity at Tarsus for about a decade until the time Barnabas fetched him to assist with the revival happening in Antioch (Acts 11:25–26). For all his strength in body and spirit, Saul was a man under authority who worked with the brethren rather than live and minister with an independent spirit.

Jonah was tossed into the sea during the great storm (Jonah 1:12–15). Paul was sent back to Tarsus due to the civil storm his presence caused in Jerusalem. Remarkably, the results were the same: peace. After Saul was shipped out of the country, then the churches had rest throughout all of Judaea, Samaria and Galilee. They were built up, walked in the fear of the Lord, the comfort of the Holy Spirit and were multiplied (9:31). It almost appears that Saul was a liability to the church and its growth; if that were the case, his sabbatical in Tarsus may have help straighten him out. He had energetic zeal; now he needed the wisdom to become effective and fruit-bearing. No doubt, he learned his lessons.

Nine: Saul of Tarsus Repents

Strategic Miracles in Lydda and Joppa (9:32–43)

With Saul safely tucked away in his native Tarsus, the apostolic spotlight returned to Peter. He *'passed throughout all quarters'* until he came to the saints at Lydda (9:32). Lydda is where St George, the patron saint of England, was martyred in 303 AD. Known as Lod in Hebrew, Lydda is on the *Shephelah* (meaning lowlands) near the intersection of the Jerusalem–Joppa road and the Afro-Eurasian highway. Today it's the location of the international airport, just as it hosted the airport in the British mandate period. Peter 'went down' from Jerusalem to Lydda because it is a steep descent on the Judaean mountains. His purpose was to visit the saints there.

At Lydda dwelt Aeneas, bedridden for eight years and sick from palsy (9:33). Without hesitation, Peter declared to him, *'Aeneas, Jesus Christ maketh thee whole: arise, and make thy bed.'* And he arose immediately' (9:34). No sooner had the word come out of his mouth that Aeneas rose immediately and was completely healed.

Just as the conversion of the Ethiopian eunuch was a strategic act of evangelism, so was the healing of Aeneas. Due to the location of Lydda, word of Aeneas' healing spread rapidly through the city and the plain of Sharon area (9:35), which included Caesarea. Many turned to Christ because of this miracle. The Greek word for 'turn' is *epistrepho*, used thirty-nine times in the New Testament, defined as 'turn', 'return', and 'convert'.[44] By extension, 'repentance' means 'to turn', 'willing to change', and 'sorry enough to quit'.

While the church at Lydda rejoiced at the healing of Aeneas, the saints in nearby Joppa were in crisis. A disciple named Dorcas (or Tabitha) lived in this seaport city, also known as Jaffa. It was here that Jonah boarded the ship to sail to Tarshish to flee from the presence of the Lord (Jonah 1:3). Dorcas did many good works and alms deeds (9:36). These things, of course, do not save you but once saved, out of love for God and others, you are motivated to do good works. Unfortunately, Dorcas got sick and died (9:37) and this plunged the Joppa church into mourning. As is the custom, her body was washed and they laid her in the upper chamber.

Acts 9:38 says, *'As Lydda was nigh to Joppa'*. To be precise, Lydda was eighteen kilometres (eleven miles) from Joppa. The Joppa disciples heard that Peter was at Lydda. In this 'state of emergency', two men were dispatched to Peter to ask him to come to Joppa immediately (9:38). This was possibly Peter's first-ever visit to this coastal city.

Peter arose immediately and went with the men to Joppa. Upon arrival, they brought him to the upper chamber where the body of Dorcas lay. The widows, who stood by and wept, showed Peter the coats and garments she had made. Note the phrase, *'while she was with them'* (9:39). The body of Dorcas was still with them but Dorcas the person was not. This is because, Biblically speaking, the real 'you' is not the physical body: it is your invisible soul and spirit. At death, these separate from the body, thus rendering it 'dead' (James 2:26).

Peter made everyone leave the room. All the weeping, though understandable, was also a distraction. He then knelt to pray. Turning to the body, he said a simple command: *'Tabitha, arise'* (9:40). She opened her eyes, looked at Peter and sat up. Peter took her by the hand, lifted her up, called on the saints and presented her to them fully alive (9:41). Imagine the excitement this caused.

The news that Dorcas had been raised from the dead was quickly known throughout all of Joppa and beyond. The result? *'Many believed in the Lord'* (9:42). Peter decided to sojourn in Joppa for *'many days'* (9:43). His host was Simon the Tanner, whose house was by the sea. The Holy Spirit was preparing an even greater mission for Peter, which will be revealed in the next chapter. The best was yet to come.

Nine: Saul of Tarsus Repents

[42] Saul of Tarsus was his legal Hebrew name and Paul his Roman name. The latter does not come into common usage until he begins his missionary journeys in **Acts 13**.

[43] The term 'Christian' appears to have come into common usage at the latter end of the New Testament period and was applied to all followers of Messiah, Jew or Gentile. This is a legitimate thing; nevertheless, it is unlikely that Saul and the very early church, which was one hundred percent Jewish for its first few years, called themselves 'Christians'.

[44] G1994 - epistrephō - Strong's Greek Lexicon (kjv). Blue Letter Bible. Accessed 17 Nov, 2023. https://www.blueletterbible.org/lexicon/g1994/kjv/tr/0-1/

CHAPTER TEN

Gentile Pentecost

Who: Peter and Cornelius

What: Start of the Gentile mission

When: Early years of the Church after Peter left Jerusalem

Where: Joppa and Caesarea

Why: Fulfilment of Genesis 12:3

How: By the power of the Holy Spirit

> *While Peter yet spake these words, the Holy Ghost fell on all them which heard the word. And they of the circumcision which believed were astonished, as many as came with Peter, because that on the Gentiles also was poured out the gift of the Holy Ghost. For they heard them speak with tongues, and magnify God.*
> —*Acts 10:44–46*

Introducing Cornelius and Caesarea (10:1–8)

We are about to witness a revolution. It started with one man, Jesus of Nazareth, and grew, with an abundance of supernatural help, into a mighty army. In the last chapter, we saw the effects of the glorious gospel and the infilling of the Holy Spirit in the life of one man, Saul of Tarsus.

In this chapter, we will see the revolution go to another level and all of this was according to God's foreordained will. It should be abundantly clear that the great commission of Christ, found in **Matthew**

Welcome Holy Spirit

28:19–20, Mark 16:15–20, Luke 24:46–49 and **Acts 1:8**, was part of God's plan to include Gentiles in the coming Messianic kingdom. However, the mother church, which was Jewish, just didn't seem to get it. They stayed in the 'Jerusalem salt shaker' until persecution broke out after the martyrdom of Stephen. By all appearances, they were in no hurry to evangelise the Gentiles, let alone add them to their numbers.

This chapter shows how God personally intervened to get no one less than Peter himself to be the chosen vessel to bring good news to the Gentiles, not in Jerusalem but in a highly heathen Gentile city and Gentile home with unkosher Gentile food. The Jewish people had waited centuries for the promise of the Spirit to be poured out (Joel 2:28-32); yet the same experience will happen to the Gentiles in a matter of moments.

Introducing Caesarea (10:1): Caesarea was the Roman administrative capital of first-century Israel. Built by Herod the Great in the 1st century BC, it was an ancient technological marvel. Its location was on the Plain of Sharon at a place called Strato's Tower. Despite its idyllic-sounding connotation ('the rose of Sharon'), the plain was sparsely inhabited during the Old Testament period. This was due to sand-choked harbours, a lack of fresh water, haunted oak forests and poor roads.

Herod performed engineering miracles; he dredged the sand out of the harbour, built solid roads to the site and piped water via aqueducts from Mount Carmel twenty kilometres (twelve and a half miles) to the north. He succeeded in building a major metropolis where only a puny sleepy fishing village had once existed.

Naming the city after his patron, Caesar, Herod's Caesarea was like a miniature Rome on the Mediterranean coast. Its infrastructure included an amphitheatre, a hippodrome and Roman temples. In this pagan milieu, God was going to let the light of the gospel and the power of the Holy Spirit shine forth.

Introducing Cornelius (10:1): Cornelius was a centurion from the Italian battalion and he lived in the city. Cornelius was a God-fearer; the

Ten: Gentile Pentecost

implication is that he and his household were more interested in the God of Israel than in the Roman gods. He was devout, gave alms and prayed to God always (10:2), which is a good start. Yet he still needed the gift of salvation that Jesus Christ gives. Before he could receive it, someone would have to tell him about it (Romans 10:14–15).

Around 3 pm (the ninth hour), he saw a vision from God of an angel approaching and calling him by name (10:3). Cornelius was understandably terrified by the appearance of the angel. He asked, '*What is it, Lord?*' The remarkable response: Your prayers and almsgiving have come up as a memorial before God (10:4).

Here is a principle to remember: when you seek God, you will find Him. When you draw closer to Him, He will draw closer to you (James 4:8). Moreover, God takes note of sincere, heartfelt prayer and benevolently motivated charity. These things do not save you, but they bring you closer to God and better position you to hear the good news. We are saved by grace through faith; it is a gift of God, not of works (Ephesians 2:8-9).

Since the prayers and alms had been remembered by God, Cornelius was commanded to send to Joppa and fetch Simon Peter (10:5). He would not be hard to find. He was dwelling at the home of Simon the Tanner, whose house was by the seaside. Peter would tell Cornelius what he ought to do (10:6). To get saved, someone has to give you the word of life with the help of the Holy Spirit.

As a wise God-fearer, Cornelius did not waste any time. As soon as the angel departed, he called two household servants, plus a devout soldier who worked among those who served Cornelius continually. After sharing the vision, this party of three were dispatched to Joppa to fetch Peter (10:7–8).

Vision from Heaven (10:9–16)

Vision is one of the results of the Spirit-infilling. Joel prophesied it (Joel 2:28; Acts 2:17) and **Acts 10** affirms it. The empowerment of the Spirit makes a person far more sensitive to the spiritual realm. When coupled with the spiritual discipline of fasting, our spiritual antennae are greatly extended. Peter was about to experience that very thing.

Peter went to the rooftop of Simon's house around noon because he wanted to pray (10:9). He probably was fasting, too. This was the day after Cornelius had had his vision and had sent the three men to Joppa from Caesarea. The men came close to Joppa at the time Peter was praying. The Holy Spirit was preparing Peter to receive them, just as He had prepared Cornelius the day before.

Peter became very hungry and decided to break his fast. He requested food and his hosts went to prepare it. While they were going to the kitchen, Peter fell into a trance (10:10). It is as if his spirit became a movie screen and he saw a vision that would transform him and the world.

In the trance, Peter saw heaven open and a vessel, specifically, a big sheet knit at the four corners, descending to the earth (10:11). Inside the sheet were all kinds of four-footed and wild beasts. In addition, there were fowls of the air and creeping things on earth (10:12). The verse does not elaborate but as we see in verse 14, the implication is that some or all of these creatures were considered by pious Jews to be unclean meat.

The voice from heaven told Peter to rise, kill and eat (10:13). Unlike Cornelius, who was instantly compliant, Peter hesitated to obey the heavenly command. Even though he was very hungry, he did not want to defile himself with unclean food (10:14). Though Peter acknowledged it was the Lord, he couldn't bring himself to change his diet.

The voice spoke to him the second time. What God has made holy, don't call otherwise (10:15). This happened three times and after each episode, the sheet was taken back into heaven (10:16).

'Kosher Peter' Accepts the Gentile Invitation (10:17–23)

Ten: Gentile Pentecost

Peter was still processing what this unusual vision meant when the delegation from Caesarea arrived. They had inquired and been told where Simon's house was and now stood at the gate. The three men asked if Simon was present in the house (10:17–18).

Peter was still meditating on the vision of the sheet and unclean animals – whom God had made clean. The Holy Spirit spoke to him that three men were seeking him. He was to arise, go downstairs and go where they went. The Spirit had sent them. Therefore, do not doubt (10:19–20). **Note**: we learned that the Holy Spirit is a divine person, not an impersonal wind, thing or 'it'. He has personality, can act, react, speak, think and possesses all the other aspects of personhood. Answered prayer, Christian growth, breakthrough and transformation can and will occur when we welcome the Holy Spirit into our hearts.

Thankfully, Peter obeyed the Spirit. He went down to Cornelius' men and affirmed that he was the one whom they sought. Then he asked them the reason for their coming (10:21).

Cornelius' call (10:22): They spoke highly of their master Cornelius. He was described as a just man, a God-fearer and an exceptional individual with a good reputation among the Jewish people. He was warned by God's angel to send for Peter and bring him into his house. Peter was expected to have a word from God for them.

Peter invited these Gentile men to spend the night at Simon the Tanner's house. It possibly was the first night in his life that Peter had slept under the same roof as Gentiles. What was unthinkable a short time ago was now made gloriously possible by the Holy Spirit. The next day, Peter, the three men and some of the brethren from Joppa accompanied them on the journey to Caesarea (10:23).

'Kosher Peter' at Gentile Cornelius' Home (10:24–35)

What we are about to witness would have been unthinkable a few days earlier. 'Kosher Peter,' who grew up in the mixed Jew and Gentile city of Bethsaida on the northeastern shore of the Sea of Galilee, was about to

Welcome Holy Spirit

do something unprecedented: enter a Gentile home and eat there. A great taboo was about to be broken. The ramifications of this would change God's relationship with humanity and from one people group to another.

The Gentile in question was Cornelius the Roman centurion. Peter had journeyed fifty-three kilometres (thirty-three miles) from coastal Joppa in the south to coastal Caesarea in the north. While awaiting Peter's arrival, in faith, Cornelius had gathered the clan and friends (10:24). They appeared to have every confidence that their guest would arrive. He did. No sooner had Peter walked into the house when Cornelius came, fell at his feet and began to worship him (10:25). Momentarily stunned at this misplaced act of respect, Peter lifted him up and said, *'Stand up; I myself also am a man'* (10:26).

Worship Christ

Peter was right in telling Cornelius not to worship him because he was only a man. Yet there is a Man who did receive worship because he was not just a man; He is the Son of God. Worship belongs to God. Yet, note that when people offered worship to the Son of Man, Son of God, Jesus Christ, He did not reject it.

Here are some Biblical examples of the appropriateness of worshipping the Son of God and the Son of Man:

- **Matthew 4:10; Luke 4:8:** Jesus says that worship belongs to the Lord our God, and Him only shall we serve. So how does He respond to worship directed at Him and what does that say about His identity and divinity?

- **Matthew 2:2, 11**: The wise men fell down and worshipped the very young Jesus (obviously, a toddler could not competently reject such a gesture, but his parents did not, either).

- **Matthew 8:2**: The leper worshipped Him and said if He was willing, he would be made clean. Christ was willing.

Ten: Gentile Pentecost

- **Matthew 9:18:** A certain ruler (Jairus) worshipped and said that his dying daughter would be healed by the laying on of his hands.

- **Matthew 14:33**: The disciples worshipped the One who calmed the storm on the lake.

- **Matthew 15:25**: The Syro-Phoenician woman worshipped the One who could heal her daughter of the evil spirit.

- **Matthew 28:9, 17**: They worshipped the risen Christ.

- **Mark 5:6**: The Gadarene demoniac worshipped Christ even before his deliverance.

- **Luke 24:52**: The disciples worshipped the risen Christ.

- **John 9:38**: The blind man who was healed at the Pool of Siloam believed and worshipped him.

- **John 20:28**: Doubting Thomas worshipped Christ after touching His hands and side; he exclaimed *'My Lord and my God'*.

- **Revelation 5:14**: The twenty-four elders and four beasts worshipped Him that lives forever and ever.

- **John 4:21–24, 10:30:** Jesus speaks of worship being directed to God and the Father. He did not ask for worship to be directed at Him but neither did He refuse it. That's because, as He proclaimed, *'I and My Father are one'*.

After meeting Cornelius at the door, Peter was astounded that many people were gathered inside (10:27). What was first called the 'Cornelius' party' would soon become the 'Holy Spirit and Peter's'.

What seemed like a simple statement was actually highlighting a revolution. Peter reiterated Jewish tradition that it was unlawful for a Jew to keep company or visit the home of a Gentile. There appears to be no cross-references to this in the Old Testament, but **John 4:9** says the Jews had no dealings with Samaritans and in **John 18:28**, the Jewish elders, after bringing Jesus to Pilate's judgement hall, would not enter in themselves lest they be defiled for the Passover. It may have been a rabbinic interpretation of clean and unclean meats applied to Gentiles.

Though Peter came from Bethsaida, a fishing village with a Gentile population on the Sea of Galilee, he apparently had never entered a Gentile home, even that of his neighbours over the fence, until the day he entered Cornelius' house. It took a vision from heaven and the prompting – even prodding – of the Holy Spirit to get him to do the unthinkable for the sake of the gospel. When he said, *'God hath shewed me that I should not call any man common or unclean'* (10:28), he was referring to the sheet vision. Thus, the promise to Abraham in **Genesis 22:18** that all the nations of the earth would be blessed through Abraham's seed, was coming to pass.

Because God spoke to Peter so profoundly by word and vision, he accepted Cornelius' invitation immediately. Then the apostle asked why he was called; he wanted to hear it from the mouth of his host (10:29).

In response to Peter's question, Cornelius prepared his answer. Four days had passed since he had had his vision. He was fasting that day and began to pray at 3 pm (the ninth hour). As he did, a man stood by him in bright clothing (10:30). If you want to draw near to God or get prompt answers, try fasting (provided you are healthy enough). Why do people fast? Because it works! One of the reasons the Korean church grew from single digits to around thirty-five per cent of the population in a little over a generation, plus hosting some of the largest congregations in the world, is because of their commitment to ongoing prayer and fasting.

Back to Cornelius and the angel. The man in white announced that his prayers were heard, and his alms were remembered before God (10:31). Because of this divine favour, he instructed the centurion to send for Simon Peter, 'who is staying at the house of Simon the Tanner whose house is by the seaside. When Peter comes to you, he will have a word from God (10:32)

Ten: Gentile Pentecost

Cornelius did not waste time; he sent for Peter immediately. The apostle did the right thing by coming to Caesarea, despite his initial misgivings. Now he had an eager and hungry audience including Cornelius, his family and guests. Seated in the presence of God, they were ultra-attentive to hear everything that God commanded Peter to speak (10:33).

The apostle was greatly moved by what he heard and experienced. He already was a changed man. Peter then reiterated a profound Biblical truth: God is no respecter of persons – in other words, He does not play favourites (10:34). As one person put it, God does not respect persons, but He does respect conditions. Fulfil His conditions, and be you Jew or Gentile, male or female, young or old, He will bless you in return. *Obedience positions you for divine blessing.* Then Peter made a profound and magnanimous declaration: in every nation, those who fear Him (like Cornelius) and do what is right are accepted of Him (10:35). Now that the wall of partition between Jew and Gentile was falling, Peter could afford to see and be part of what was God's plan all along: that through Abraham and his 'seed' (Galatians 3:16 states that Jesus Christ is the 'seed' of Abraham), all nations of the earth shall be blessed.

A Sermon for the Gentiles (10:36–43)

Though speaking to Gentiles in a very Gentile, heathen city like Caesarea, Peter told them the message given to the children of Israel: peace by Jesus Christ, who is Lord of all (10:36). As Isaiah had prophesied, the coming king is known as the Prince of Peace (also 'the mighty God' and 'Everlasting Father' in Isaiah 9:6). This Word of Peace through Jesus was published throughout all Judaea, but first began in Galilee, after the baptism of John was preached (10:37). Galilee, in the north of the country, of course, is where Jesus grew up and was the main stage of His ministry.

The word is amplified. God anointed Jesus of Nazareth with the Holy Spirit and power. As a righteous man, He went about doing good and healing all who were oppressed by the devil, because God was with him

Welcome Holy Spirit

(10:38). To seal his credibility, Peter affirmed this testimony as a first-hand witness. The apostle saw everything Christ did in the 'land of the Jews' (Judaea) and Jerusalem. They slew Him by hanging on a tree (10:39). **Deuteronomy 21:23** tells us *'for he that is hanged (on a tree) is accursed of God'*.

Jesus' death was not the end of the story. God raised Him back to life on the third day. The risen Christ was openly manifested (10:40). Yes, Jesus Christ, crucified and raised to life, was witnessed, but not by all the people. Those who witnessed the resurrected Christ were chosen ahead of time by God (10:41). That included the apostles, who ate and drank with Him after His resurrection.

God commanded the Church to preach to the people and testify that Jesus, the risen Christ, was ordained of God to be the judge of the living and the dead (10:42). Not only did the apostles witness Christ, but so did the prophets who went before them. They testified that in His Name, all who believe in Him would receive remission of sins (10:43). Yes, sin is forgiven and cleansed, not by good works that we *do* but by what Christ has *done* on the cross.

> LESSON FOR LIFE: Peter's sermon to Cornelius affirms that Jesus will either be your Saviour or your Judge – the choice is yours.

Gentile Pentecost (10:44–48)

After giving a simple gospel message, what happened next shocked even Peter himself. Remember that they are in Caesarea, a heathen city and not Jerusalem, the holy city. What holy people in the holy city waited centuries for, mere Gentiles in a heathen city received within minutes. Without an appeal, an altar call or filling out a decision card (nothing wrong with these things, though), while Peter still spoke, the Holy Spirit 'fell' on Cornelius and those in his house (10:44).

Remember, even Jesus' own apostles had to wait for ten days after Christ's ascension to be baptised in the Spirit. Cornelius' house received

Ten: Gentile Pentecost

it immediately. The last shall be first and the first last. **Luke 10:23–24** says,

> *And he turned him unto his disciples, and said privately, "Blessed are the eyes which see the things that ye see: For I tell you, that many prophets and kings have desired to see those things which ye see, and have not seen them; and to hear those things which ye hear, and have not heard them.'*

'They of the circumcision which believed' is a reference to Jewish believers, what we now call 'Messianic Jews'. These Messianics were astonished – all of them. Why? Because the once 'unclean' Gentiles received the same gift of the Holy Spirit as they had (10:45), and in a fraction of the time.

How did the Messianic Jews who accompanied Peter know that the Gentiles had received the Holy Spirit? Good question. The Holy Spirit is invisible and the work He does begins in the heart. So how will you know? One way to put it is that the Spirit of God is big and powerful; thus, if He comes into your life in fullness and power, it is impossible to hide it. He doesn't enter your life through some rear door and sit quietly in the back row. When He comes, there will be a manifestation.

What can that be? It says that the Jewish believers heard the Gentiles speaking in tongues and magnifying God (10:46). This was the same manifestation the Jewish believers had on the day of Pentecost (Acts 2:4). It is the same manifestation the Ephesian disciples would also have (Acts 19:6). Though the text does not explicitly state this, there is a strong possibility that this was the same manifestation found among the Samaritan disciples (Acts 8:17–18), and also Saul of Tarsus (Acts 9:17–18; 1 Corinthians 14:18).

Speaking in tongues was the sign the apostles received themselves that they were filled with the Spirit, it was the sign they saw in others and no other consistent sign was expected or offered. Of course, there are other types of evidence of a person being filled with the Spirit, but this is the one that happens immediately and consistently. Please don't make your theology based on your experience – or lack of it – but on what the Word says. **Acts 2:4** says they were all filled and they all spoke in other tongues. God does not play favourites. What He does for others, He will do for you. Remember **Psalm 81:10:** '*... open your mouth wide, and I will fill it.*' That is the key.

Since these Gentiles received favour from God because of their hunger, humility and faith, and this was manifested by the outpouring of the Holy Spirit, it was time to 'seal the deal' by having them water baptised (10:47). It was obvious to the Jewish believers that the Gentiles had received the Holy Spirit in the same manner that they had and it would be wrong to deny them further induction. While we would think that the proper order of events is repentance, faith, water baptism and Holy Spirit baptism, God can change the order, as He did here. Yet note that water baptism followed immediately after conversion and the Holy Spirit baptism.

> LESSON FOR LIFE: Like the wind, born-again, Spirit-filled Christians must go where the Spirit leads, not where flesh and tradition dictate.

No one could come up with a good reason why the Gentiles should not be baptised, so Peter ordered that they be baptised immediately – and they were. Gentile Pentecost had come and, like an Australian bushfire, spread rapidly all over the ancient world. Its growth in the modern world since 1901 has ushered in the greatest revival the world has ever seen.

Peter was asked to stay on in Caesarea, which he did (10:48). However, he would face stiff questioning when he returned to the Jewish church in Jerusalem. We will get a taste of this in the next chapter.

CHAPTER ELEVEN
Revival at Antioch
(and the Birth of 'Christianity')

Who: Peter and Barnabas

What: Explains Caesarea event, reaches out northward

When: After Gentile Pentecost at Caesarea

Where: Jerusalem and Antioch

Why: Fulfilment of Acts 1:8

How: By the power of the Holy Spirit

> *Then departed Barnabas to Tarsus, for to seek Saul: And when he had found him, he brought him unto Antioch. And it came to pass, that a whole year they assembled themselves with the church, and taught much people. And the disciples were called Christians first in Antioch.*
> — **Acts 11:25–26**

What Happened in Caesarea? (11:1–18)

Without exaggeration, Gentile Pentecost at Cornelius' house changed everything. No longer was the family of God limited to a particular ethnicity and law; now the Holy Spirit was adopting Gentiles by grace and truth. This chapter starts in Jewish Jerusalem, home of the mother church, and ends in the third most important city of the Roman Empire,

Welcome Holy Spirit

Antioch. This thriving, multi-ethnic metropolis would become the headquarters of the growing Gentile church movement. It, more than Jerusalem, would host the missionary church. Antioch could be considered the birthplace of Christianity for reasons we will discuss shortly. But for now, we will head back to Jerusalem.

The apostles and brethren in the region of Judaea, which by implication means they were predominantly Jewish, heard that the Gentiles had received the word of God (11:1). This should have been cause for great rejoicing. Yet apparently it was not. When Peter 'was come up' to Jerusalem (you never go 'down' to Jerusalem, only 'up'), *'they that were of the circumcision'*, meaning the Jewish believers, confronted him (11:2).

What was their problem? They objected that Peter had gone to the home of the uncircumcised (Gentiles) and had eaten with them, meaning he probably consumed un-kosher food (11:3). They overlooked the fact that the Lord Himself wanted them to be His witnesses to the ends of the earth, something the Jerusalem church was slow to comply with. The same God who can declare all meats to be clean can and does the same for people.

Though the reaction of the Jewish believers was emotive and extreme, Peter was a man under authority. So, he told the story of his own personal transformation which led to a revival in Caesarea (11:4). First, he began the account with his time of prayer in Joppa. Nothing wrong with that: he was praying, and it happened to be a Jewish city. Then he fell into a trance and saw a vision: a vessel descended in the form of a great sheet let down by its four corners and it presented itself right in front of him (11:5). As he looked at the sheet, inside were four-footed beasts of the earth, wild things, creeping things and fowls of the air. These are animals he rarely saw and never ate because of their unclean status in Mosaic law (11:6).

As shocking as this vision was, the command was even more so: get up, Peter, slay and eat (11:7). Remember, it was lunchtime and he was

Eleven: Revival at Antioch

hungry. As reported in Chapter Ten, Peter refused the Lord's command. He affirmed that nothing common or unclean had ever entered his mouth (11:8). This is like the proverbial (self) pat on the back. The heavenly voice spoke a second time: what God has cleansed, never call common, unclean or unholy (11:9). In case the point was lost on Peter, the vision appeared three times and then the sheet returned to heaven (11:10). When God speaks once, that is sufficient; twice, it is urgent; thrice, it's revolutionary.

Immediately after seeing this vision, three men came to him from Caesarea (11:11). The timing couldn't have been more perfect. This is a most significant point: the Holy Spirit Himself told Peter to go with these men to Caesarea and he was to doubt nothing. This is another affirmation of the divine personhood of the Holy Spirit. So, Peter proceeded in faith with the six men accompanying him to Cornelius' house (11:12).

Peter turned the narrative from his to Cornelius' perspective. He saw an angel in the house who told him to send his servants to Joppa and call for Simon Peter (11:13). The reason to bring the apostle to Caesarea so he could tell Cornelius and his household the way of salvation (11:14). Note that Cornelius was already recognised as a just, generous, charitable, God-fearing man; yet, despite these commendations, he still needed the gospel of Christ. Peter had the words of life for him and all who were present in the house.

> LESSON FOR LIFE: Repentance precedes salvation and repentance precedes revival. When you repent to God and believe Christ's gospel, you pass from death to life (John 5:24).

While Peter gave the words of life, the Holy Spirit *'fell on them, as on us at the beginning'* (11:15). When was the beginning? **Acts 2**, the Day of Pentecost. Just as the Holy Spirit had filled the Jewish believers that day in Jerusalem, so now He filled the Gentile believers in Caesarea, in the same manner, and with the same evidence – speaking in tongues (10:46).

Welcome Holy Spirit

When Peter witnessed this Gentile Pentecost, he remembered the words of Jesus in **Acts 1:5**: *'John indeed baptized with water; but ye shall be baptized with the Holy Ghost.'* God keeps His word! Peter and his companions could not argue with reality. God had given to the Gentiles the same gift He had given to the Jews who believed in Jesus. Peter concluded: 'So who am I that I should oppose what God is doing?' (11:17)?

After hearing this moving testimony, the Jewish believers could not argue anymore. They made a simple but profound declaration: they held their peace, gave up their contention and glorified God, proclaiming that the Lord had granted the Gentiles repentance unto life (11:18). It took a while but the penny finally dropped – through the 'seed of Abraham', all the nations would be blessed (Genesis 22:18). Yes, the gospel is for both Jews and Gentiles.

Road to Antioch (11:19–24)

Because of the persecution that had broken out against the Jerusalem church after the death of Stephen (Acts 7), the believers had scattered far and wide. They went to Phoenicia (Lebanon), Cyprus and Antioch. However, at this point, they only preached the gospel to Jews (11:19). Fortunately, the fishing net was expanded and there were men from Cyprus and Cyrene (in Libya) who came to Antioch. They preached Jesus to the 'Grecians' or Hellenists (11:20) and Gentiles. God's hand was on these men and many people repented and came to faith in Christ (11:21). Antioch proved to be a very fertile field for the gospel.

When the Jerusalem church heard of this revival, they sent one of their best men, Barnabas (11:22). He headed to Antioch but may have also ministered to the other churches on the way. Barnabas had to see for himself first-hand what was happening in that great city. He was very glad when he saw the grace of God in action: a thriving church in a thriving city. He exhorted the Antiochian believers that with one *'purpose of heart they would cleave unto the Lord'* (11.23).

Eleven: Revival at Antioch

The move of God in Antioch was greatly aided by Barnabas, the key leader. He had an enviable reputation. He was called a good man, full of the Holy Spirit and full of faith. This is a great combination, so take a person like Barnabas during a time of great grace, and it is no wonder that *'much people was added unto the Lord'* (11:24).

> LESSON FOR LIFE: Despite the trauma over the martyrdom of Stephen, God used the persecution to spread the gospel to Antioch and the world.

Birth of 'Christianity' (11:25–29)

Noble Barnabas was God's chosen vessel in Antioch, with many souls coming to faith in Jesus. Yet the revival there was becoming too much for him to handle on his own. So, he made a trip to the region of Cilicia and the city of Tarsus. His mission was to find Saul and bring him to Antioch to help (11:25). Remember that Saul had been sent by the Jerusalem church back to Tarsus because his life was in danger (9:30). Though a strong-willed man, he also respected authority. His decade-long sojourn in Tarsus continued until the day Barnabas came to recruit him as a chosen labourer in the revival at Antioch.

When Barnabas found Saul, he promptly agreed to return with him. Together for one year, this dynamic duo assembled in the church and taught many people. After all, disciples need to be taught; without that, it is hard to be a disciple. Then we learn that the disciples were first called Christians in Antioch (11:26).

The word 'Christian' or 'Christians' is used only three times in the Bible (Acts 11:26; 26:28; 1 Peter 4:16). The term in Greek is χριστιανός, *christianos,* meaning 'followers of Christ'. It was not a name the Jews used since it would be a tacit admission that Jesus of Nazareth was the Messiah, something their rabbis insisted was not the case.

Welcome Holy Spirit

The Gentiles are the ones who used this name towards the followers of Jesus. It was not meant as a compliment initially but eventually became a badge of honour. In *Vine's Expository Dictionary of New Testament Words*, it says, 'Tacitus, writing near the end of the first century, says, 'The vulgar call them Christians. The author or origin of this denomination, Christus, had, in the reign of Tiberius, been executed by the Procurator, Pontius Pilate'.[45]

Paul is blamed, usually by unbelieving 'scholars', for being the founder of Christianity. This is to imply that his epistles are contrary to the teachings of Jesus. The fact is it is Jesus, not Paul, who promised to build His church (Matthew 16:18).

While not everyone will agree, the meaning of 'Christian' can also imply that a follower of Christ is a 'little Christ'. Since Jesus is 'the Anointed One', we therefore are little anointed ones. As those who follow the Master, it should be our goal to emulate His actions: everything He did was anointed in word and deed. He was even anointed for burial (Mark 14:8). Thanks to the baptism and fullness of the Spirit, we, too, can speak and act in His anointing, too (Mark 14:12).

In the days of the revival at Antioch, prophets came from Jerusalem (11:27), a distance of five hundred and two kilometres (three hundred and twelve miles). One of the Jerusalem prophets Agabus said there would be a worldwide dearth, and this was fulfilled in the days of Claudius Caesar (11:28).

There was an overwhelmingly generous response from the saints in Antioch. According to their ability, they determined to send relief to the brethren dwelling in Jerusalem (11:29). This is an example of the 'offspring church' helping the 'mother church'. The charitable gift was to be taken by hand through Barnabas and Saul. The Antioch church was doing well enough that these two Jewish pillars could be sent on a mission of mercy and the local congregation would continue to flourish. That flourishing came at a price, as we will soon find out.

Eleven: Revival at Antioch

LESSON FOR LIFE: The name 'Christian' may have been coined in derision, but it now shines like a star on the greatest divine-human endeavour in history.

---

[45] Vine, W. Christian - Vine's Expository Dictionary of New Testament Words. Blue Letter Bible, quoting Tacitus, *Annals*, xv. 44. Last modified 24 June 1996. Accessed June 2017.

CHAPTER TWELVE

Growing Persecution, Growing Church

Who: Peter, Herod and an angel

What: Official persecution and deliverance

When: Passover season

Where: Jerusalem and Caesarea

Why: Church was growing

How: Abusive temporal power, and prayer

> *Now about that time Herod the king stretched forth his hands to vex certain of the church. And he killed James the brother of John with the sword ... But the word of God grew and multiplied.*
> — **Acts 12:1–2, 24**

Death and Deliverance (12:1–19)

It was destined to happen. Just like in the ministry of Jesus, the favour, success and growth of the early church were bound to attract the envy and displeasure of the ruling elites; prodded by the invisible spiritual forces of darkness (Ephesians 6:12). Along with joy and fearlessness, the apostles and their followers were constantly in trouble. Ultimately, this was nothing less than a clash of kingdoms: the kingdom of darkness of this world attacks the kingdom of heaven and light. The dark will lose but it shall not descend into the abyss without a fight.

Welcome Holy Spirit

Persecution broke out against the Jerusalem church after Stephen's death in **Acts 7**. The people scattered but the apostles did not (8:1). Now King Herod Agrippa I, grandson of Herod the Great and nephew of Herod Antipas, tetrarch of Galilee, decided to go after the heads of the church (12:1). Agrippa would soon become persecutor-in-chief. Things would get serious and ugly. Another martyr comes into the narrative: James, the brother of John, the son of Zebedee. He was killed by the sword (12:2). No further details are given. Thus, Jerusalem, the city that killed the prophets was starting to kill apostles, too.

Herod saw that the murder of James pleased the Jews, so he decided to get the 'big fish', Peter (12:3). It was the days of unleavened bread. Violence can increase during times of religious holidays. The 'Nazarenes' and 'The Way,' terms used to describe the all-Jewish early church, were still considered part of the Jewish people. Yet even at this juncture, the schism between the church and synagogue began to appear. It would become a rupture after the Roman destruction of Jerusalem and Herod's temple in 70 AD.

Peter was arrested and imprisoned. He was being watched by four quaternions of soldiers (12:4). According to *Vine's Expository Dictionary*, 'A "quaternion" was a set of four men occupied in the work of a guard, two soldiers being chained to the prisoner and two keeping watch; alternatively, one of the four watched while the other three slept. The night was divided into four watches of three hours each; there would be one "quaternion" for each watch by day and by night.'[46] This means that Peter was well-guarded and after Easter/Passover (*Pesach*) would be brought out to the people. So, the apostle would be observing the days of unleavened bread from prison.

However, this dire development was met with a wise spiritual response. The early church gave continuous prayers to God on Peter's behalf (12:5). Since the church knew that the apostles were now the new target, they prayed in a concerted way for Peter which they may not

Twelve: Growing Persecution, Growing Church

have done in the same measure for James. Peter's miraculous deliverance would be the result.

Herod Agrippa I was getting ready to present Peter to the people, ostensibly to condemn and execute him. Please note that the same night, Peter was sleeping. Instead of worrying and fretting about his fate, he was able to sleep like a baby. Peter had obviously learned to have the peace of God that surpasses all understanding (Philippians 4:6-7). This peace is freely available to all God's children (John 14:27).

Peter was between two soldiers, bound with the two chains (12:6). There was a keeper at the door. Most probably, as a result of the continuous prayers of the saints (12:5), the angel of the Lord came to Peter and a bright light shined in the prison. The angel struck Peter on the side to wake him up – that's how soundly he slept. He told him to rise up quickly. At that point, the chains fell off his hands (12:7). The angel told him to get dressed and put on his sandals, which he did. 'Put your garments on and follow me', said the angel. Peter obeyed (12:8).

> LESSON FOR LIFE: In Acts 12, God delivered His two apostles: James into His presence and Peter from prison.

Peter followed the angel out of the cell and the prison. Yet he was having a hard time believing this was really happening to him; perhaps he was in a trance (12:9), seeing a vision as he did in Chapter 10. Everything happened so quickly. It was a long journey to get out of the prison. They had to pass through the first and second wards. Then they reached the iron gate that led to the city, which opened up of its own accord (obviously by the power of God; gates don't open themselves). They went out of the prison, passed through one street and then, violà, the angel of the Lord disappeared (12:10). Peter was now on his own and a free man.

After all these wonderful events, Peter realised that he was not seeing a vision; this was reality. He said that he knew of the certainty that the

Welcome Holy Spirit

Lord had sent his angel and delivered him from the hand of Herod and from *'all the expectation of the people of the Jews'* (12:11). This phraseology almost makes Peter sound like a Gentile; the fact is, he was as much a part of the Jewish people as any Pharisee or Sadducee. Yet the rift between the church and synagogue would continue to grow until it became a very messy divorce.

After pondering these things, Peter went to the house of Mary, the mother of John Mark, where many were praying for him (12:12). His arrival at her doorstep was an answer to their prayers. Peter began to knock at the gate. A young woman named Rhoda heard the knock and came to hear who it was (12:13).

Peter did not just knock at the door; he also used his voice to get attention. When Rhoda recognised Peter's voice, she got so excited that she ran and told the people assembled inside that Peter was standing at the gate (12:14). The one problem was she failed to open the gate and let Peter in.

Amazingly, people could be praying for a miracle and when it finally happens, they don't believe. Remember that there were doubts about the risen Christ, even though He was standing right in front of them with scarred hands. This appears to be the case in the deliverance of Peter. Now that the prayer for Peter's deliverance was answered, they refused to believe the persistent testimony of Rhoda. Their response: it couldn't be Peter, but perhaps it is his angel (12:15). Well, yes, an angel was involved, but it was truly Peter.

Peter had no choice but to keep knocking. This reminds us of the words of Jesus regarding prayer: ask, seek and knock (Matthew 7:7). In the original Greek, it means we are to ask, and keep asking; seek, and keep seeking; and knock, and keep knocking. That's what Peter did. So when they finally opened the door and saw it really was Peter, they were astonished (12:16). Understandably so.

Twelve: Growing Persecution, Growing Church

Peter told them to hold their peace so he could recount his miraculous story of deliverance. Apparently, in their astonishment, they made a lot of noise of excitement. So, Peter gave the details and commanded them to show these things to James, and to the brethren. James was known as 'James the Just' and was probably the biological half-brother of Jesus, a key leader in the Jerusalem church and the author of the New Testament epistle that bears his name. After speaking, Peter departed from Mary's house and went to an undisclosed location (12:17).

When the day dawned, there was a big stir among the soldiers (12:18). After all, there had been up to sixteen of them involved in guarding Peter and yet, despite their extensive precautions, he had disappeared from the prison. Herod sent for Peter to be presented to the people. To his chagrin, he discovered that he had escaped from the prison.

After examining the prison keepers, he was convinced that they were negligent and commanded that they should be executed. This could be from two to sixteen soldiers who would lose their lives because of this incident. From what we read in Acts, Agrippa I was ruthless and tyrannical like his grandfather, Herod the Great.

After the command was given, Herod went down from Judaea to Caesarea (it is a literal descent from the mountains to the coastal plain, which includes the Plain of Sharon). He abided there (12:19), and it would be to his undoing.

The End of Agrippa I (12:20–25)

In Caesarea, King Herod Agrippa I planned a meeting with representatives from Tyre and Sidon. These cities were located in Phoenicia, Israel's maritime neighbour to the north. Historically, the Phoenicians provided shipping for the agrarian Israelites and they in return supplied food. Herod was angered with the Phoenicians (the reasons are unknown), and since they realised they were biting the hand that fed them, they needed to make peace. With one accord they secured the service of Blastus, the king's chamberlain, and befriended him to be an intermediary for them (12:20). They wanted peace with Herod so that their food supply would continue uninterrupted.

On a specific day, Herod came to his throne, sat upon it and was dressed up in splendid royal apparel. He began to give an oration to them (12:21). To win over Herod, the Phoenicians acted like sycophants by making an incredible statement: *'It is the voice of a god, and not of a man'* (12:22). Much action happened in one verse. The angel of the Lord smote Herod for taking the glory for himself and not giving it to God. The consequences were frightening: he was eaten by worms and died (12:23). After taking innocent lives as he had, Herod was reaping what he sowed.

Flavius Josephus (37-100 AD) was a famous Jewish historian of the first century AD. He wrote an interesting account of the death of Herod Agrippa I in his book, *Jewish Antiquities*. Here is an excerpt from when the Phoenicians called him a god:

> *Upon this the king did neither rebuke them, nor reject their impious flattery ... A severe pain also arose in his belly, and began in a most violent manner. He therefore looked upon his friends, and said, 'I, whom you call a god, am commanded presently to depart this life; while Providence thus reproves the lying words you just now said to me; and I, who was by you called immortal, am immediately to be hurried away by death. ... And when he had been quite worn out by the pain in his belly for five days, he departed this life, being in the fifty-fourth year of his age, and in the seventh year of his reign.'*[47]

Herod, the great persecutor of the apostles, was dead by the hand of God. More importantly, the Word of God grew and multiplied (12:24).

Almost as an afterthought, Barnabas and Saul were returning from Jerusalem, having delivered the charitable donation that was sent by the church at Antioch. They decided to take young John Mark with them

Twelve: Growing Persecution, Growing Church

back to Antioch (12:25). Remember, it was his mother Mary's house where the apostles and believers had gathered to pray for Peter. John Mark was exposed to lots of prayer and also rubbed shoulders with key leaders of the church; despite several key setbacks, prayer and mentoring helped Mark to make a comeback. We will see two of these chief mentors in action as we proceed to **Acts 13**.

---

[46] Vine, W. Quaternion - Vine's Expository Dictionary of New Testament Words. Blue Letter Bible. Last modified 24 June, 1996. https://www.blueletterbible.org/search/Dictionary/viewTopic.cfm. 3 June 2017.

[47] http://www.bible-history.com/herod_agrippa_i/HEROD_AGRIPPA_IJosephus_Account_of_Agrippas_Dea.htm. 3 June 2017, quoting Josephus, *Jewish Antiquities* (19.343-350).

Part Four

Holy Spirit Power

To the Ends of the Earth

CHAPTER THIRTEEN
From Saul to Paul
(The Birth of Global Mission)

Who: Saul and Barnabas.

What: First Missionary Journey, commanded by the Spirit

When: around 47 AD

Where: Cyprus, Pamphylia and Lycaonia

Why: To build God's kingdom

How: By the power of the Holy Spirit

> *As they ministered to the Lord, and fasted, the Holy Ghost said, Separate me Barnabas and Saul for the work whereunto I have called them. And when they had fasted and prayed, and laid their hands on them, they sent them away.*
> — *Acts 13:2–3*

Set Apart for Mission (13:1–7)

One of the most momentous and important events was about to happen. Saul of Tarsus, from the stock of Israel, the tribe of Benjamin, a Hebrew of Hebrews, a Pharisee and – most importantly – a follower of Jesus the Messiah, was about to have a name change. Or, more likely, he will put aside his Hebrew name, *Shaul*, and begin to use his Roman name, Paul. Why? Because the Holy Spirit was about to do with him what God

Welcome Holy Spirit

intended all along: through the 'seed of Abraham', all the nations of the world would be blessed. Jesus Christ is that seed and Paul – the most Jewish man you can imagine – was bringing this good news to the world of the Gentiles. This taking of the gospel beyond Israel was destined to turn the world upside down (Acts 17:6) and bless all nations.

It all began with a 'waiting on God' session at the church in Antioch. The lost art of 'waiting' is not passive but active: prayer, fasting, personal devotions of Bible study, meditation, praise and worship. In such an atmosphere, God is destined to speak. And those who wait, listen and obey will not fail to get to the next level (Isaiah 40:31).

Antioch, a major city, hosted a major church dominated by Gentile members. There were key people based there called 'prophets' and 'teachers'. The prayer meeting was replete with illustrious leaders. These included Barnabas, Simeon (Niger), Lucius of Cyrene in Libya, Manaen who grew up with Herod the Tetrarch (implying he was an older man) and Saul of Tarsus (13:1).

All of these significant men came together to minister to the Lord. It does not say what that 'ministry' was, but no doubt it included prayer, fasting, praise and worship. During this process, the Holy Spirit spoke directly to the leader: *'Separate for me Barnabas and Saul for the work that I have called them'* (13:2). They were being sanctified for the honourable, glorious and ultimately successful mission to the Gentile world. (**Note**: Since Saul and Barnabas were key teachers and leaders of the church at Antioch, the fact that they were released from local church work to do international outreach points to the effectiveness of their ministry: their Antioch disciples were raised up to take their place. Great leaders work themselves out of a job so their disciples can fill the gap).

How did the prophets and teachers respond to the Holy Spirit's clear directive? These anointed men acted immediately. They prayed, fasted and practised the *'laying on of hands'*. As we learned, the latter is one of the six fundamental doctrines of the Christian faith as mentioned in **Hebrews 6:1**. After this, the two apostles were sent away (13:3), possibly

Thirteen: From Saul to Paul

on the very day the Spirit spoke. Thus began the first of three recorded missionary journeys and the formal commencement of global mission.

Though the anointed brothers of Antioch sent the apostles away, the text says, *'being sent forth by the Holy Ghost'* (13:4). God often uses people to fulfil His will, but ultimately He is the one who appoints and sends apostles, as well as commissions Christians in general for kingdom ministry.

The two apostles departed from the port city of Seleucia, known as Seleucia Pieria and Seleucia by the sea. This was Antioch's outlet to the Mediterranean. In a sense, this spot is the launching pad of Saul's missionary ministry and Christian mission in general. It is about thirty kilometres (nineteen miles) southwest of Antioch. Today it is in ruins. From here, the apostles, with John Mark, son of Mary of Jerusalem, sailed to the island of Cyprus, also to the south-west (13:4). Upon their arrival, they went to the city of Salamis, they preached the word of God in the synagogues (13:5) and John Mark assisted them.

From there, they travelled across Cyprus to a place called Paphos (13:6). In Paphos there was a false prophet and sorcerer named Bar-jesus (which means 'son of Jesus' but, of course, not the Messiah). He would try to be the spoiler when it came to the presentation of the gospel. He would do his best to choke the 'good seed of God's Word before it had a chance to take root in the heart'.

The apostles encountered a man named Sergius Paulus (13:7). He was a deputy to the country, a prudent, significant man, who eagerly wanted to hear the message of Barnabas and Saul. Bar-jesus will try to torpedo the gospel message.

LESSON FOR LIFE: If you want a directive Word from the Lord, then begin to minister to Him with prayer, praise and fasting and you will get your answer (Acts 13:2).

Welcome Holy Spirit

Defeating a Foe (13:8–13)

This would be the first of many attempts to thwart the ministry of the apostles and their life-giving message. The road to spiritual success is paved with spiritual opposition. This opposition comes from the spiritual forces of darkness (Ephesians 6:12), using human opponents as the frontmen. The devil knows his territory is under threat and time is short, so he will use his minions to cause all the trouble they can. Of course, they will all fail in the end.

Understanding that the ultimate source of opposition is spiritual and satanic makes us more willing to forgive our human foes. Bar-jesus, whose name was also Elymas, a sorcerer and servant of Satan, stood against the apostles and sought to stop the deputy, Sergius Paulus, from coming to faith (13:8).

Then Saul, (who also is called Paul) … ' (13:9). The name of Paul is used one hundred and fifty-seven times in the New Testament. It is this verse where it is used for the very first time.[48] Paul was Saul's Roman name, which he, having been born in the Diaspora, may have received at birth. Now that he was ministering to the Gentiles, using his Roman rather than Hebrew name was appropriate. From now on, as an apostle–missionary, this is the name he will be using. This verse says that Paul was filled with the Holy Spirit and set his eyes on his opponent, Elymas (13:9). Boldness is one of the results of being filled with the Spirit (4:31).

Elymas was going to receive a mouthful and more from Paul. He was told of being subtle (crafty and cunning) and mischievous. In addition, Elymas was called a 'child of the devil', the enemy of all righteousness. Would he ever cease to pervert the right ways of the Lord (13:10)? Yet Paul wasn't going to wait for the answer.

The hand of the Lord was now against the sorcerer. He would be blind and not see the sun for the season. It seems that the divinely inspired blindness was a temporary punishment for his evil ways. No sooner was this said that there fell on Elymas a mist and darkness, and

Thirteen: From Saul to Paul

he now sought for someone to lead him by the hand (13:11) – the blind leading the blind.

After this amazing demonstration of authority and power by Paul, the deputy, Sergius Paulus, saw what was done and became a believer. He was 'astonished at the doctrine of the Lord' (13:12). Why? As it says in **1 Corinthians 4:20,** *'For the kingdom of God is not in word, but in power.'* **Luke 4:32** speaks of the ministry of Jesus: *'And they were astonished at his doctrine: for his word was with power'*. That's how it should be with us today, thanks to the Holy Spirit.

After this great victory in Cyprus, the apostles were about to have a shock development, an unexpected transition. From Paphos in Cyprus, Paul and his company set sail north to the mainland of Asia Minor, the province of Pamphylia and the town of Perga. Young John Mark, their protege, left the apostolic team and returned to Jerusalem (13:13). No reasons, explanations or apologies were offered. This act would be a cause of serious contention between Paul and Barnabas when the second missionary was about to be launched (15:36-41). Despite the current disappointment, a great adventure and much spiritual fruit awaited this dynamic duo.

> LESSON FOR LIFE: The answer to spiritual opposition is the Word of God accompanied by the power of the Holy Spirit.

Revival in Antioch in Pisidia (13:14–52)

The apostles, minus John Mark, travelled from Perga on the coast north to a place called Antioch in Pisidia. This city is not to be confused with Antioch on the Orontes River, also known as Syrian Antioch. (There were several cities with this name, but the one on the Orontes we are already familiar with. In church history, Syrian Antioch became one of five patriarchates with Rome, Jerusalem, Constantinople and Alexandria).

As was their custom, Paul and Barnabas went to the synagogue. At this point, they merely attended *'and sat down'* (13:14). After the customary reading of the Bible, especially the law and the prophets, the rulers of the synagogue sent a message to the visiting apostles: 'If you have a word of exhortation for the people, please share it' (13:15). This was an opportunity too good to miss. A door for the gospel had now opened – and very quickly.

Paul rose to speak and gestured with his hand. He addressed two categories of people: men of Israel who were ethnic Jews and proselytes, and those who 'fear God', namely, the God-fearers (13:16). These were Gentiles who respected the superior moral, ethical and spiritual standards of the God of Israel but had not converted to Judaism by circumcision and law-keeping. Proselytes were Gentiles who converted to Judaism and were circumcised and committed to keeping the law of Moses.

Like Stephen in **Acts 7**, Paul was going to recite some Israelite history. He said that the 'God of this people Israel chose' our fathers, namely the patriarchs Abraham, Isaac, and Jacob. This 'choosing' was called 'election'; it was not an act of favouritism but of calling for holy purposes. 'Favouritism' blesses only the object of favour, often at the expense and detriment of others. 'Calling' blesses the chosen so they can be a blessing to everyone. God chose the patriarchs to be a blessing. He then exalted the people of Israel when they were strangers in the land of Egypt (13:17). With a strong arm, He brought them out of the land of bondage.

God had to put up with their (lack of) manners in the wilderness for forty years (13:18). This journey, which should have only taken forty days, was prolonged because of their sin and disobedience. God helped Israel destroy seven nations in the land of Canaan: the Hittites, Girgashites, Amorites, Canaanites, Perizzites, Hivities and Jebusites (Deuteronomy 7:1). Then He divided their land by lot (13:19). Despite Israel's disobedience in the wilderness, God was faithful to His promise of the land to Abraham and his descendants.

Thirteen: From Saul to Paul

After the conquest of Canaan, God gave Israel judges who delivered them from their oppressors. Remember, however, the oppression was self-inflicted – the **Book of Judges** is summarised by this simple phrase: *'every man did that which was right in his own eyes'* (Judges 21:25). During this four-hundred-and-fifty-year period, there were cycles of moral anarchy. First, there was sin and backsliding. Then the Lord allowed His people to be oppressed by foreigners. This is not done out of hatred but love. **Proverbs 3:11–12 (NKJV)** declares, *'For whom the Lord loves, He corrects, just as a father the son in whom He delights'*. From the depths of distress and anguish, Israel cried to the Lord. His response was to raise up judges to deliver His people. Once delivered, Israel served the Lord as long as the victorious judge lived. Once they were gone, Israel returned to its fallen ways and the cycle began all over again. This continued until the time of Samuel (13:20), the greatest prophet of Israel since Moses.

During the time of Samuel, Israel desired a king like all the other surrounding nations. So, God gave them their request in the form of Saul, the son of Kish, from the tribe of Benjamin, for forty years (13:21). He started well, with goodwill and favour with God and man. Yet, Saul made some disastrous decisions and God regretted making him king. His murderous reaction to his successor, David, the son of Jesse, recorded in detail in **1 Samuel**, caused him to be remembered in infamy. In the end, the Lord refused to answer his cries.

> LESSON FOR LIFE: You cannot leverage towards a brighter future until you know and understand your past.

This lesson on Israelite history continued with a focus on one of the key figures of the Bible: David. One of the greatest commendations bestowed on a mere mortal is that he was a man after God's own heart. This was given to David, the son of Jesse. God removed backslidden Saul from being king of Israel. Because of David's exemplary attitude towards God, the Lord said that this special man will *'fulfil all my will'* (13:22).

Welcome Holy Spirit

Though stated succinctly, this is a major point. *'God according to his promise'* means David's Covenant of **2 Samuel 7** and **1 Chronicles 17**, one of the major binding agreements of Scripture. God promised to give David a son to rule on his throne forever. David's Son would also simultaneously be God's Son, too. Paul affirmed that God kept His promise to David by giving to Israel a Saviour named Jesus (13:23).

Before Jesus was revealed to Israel, God used the forerunner, John the Baptist. John's was a baptism of repentance for all the people of Israel (13:24). The purpose of this baptism was to point to the coming of Messiah, Who would also baptise with the Holy Spirit and fire. The Holy Spirit baptism by Messiah was mentioned in all four gospels and **Acts 1**.

After fulfilling his duty, John asked of the people: Who do you think I am? Take note: I am not He, the Messiah. He comes after me. I am not worthy to even loose his sandals off His feet (13:25). Such humility is admirable, yet also very true to John and us all. Messiah is the Holy One of God.

Ready to hit home and hit hard, Paul told the people they were recipients of the word of salvation (13:26). Addressing a range of people – men, brethren, children of Abraham and God-fearers – the apostle declared, to every one of *'you is the word of this salvation sent* (13:26)'. You are blessed with a priceless message but with that blessing comes a responsibility to repent and believe.

Those who dwelt at Jerusalem, including the rulers, had fulfilled prophecy by condemning Christ (13:27). How could these people, who were very knowledgeable in the law of Moses, do such an evil thing? It says they did not know Him, and they did not know and understand the words of the Hebrew prophets, even though they are read every sabbath day. Yet God used their ignorance to fulfil His prophetic purposes.

Christ was sinless so there was *no cause of death* to be found in Him (though He was accused of blasphemy because, at the Sanhedrin trial, he was forced to admit He would be at the right hand of God, therefore

Thirteen: From Saul to Paul

implying He was divine). Yet despite His innocence, they pressed on to have Him condemned and slain by Pilate (13:28), the only man who had the authority to condemn and execute a prisoner.

By betraying and crucifying Christ, perpetuating the greatest injustice in history, the religious leaders plus Pontius Pilate were fulfilling Bible prophecy (Psalm 22; Isaiah 53; Zechariah 12, etc.). This was Christ's passion: the Scriptures had to be fulfilled, no matter the pain, the cost or the humiliation. After He declared from the cross, 'It is finished', He died. Then the Romans took Him down from the tree (the cross) and put Him in a sepulchre (13:29). Tragic and unjust as the trial and crucifixion were, they led to a greater purpose of divine origin.

The resurrection of Jesus changed everything! It replaced defeat with victory, death with life and darkness with light. **Note**: it was God Himself who raised Jesus from the dead (13:30). Without this event, there would be no forgiveness of sins, no new birth and no Christian Church.

After His resurrection, Christ was seen for many days by the (apostolic) witnesses who came up with Him from Galilee to Jerusalem (13:31). These same apostles bore witness of the resurrection to the people. The fact that Jesus was seen by them during forty days helped to reinforce the surety and credibility of their witness.

As a result of all this Israelite history, culminating in the resurrection of Jesus, Paul now declared to them the glad tidings (13:32) – the gospel – about the promises made to the fathers (patriarchs). Part of the good news is that God made and kept his wonderful promises. The proof of this was His raising Jesus from the dead (13:33). Paul then quoted **Psalm 2:7**: *'Thou art my Son, this day have I begotten thee'*. And more quotes from the Bible were on the way.

To prove the point that Jesus rose from the dead and will never die again, Paul quoted from **Isaiah 55:3**: *'Incline your ear, and come unto me: hear, and your soul shall live; and I will make an everlasting covenant with you,*

Welcome Holy Spirit

even the sure mercies of David' (13:34). This link to David is given as proof that Christ would not see the decay of death.

Now he quoted **Psalm 16:10**: *'For thou wilt not leave my soul in hell; neither wilt thou suffer thine Holy One to see corruption'* (13:35). Although this is a psalm of David, the promise is actually to the Son of David, as we are about to see. Here is an amazing phrase: David *'served his own generation by the will of God'* (13:36), which is what we should all do. If we leave a Godly legacy, then we serve future generations, too, not just our own. After David served his generation, he *'fell on sleep'* (died) and was *'laid unto his father'*, and saw corruption (13:36), meaning his body decayed. The promise of **Psalm 16:10** was not for David but for his Son, Jesus. The One whom God has raised from the dead did not decay (13:37) nor will He ever die again. This is good news for all of us and the heart of the gospel.

> LESSON FOR LIFE: All sacred Biblical history points to Jesus and He fulfils all promises, prophesies and expectations.

Paul became emphatic because he was about to give a 'call to action'. How will the people at the synagogue at Antioch in Pisidia respond? *'Be it known unto you, therefore'* (13:38) – be very clear about what you have just heard. Men and brethren, through Jesus Christ of Nazareth, Son of God, crucified, risen from the dead, is the only enduring means of obtaining forgiveness of sins (13:38), the new birth and the gift of eternal life.

By Him, and Him alone, those who believed are justified by all things. Justification means to be declared not guilty and also declared righteous in the sight of God. Such justification was not possible by mere observance of the law of Moses (13:39), especially since the law has no power to save. It does a great job, however, outlining God's high and holy standards which shows us how unrighteous we truly are; like a mirror, it shows our wretchedness and dire need for the Saviour.

Thirteen: From Saul to Paul

With the great promise of the gospel is a solemn warning. Make sure the following prophesied condition does not apply to you (13:40). The prophet Habakkuk in **Habakkuk 1:5** said, *'Behold ye among the heathen, and regard, and wonder marvellously: for I will work a work in your days, which ye will not believe, though it be told you'* (13:41). Don't be so stubborn and blind that you miss what God is doing because failure to receive the gospel will be catastrophic.

Though some, perhaps many, of the Jews left the synagogue at Antioch in Pisidia, the Gentiles begged Paul to return on the next sabbath day (13:42). He would keep this appointment.

Because of his words, guided by the Holy Spirit, not only did the Gentiles want him to return, but now many Jews and religious proselytes followed Paul and Barnabas. The fact that they followed the apostles showed that they received the grace of God. The apostles' advice: continue in the grace of the Lord (13:43). We should do likewise.

> LESSON FOR LIFE: All who proclaim the gospel do not merely tell the story of Jesus but require a response to the good news. Don't let the fish off the hook.

After one week, on the next sabbath day, almost the whole city came to the synagogue to hear God's Word (13:44). This is a good sign when people are hungry for the Word and thirsty for the Holy Spirit. But such ministry success will attract a carnal pushback, as we are about to see.

When the impenitent Jews saw the crowds, they were *'filled with envy'* (13:45). Opposition to the gospel was not exclusively a Jewish thing; however, what we learn is that being a physical descendant of Abraham does not guarantee a minimal level of spirituality, obedience or openness. Without the new birth and indwelling of the Holy Spirit, the person – male or female, Jew or Gentile – will still be 'in the flesh', even if they are religious – often because they are religious. This opposition, as was often the case, came from envy and manifested with evil words and actions towards God's servants. In this instance, they contradicted Paul and blasphemed.

Rather than being intimidated by the spirit of opposition, Paul and Barnabas, filled with the Holy Spirit, *'waxed bold'* (13:46). An amazing statement followed: it was necessary that you, the Jews, receive the word of God first. This theme of 'to the Jew first' is reiterated three times in Romans (1:16; 2:9; 2:10). They were given the first opportunity to receive the words of life. However, they rejected the gospel and judged themselves 'unworthy of everlasting life' (13:46). Sobering words. So now, it is time for the Gentiles to hear, receive and be blessed.

Notice that Paul ministered in the synagogue by history and Scripture, two things that the Jewish people would understand better than others. Paul quoted from **Isaiah 49:6:** *'And he said, "It is a light thing that thou shouldest be my servant to raise up the tribes of Jacob, and to restore the preserved of Israel: I will also give thee for a light to the Gentiles, that thou mayest be my salvation unto the end of the earth".'* (13:47). God's intention from day one was to bless all nations, not just one.

Instead of feeling like second-class citizens, Paul's words encouraged the Gentiles to see that they were very much part of the plan and heart of God. They were glad and glorified the Word of the Lord. Then came the phrase, *'and as many as were ordained to eternal life believed'* (13:48). The Sovereign hand of God is involved when we turn to Christ in faith, and He is not surprised when we do.

The move of God in Antioch in Pisidia caused the Word of the Lord to spread throughout all the neighbouring regions (13:49). This is how it should be. The apostles' unbelieving opponents were not going to go away quietly. They strategically chose people of great influence to join their side, including the *'devout and honourable women'* (13:50) and the chief men of the city. In partnership with the local leadership, they raised persecution against the apostles and expelled them from the area (13:50).

Thirteen: From Saul to Paul

Rather than lick their wounds and act like victims, the apostles demonstrated a gesture of contempt against their opponents. They shook off the dust from their feet as a witness against them (13:51). Jesus spoke about doing a similar action if a city did not repent. **Mark 6:11** says, '*And whosoever shall not receive you, nor hear you, when ye depart thence, shake off the dust under your feet for a testimony against them. Verily I say unto you, It shall be more tolerable for Sodom and Gomorrha in the day of judgment, than for that city*' (see also Matthew 10:14–15; Luke 9:5; Luke 10:11). The apostles decided to move on, and they went to Iconium.

Though the apostles were no longer with the new church plant at Antioch in Pisidia, the Holy Spirit was. The disciples (which is what every believer should be) were filled with joy and the Holy Spirit (13:52). As the fruit of the Spirit, ceaseless joy can be your experience in all circumstances.

The apostles were again on the road. Led by the Spirit, they were on their way for more fruit – and fight – as they made their way across Asia Minor. How they conducted themselves will be an example for us all.

> LESSON FOR LIFE: When opposition confronts the Godly, it is a great sign that they are doing something right.

---

[48] "KJV Search Results for "Paul"." Blue Letter Bible. Accessed 22 Aug, 2024. https://www.blueletterbible.org//search/search.cfm?Criteria=Paul&t=KJV#s=s_primary_0_1

CHAPTER FOURTEEN

Triumph and Trouble
(End of the First Missionary Journey)

Who: Saul and Barnabas

What: Apostolic mission work

When: During the first missionary journey

Where: Iconium, Lycaonia, Pamphylia, Antioch in Pisidia

Why: To build God's kingdom

How: By the word of God and the power of the Holy Spirit

> *And thence sailed to Antioch, from whence they had been recommended to the grace of God for the work which they fulfilled. And when they were come, and had gathered the church together, they rehearsed all that God had done with them, and how he had opened the door of faith unto the Gentiles.*
> — *Acts 14:26–27*

Triumph and Trouble in Iconium (14:1–7)

Having been duly expelled from Antioch in Pisidia, the apostles embodied that great British wartime slogan: keep calm and carry on. They found their way into a new harvest field called Iconium. Known today as Konya, this important city had a synagogue of the Jews. Paul and Barnabas went there, presumably on the sabbath day, and there was an exceedingly big response to the gospel message: a great multitude of Jews and Gentiles came to faith (14:1). That's the good news.

Wherever you sow the wheat, the enemy will come and plant the tares (Matthew 13:25). The Jews who did not believe were stirred up, just like in Antioch in Pisidia. They provoked the Gentiles and turned them against the apostles and the local brethren (14:2). While the text does not say, chances are these newly minted opponents were stirred by the same spirit of envy as those in the previous place.

Despite the bad press, the apostles continued in the area for a long time (14:3). They spoke boldly in the Name of the Lord. They testified of the word of His grace. Their hands were used in signs and wonders. Both the boldness and miracles were made possible by the Holy Spirit's anointing. This resulted in more salvations ... and more opposition. Amazingly, the opposition was so hardened that even miracles did not move them to believe.

> LESSON FOR LIFE: It is impossible to please all the people all the time; wisdom decrees that you use your energies to please God alone.
> **Proverbs 16:7**: *When a man's ways please the LORD, he maketh even his enemies to be at peace with him.*

As it turned out, the multitude of the city was divided (14:4). Part-sided with the unbelievers and part-sided with the apostles (believers included both Jews and Gentiles). Hateful opposition is often irrational. There is no logical or justifiable reason for their stance but they persist anyway. Oftentimes, they resort to insults and blasphemies. When this does not stop the work of God, then they go to the next step and threaten physical violence (14:5). Demonic forces move upon people's carnal nature to produce this kind of response. So the Gentiles and Jews, along with the rulers, wanted to assault and stone the apostles.

Wisdom decrees that you choose your battles carefully. There are times to fight and there are times to flee; may we have the wisdom to know which pathway to take. In this case, the apostles knew they were

Fourteen: Triumph and Trouble

in mortal danger and they fled to the region of Lycaonia, to places known as Lystra and Derbe (14:6) and the outlying regions. In Lycaonia the apostles did what they had done from Day One on this first missionary journey: they preached the gospel (14:7). Like all the other places they had been before, there would be triumph and trouble.

Triumph and Trouble in Lystra (14:8-20)

At Lystra there was a certain man, impotent in his feet, a cripple from birth, and had never walked in his life (14:8). That was the obvious problem. The deeper, greater issue is that he was a sinner in need of sovereign grace and salvation. He would get both issues addressed thanks to the visit of the apostles. The lame man listened to the words of Paul. No doubt, Paul was quoting Scripture and faith was rising in the man's heart. As Paul looked at him steadfastly, he perceived that this lame man had faith to be healed (14:9). This is key since Jesus Himself says that your faith has made you whole (Mark 5:34; 10:52)

Confession, command, and/or declaration activate faith, provided it is per His Word and will. Paul was going to make both a confession and a command to the lame man. He says in a loud voice. 'Stand upright on your feet' (14:10). Before he could reason, rationalise, and talk himself out of his healing, the lame man obeyed. Next thing, he not only walked for the first time but he was also leaping before God (14:10). This miracle would get everyone's attention yet lead to some misguided actions.

There was no doubt that a notable miracle had occurred. However, the response by the people of Lystra was a problem. Once the lame man was healed, the locals said in their own language, that the gods had come down in the form of men (14:11). Note they said 'gods,' meaning they were polytheists and pagans. Didn't the ancient Greeks make gods in the likeness of men?

Now came time to 'worship.' Barnabas, the amiable, kind, gracious man who encouraged many, was now called after the god Jupiter. Paul was labelled Mercury because he was the spokesman (14:12). All of this happened so quickly that it caught the apostles off guard.

What happened next was beyond the pale. The people of Lystra, led by the priest of Jupiter who was before their city, brought the paraphernalia required for sacrifice: oxen and garlands were brought to the gate (14:13). They were about to have a time of 'worship' before the people. The miracle that was meant to be a blessing had spawned a spiritual state of emergency.

Paul and Barnabas were horrified at this response; they tore their garments as a sign of mourning, and cried out to the people (14:14), asking, 'Why are you doing these heathen practices? We are merely men, of like passions with you.' Their preaching was that they should turn away (repent) from their vain practices and come to the living God. He is the Creator who made heaven, earth, the sea, and all things therein (14:15). In the past, God tolerated the nations (Gentiles) walking in their own ways (14:16). This is because of God's long-suffering, which means He is legendarily patient. However, the status quo cannot and will not remain forever; the heavenly kingdom is on the way and its roads are paved with holiness.

The apostles continued their plea. Despite the heathenism of the Gentiles, God left a witness of Himself throughout history. He did good to the people on earth. God provided rain from heaven to water the crops and gave them fruitful seasons (14:17). This means that people were filled with good food and gladness. All of this is a blessing from God and the chief reason we say grace at the meal table. We not only bless the food; we also bless God who provided it.

What was the result? Despite these many authoritative and graceful sayings from the apostles, the act of animal sacrifice was narrowly averted (*scarce restrained they the people*) (14:18). However, a greater storm was on the horizon.

Fourteen: Triumph and Trouble

The apostles' opponents went out of their way to persecute them. A coalition of Jewish unbelievers from Antioch in Pisidia and Iconium assembled together and came to Lystra. Their goal was to stop Paul. They spoke to the people and persuaded them that this god-like person was an evil man. Their slander proved to be satanically effective. The people turned on Paul and stoned him. Then they dragged his body out of the city, believing he was dead (14:19). He experienced the very same punishment Stephen did in **Acts 7.**

Did you notice something strange: the same people who worshipped Paul shortly before now stoned him? The same Jerusalem that welcomed Jesus on His Palm Sunday Triumphal Procession crucified Him a few days later.

Please note another miracle happened. The disciples of the LORD stood around the body of Paul. To their amazement, he also rose up, came into Lystra, reunited with Barnabas and the next day travelled to Derbe (14:20), around fifty kilometres (thirty miles) away. Was Paul actually dead or merely wounded? It is hard to tell from the text but there is a chance Paul actually died from the wounds of the stones and came back to life again. After all, stones are heavy and lethal. Either way, the disciples had just witnessed a miracle even greater than the healing of the lame man. Perhaps the reason Paul did not stay dead is because he had not yet 'finished the course' God had set for him (2 Timothy 4:7).

> LESSON FOR LIFE: People pleasers, take notice. People can change their minds about you in an instant but God never changes.

Full Circle (14:21–28)

After a turbulent response to the gospel in Asia Minor, Derbe seemed to be smooth sailing. The apostles preached the gospel in that city and taught many. If there was opposition in Derbe, it is not mentioned. After teaching the multitudes, the apostles fearlessly returned to the other cities where they had been seriously mistreated: Lystra, Iconium, and

Welcome Holy Spirit

Antioch in Pisidia (14:21). Without explicitly stating the fact, life in the Holy Spirit gives you boldness to face people and places that have been a source of pain in the past.

The reason the apostles returned to these hot-spot cities was *'confirming the souls of the disciples'* (14:22). This is an apostolic and pastoral function and of necessity because in these troublesome places were Christian congregations who needed care. The apostles told them to *'continue in the faith'* and added this caveat: *'We must through much tribulation enter into the kingdom of God'* (14:22). This is true though Paul experienced exceptional suffering, as the Lord predicted (9:16).

What else did the apostles do in these new churches they planted? They ordained elders in every church. There was prayer and fasting. Finally, they committed these churches to the Lord, in whom they put their trust (14:23). The apostles could not stay with all these churches but the Holy Spirit did.

The apostles were on the move. Travelling southward towards the Mediterranean Sea, they passed through Pisidia and came to the region of Pamphylia. They preached the word in Perga and came to Attalia, a seaport (14:24-25). From Attalia, Barnabas and Paul sailed to Antioch on the Orontes (Syrian Antioch), where they began this journey and were *'recommended to the grace of God'* for the work they were called to do (14:26).

The apostles shared with the great church at Antioch about the wonderful things God had done (Acts 13–14). The main message was that God had opened the hearts of the Gentiles to receive the gospel of Christ by faith (14:27). Indeed, it was a bumper harvest.

The first missionary journey was now completed. Paul and Barnabas had gone full circle from Syrian Antioch to Cyprus to Asia Minor back to Antioch. Though it had its troubles, the journey was a big triumph, especially in the fruitful harvest field of the Gentiles.

Fourteen: Triumph and Trouble

There was no quick return to the mission field. Barnabas and Saul remained in Syrian Antioch for a long time (14:28). Thus ended Paul's first missionary journey but it would not be his last. Yet before he returned to the mission field, a serious controversy erupted regarding Jewish and Gentiles believers. The church leaders needed the wisdom of Solomon to solve it. Fortunately, someone greater than Solomon came. Learn all about it in the next chapter.

LESSON FOR LIFE: No demonic opposition can stop you from fulfilling your call when you persevere in God's grace and the power of the Holy Spirit.

CHAPTER FIFTEEN
The Council of Jerusalem

Who: Judaisers versus Apostles

What: Troubled the Gentile believers

When: In-between the first and second missionary journeys

Where: Syria and Judea

Why: Decide the status of Gentile believers

How: Word of Wisdom from the Holy Spirit

> *For it seemed good to the Holy Ghost, and to us, to lay upon you no greater burden than these necessary things; That ye abstain from meats offered to idols, and from blood, and from things strangled, and from fornication: from which if ye keep yourselves, ye shall do well. Fare ye well.*
> — *Acts 15:28–29*

A Word of Wisdom (15:1–12)

While there was a gap of time between the first and second missionary journeys, Paul and Barnabas were not idle. The thriving church at Antioch commanded much of their attention. And now the mother church had a great challenge that, if not handled with sensitivity and wisdom, could powerfully rupture the early church. It would be the first of many such internal challenges throughout church history.

In the great gospel harvest field, there is always the danger of weeds among the wheat. While Paul and Barnabas were still in Antioch, certain men came down from Judaea and taught the brethren they could not be saved unless they were circumcised after the manner of Moses (15:1).

Welcome Holy Spirit

Paul and Barnabas, the leaders in Antioch, had a big dispute with these teachers (often called Judaisers, who wanted Gentiles to become Torah-observant Jews before they could become Christians). This matter was not going away nor dying a quiet death. So, it was decided that Paul and Barnabas with other key people would go to Jerusalem and discuss this matter with the apostles and elders there (15:2).

On the road from Antioch to Jerusalem, the apostles passed through Phoenicia and Samaria. In these places, they declared that the Gentiles were coming to faith in the Messiah (15:3). Unlike the terse reaction of the Jerusalem apostles in **Acts 11**, these people were full of great joy when they heard the news.

> LESSON FOR LIFE: Wherever you see the wheat growing, there will also be the tares. God will deal with both in His own way and time.

Upon the arrival of the Antiochian delegation to Jerusalem, they were received by the church, apostles and elders. The first order of business was to declare all the things that God had done with them (15:4). After the testimonials, *'certain of the sect of the Pharisees which believed'* (15:5) laid their cards on the table. Note that not all Pharisees were the enemies of Jesus and the church. Paul was a Pharisee (23:6) and now an apostle for Christ and so were some others. Nevertheless, they had strong opinions which needed to be addressed. Without a resolution, the ancient church could be seriously split. The certain believing Pharisees said that Gentiles who came to faith in Messiah needed to be circumcised and keep the law of Moses (15:5) in order to have eternal salvation in Messiah. In other words, they needed to convert to Judaism and be like the proselytes before they could enter into the Messianic community of faith. After this audacious statement, the apostles and elders came together to consider this matter. It was of the utmost urgency (15:6). Thus commenced the council of Jerusalem, the first of several key gatherings throughout church history that helped determine the direction of the Lord's people.

Fifteen: The Council of Jerusalem

This contentious issue affected the entire Christian church and there was *'much disputing'* (15:7). Peter, the leader, rose up and addressed the *'men and brethren'* (15:7). He reminded them that God had chosen him, perhaps the very first, to take the word of the gospel to the Gentiles (15:7). The result of that was that they believed. He was referring to the transformational events that had happened in **Acts 10** with the conversion of Cornelius, the Roman centurion, in Caesarea.

Peter made an insightful statement: God knows the hearts (15:8). His X-ray vision cuts through the surface and superficial and gets to the core of the matter. God had validated the Gentile believers in their new faith. He had done this by giving them the Holy Spirit, just as He had done to the Jewish believers on the day of Pentecost (15:8). Remember, in **Acts 10**, while Peter was still preaching, the Holy Spirit had come upon Cornelius and the other Gentiles. How did they know that this had happened? They heard them speak in tongues and magnify God (10:44–46). **Note**: Cornelius and company had not been circumcised, had not yet been baptised and had not overtly kept any of the law of Moses. Nevertheless, God had blessed them with the same Holy Spirit in the same manner as He had done with the Jewish believers in **Acts 2**. Before God, there was no difference between Jewish and Gentile believers. God had purified the Gentiles' hearts by faith (15:9).

Then Peter came straight to the point: why were they going to tempt God? How did they do that? By putting a yoke upon the neck of Gentile disciples which neither the Jews past nor Jews present had been able to fulfil (15:10). If Jews struggled to keep the law of Moses, which cannot save a person anyway, why were they requiring it of Gentiles who already had received the blessing of God? We, both Jew and Gentile, are saved by the grace of our Lord Jesus Christ (15:11). Religious works can't deliver salvation.

After hearing about the grace of God in one Gentile house, namely Cornelius, the members of the council turned to Paul and Barnabas. They were in attentive silence as the two apostles shared about their great adventures in evangelism and church planting. A multitude of

Gentiles came to faith in various cities, all without circumcision or the Law of Moses (15:12). Without realising it, a new dispensation had dawned: God's long-term plan of saving the Gentiles had finally come to pass.

The Word of Wisdom in Action (15:13–34)

According to **1 Corinthians 12**, there are nine supernatural 'gifts of the Holy Spirit'. Christians should not be ignorant of these gifts (1 Corinthians 12:1); they are given for the benefit of everyone (1 Corinthians 12:7); distributed through the believer at the discretion of the Holy Spirit (1 Corinthians 12:11); and believers should earnestly seek the best gifts (1 Corinthians 12:31). There are three gifts of power: faith, miracles and healing (the latter described as 'gifts', plural); three gifts of exhortation: a message in tongues, interpretation of tongues and prophesying. Finally, there are three gifts of revelation: discerning of spirits, word of knowledge and word of wisdom. It is the latter we will focus on.

A word of wisdom is a supernatural infusion of divine wisdom when facing a difficult and seemingly unsolvable problem. Solomon demonstrated the word of wisdom when he rightly discerned between the two harlots who was the real mother of the living child (1 Kings 3:16–28). Paul displayed the word of wisdom when he counselled the ship captain during a potentially fatal storm at sea; this spiritual gift saved the lives of all two hundred and seventy-six passengers (Acts 27:21–25, 37).

We will see another example of word of wisdom in this chapter. The early church faced its greatest crisis yet, and it was not from outside persecution but internal sectarian divisions. Without God's wisdom, the church could have been split asunder. The word of wisdom would save the day, and God used the mouth of James to deliver it.

James the Just was an important leader in the Jerusalem church. He stood up and invited the men and brethren to listen to him (15:13). The

Fifteen: The Council of Jerusalem

Book of James is called the 'mini-Proverbs of the New Testament' because of its wise, pithy sayings. The man himself will have a word of wisdom from the Holy Spirit at this critical hour for the church.

James recounted how Simeon[49] declared the visitation of God upon the Gentiles which resulted in separating for Himself a people called by His name (15:14). Just as God had separated the Israelites for Himself, He had done the same with the Gentiles. This testimony of Gentile salvation agreed with the words of the prophets (15:15). This is like the Biblical maxim where two or three are sufficient to be a credible witness.

Then the message spoke of a prophecy from **Amos 9:11–15**, taken from the Septuagint (LXX),[50] referring to the Tabernacle of David (15:16). The context is about the last days, including a prophecy of the regathering of Israel from captivity into the promised land, where they will settle and never be uprooted (Amos 9:15). The interpretation of this reference to the Tabernacle of David is varied; yet, it implies restoration, redemption, Messiah and ultimately salvation.

In Amos, it speaks about the remnant of Edom, in Acts of men (in Hebrew, *Edom* is close to *Adam*, which means 'man') but either way, the Gentiles are being caught in the dragnet of God's salvation: *'and all the Gentiles, upon whom my name is called'* (15:17). The salvation of the Gentiles was not some new innovative idea. It was part of God's plan from the very beginning (Genesis 12:3, 15:18; 22:17-18). That is why it made perfect sense to send the gospel to both Jews and Gentiles alike, and we should not be surprised that the Gentiles were responding so positively.

James was about to render his judgement, which carried a lot of authority. The over-arching principle was that they should not make it hard for the Gentiles who were coming to faith (15:19). 'Don't add a heavy burden to them. Let's write them a letter and ask them to keep four simple commands. Please abstain from the following four things:

Welcome Holy Spirit

1) **The pollution of idols:** Avoid idolatry and eating meat offered to idols or attending heathen feasts. Idolatry brings bondage and is an abomination to God.
2) **Fornication** (Greek *porneia*, from where we get the word 'pornography'): Fornication is not just an unmarried couple having sexual intercourse; it also includes adultery, incest, temple prostitution and all forms of sexual uncleanness and activity outside of God's design.
3) **Strangled meat:** The purpose of strangling is so that no blood is shed; it is retained inwardly and thus makes the meat defiled.
4) **Blood: Genesis 9:4** says, *'But flesh with the life thereof, which is the blood thereof, shall ye not eat'* and **Leviticus 17:11** declares, *'For the life of the flesh is in the blood: and I have given it to you upon the altar to make an atonement for your souls: for it is the blood that maketh an atonement for the soul'* (15:20).

Note: The Jewish apostles implicitly rejected the doctrine of the Judaisers. They were not requiring circumcision, sabbath-keeping or other details of the Mosaic law. The reason is that grace through faith was the road to salvation and the Gentiles were embarking on it. This simple four-fold recommendation of James, which was ratified by the Council, was a word of wisdom from Almighty God. The Gentiles were treated with respect and not burdened with requirements that the Jews themselves had struggled to keep.

James provided a 'win-win' for all followers of Messiah, Jew and Gentile. He then remembered Moses, a highly honoured figure to the Jews. James reminded the council that every sabbath day in every city with a synagogue, Moses' writings were being read. Everyone could derive benefit from his words (5:21).

Now that the Holy Spirit had spoken through James, it was time to send the Gentile believers a letter. This liberating message would be carried back to Antioch, the seat of a great Gentile church, by Paul and

Fifteen: The Council of Jerusalem

Barnabas, as well as two Jerusalem-based men, Judas Barsabas and Silas (15:22).

The letter began by identifying the senders: the Jerusalem apostles, elders and brethren. They sent greetings to Gentile brethren in Antioch, Syria (15:23) and Cilicia (Asia Minor).

After the salutation came the main message. They heard that 'certain' (nameless) men came out from them (Judaea) and gave the Gentile church disturbing words that troubled their souls. Their worrying message: 'You must be circumcised and keep the law of Moses'. The apostles had never sent these people nor given such a command (15:24), even though the Judaisers invoked their name.

The Jerusalem Council did more than send a letter – they dispatched beloved, credible and honourable men to accompany Barnabas and Paul. These brothers were genuine men of God: indeed, Judas and Silas had risked their lives for the Lord Jesus Christ (15:25–26). They were authorised messengers from Jerusalem, not like the Judaisers who had come earlier. As the latter troubled the Gentiles' souls, the authorised men blessed them; as the latter were legalistic, the apostles gave grace; as the latter brought bondage, Judas and Silas proclaimed liberty. Their initial purpose was to confirm the words of this letter and amplify the message verbally (15:27).

Yet the unspoken message was even more profound: the Jerusalem Church spoke to the Gentiles through their actions. The message went like this: You Gentile believers, once despised and estranged from the commonwealth of Israel, are important to God and us. We proved this when we convened a church council, gave a Spirit-inspired magnanimous ruling, and then sent you our very best men. You know that God cares because we care, and we proved it.

Yes, you can get the message in a book, letter, television, internet or email. Yet there is nothing like getting it incarnationally, through a visitation in-person by Godly men and women.

Welcome Holy Spirit

Now we get to the heart of the message. The Jerusalem Council, composed of the apostles and elders of the Jerusalem Church, was about to announce their ruling, not unlike a Supreme Court decree. The letter introduced the conclusion by saying it seemed good to the Holy Spirit and the Council to not burden Gentile believers further than these four necessary things. They reiterated the four-fold prohibition against eating meat offered to idols, eating blood and strangled meat, and abstaining from fornication (15:29). These four prohibitions were far more reasonable and manageable than demanding that Gentile Christians keep the six hundred and thirteen Mosaic laws. If they observed these four prohibitions, they would do well. Armed with this information, the foursome departed from Jerusalem and journeyed northward to Antioch. They gathered the people together and read to them the above epistle (15:30).

The Judaisers that had come before had created great upset and confusion among the Gentile believers at Antioch and elsewhere. Now these four anointed apostles came with the letter from the Council of Jerusalem bringing peace and joy. When the letter was read, the Gentile believers rejoiced at the comfort the letter brought (15:31). What a relief! Words that are inspired by the Holy Spirit bring light, life and peace. Any teaching that is false or a mixture of true and false will not bring such results. Along with Paul and Barnabas, Judas and Silas, who were prophets, strengthened the Gentile believers with their many anointed words (15:32). Genuine ministry builds up the Body of Christ.

Judas and Silas stayed in Antioch for a while, possibly longer than they expected, and then were released to return to the apostles who sent them (15:33). Nevertheless, Silas got a sense that he should remain (15:34). It is a good thing that he did. His continued sojourn in Antioch was a divine appointment that set him up to be part of the next great gospel adventure: the second missionary journey.

Fifteen: The Council of Jerusalem

Paul and Barnabas Separate (15:35–41)

Paul and Barnabas also decided to stay in Antioch for the time being (15:35). During that period, they were teaching and preaching the word of God, along with *'many others also'*. After some time, Paul proposed to Barnabas that they retrace their steps from the first missionary journey. The goal was to see the progress of the young churches they planted (15:36). Barnabas agreed, but they would not make the journey together. Here's why.

Barnabas added a 'P.S.' to his agreement. He wanted to take John Mark on this journey (15:37). Paul disagreed. He said it was not a good idea to take John Mark with them. He had started the first missionary journey and travelled throughout Cyprus with them, but once they had arrived in the Asia Minor region of Pamphylia, he deserted them and returned to Jerusalem (13:13). In Paul's mind, such irresponsible behaviour disqualified him from making another missionary journey.

We know that Paul had a strong personality, but was Barnabas the same? Apparently yes. The two apostles could not resolve their disagreement. The contention between them was so great that they decided to separate from each other. Barnabas took John Mark by the hand, and they sailed to Cyprus (15:39), where the former came from. Thus ended a very effective apostolic partnership.

It is good that the Word of God does not do a whitewash of Biblical heroes. It shows their essential humanity along with their spiritual fruit. Of interest is that while Paul rejected the inclusion of John Mark in his ministry team, he would have a definite change of heart near the end of his life. In **2 Timothy 4:11**, he requests Timothy to bring John Mark to him because *'he is profitable to me for the ministry'*. Paul changed his mind because John Mark had become a changed man. Thanks to his mentoring by Barnabas and Peter, his vision, Godly friendships, prayer and persistence, John Mark became the apostle to Africa in Alexandria and wrote the second gospel which bears his name.

Welcome Holy Spirit

Paul, having parted from Barnabas, chose to take Silas with him instead. They were commended by the brethren at Antioch to the grace of God and released to the mission field. Duly deployed from Antioch, Paul and Silas travelled through Syria and Cilicia, the very regions he had visited on the first journey. Wherever they went, they built up the churches (15:41).

While Paul 'lost' Barnabas, he not only gained Silas but on this trip, he would birth a spiritual son who would follow him to the end. We will meet this 'son' in the next chapter.

> LESSON FOR LIFE: Human failure can be regrettable, but in the end, it will not stop the will of God and the work of the Holy Spirit.

---

[49] While the text says 'Simeon,' and other translations say the same, it could be another way of saying Simon Peter. The wording certainly applies to him.

[50] The Septuagint, LXX (70), dated 285 BC, was the first major translation of the Hebrew Bible (Old Testament) into Greek, the *lingua franca* of the ancient world. Now the word of God was available and understandable to the vast majority of people. It was the Bible of the early church and liberally quoted in the New Testament.

CHAPTER SIXTEEN

The Gate of Europe

Who: Paul, Silas, Timothy and Luke

What: Brought the gospel to Europe

When: The second missionary journey, stage one

Where: Lystra, Troas and Philippi

Why: A follow-up apostolic visit and a missionary one

How: Guidance and empowerment of the Holy Spirit

> *And a vision appeared to Paul in the night; There stood a man of Macedonia, and prayed him, saying, Come over into Macedonia, and help us. And after he had seen the vision, immediately we endeavoured to go into Macedonia, assuredly gathering that the Lord had called us for to preach the gospel unto them.*
> — *Acts 16:9–10*

Introducing Timothy (16:1–8)

Paul returned to Lystra and Derbe, fearlessly. Remember it was at Lystra where he was worshipped one day and stoned the next – probably to death (14:19). Nevertheless, he would not be deterred from visiting the city and region again. There, on his third visit, the apostle would be more than compensated with a great blessing for the bruising he experienced earlier. Paul's reward was a young man called Timothy, a disciple of the Lord. His mother was a believing Jewess but his father was a Gentile (16:1), ostensibly not a believer. Out of the womb of tribulation was birthed a relationship that would impact eternity. Timothy would become Paul's protege, son and successor.

Timothy had a good reputation with those in Lystra and Iconium (16:2). It is always wise before entering into a partnership, whether it be work, ministry or marriage, to hear from the people who know the individual best. In today's 'smoke and mirrors' world, it is easy to put on a facade for the short-to-medium term that can deceive the unsuspecting. Your greatest protection from the heartache of wrong alliances is to heed the voice of the Holy Spirit and get credible references. Timothy received the 'thumbs up' from the brethren in these two cities.

Before their ministry partnership could commence, Paul did something that seemed puzzling and contradictory to the Jerusalem Council: he had Timothy circumcised (16:3). This simple statement could easily be overlooked but it raised some serious problems. In the previous chapter, we learned how Gentiles were not to be circumcised as a pathway to salvation. Now, here is Timothy getting circumcised. What's going on? Paul had a wise logic here without contradiction. If you, as a Gentile, submit to circumcision thinking it will get you saved, then you are mistaken. In Timothy's case, his Jewish mother made him 'Jewish enough'. Yet his father was a Gentile (16:3), thus implying he was 'uncircumcised' (which he was). He was called to win Jews and Gentiles to Christ. So, in order to even get a hearing with Jews, he needed to be circumcised as a point of contact and identity, not to 'fulfil the law'.

We are to be all things to all men, that by all means, we might win some. In **1 Corinthians 9:20**, Paul says, '*And unto the Jews I became as a Jew, that I might gain the Jews.*' That's what this was about. Perhaps it is like early missionaries to China wearing pigtails or to the Muslim world covering the head. Also, remember Paul had enough trouble with unbelieving Jews in Lystra and Iconium; he did not want to invite bonus trouble by having 'Jewish enough' Timothy work with him as an uncircumcised apostle.

Sixteen: The Gate of Europe

The encouragement of having Gentile believers remain uncircumcised (read Galatians on this) did not necessarily apply to Jews who believed, and Timothy was one of them. (Though apostles to the Gentiles were ministering in synagogues, they had to accommodate Jewish sensitivities to have a fighting chance to win them to Messiah).

As they travelled throughout Asia Minor, the apostles delivered the same Jerusalem Council letter that had been read at Antioch (16:4). They did this without a hint of contradiction. It says that the churches, especially those who received this letter, were 'established in the faith' and 'increased in number daily' (16:5). Wise oversight, sound doctrine, dynamic spiritual life of prayer and the Holy Spirit are the ways we can see the churches established and growing.

The apostles were travelling through the regions of Phrygia and Galatia in Asia Minor. The Holy Spirit had forbidden them (Greek κωλύω, *kolyo*,[51] found six times in the New Testament and defined as 'hinder', 'forbid', 'prevent', 'deny' and 'refuse') to go into the Roman province of Asia (16:6). This is western Asia Minor where Ephesus is located; it does not mean the entire continent we call Asia. If God wants us to go into 'all the world' with the gospel, why is there a prohibition by the Holy Spirit? Because God's will must be fulfilled according to His terms, timing and territory. God wanted them to go to Europe first before Asia. At Mysia in north-western Asia Minor, they wanted to go north-east to the region of Bithynia, but the Spirit said 'No' (16:7). It was as if they were cornered. They couldn't go to Asia, they couldn't go to Bithynia, so where should they go? They would soon get an answer.

> LESSON FOR LIFE: Take heart, O person of faith. When God closes one door, it is only so that He can open another better and more timely door for you.

When the doors closed, Paul and Silas went to Troas (16:8) near Troy, the scene of the legendary Trojan horse, and there they would receive divine direction for the next step of their missionary journey.

Welcome Holy Spirit

The Macedonian Call: Philippi (16:9–15)

God the Holy Spirit closed the doors – for now – to Bithynia and the Roman province of Asia; this means He had something else in mind. For the faithful, when one door closes, another opens. While pondering their next move, Paul had a night vision of a man from Macedonia. He invited the apostles to come and help them (16:9). Dreams and visions are all part of life and ministry in the Spirit (Joel 2:28; Acts 2:17). No time was wasted. Once Paul saw the vision, 'immediately' they planned to go to Macedonia in Europe, which was across the Aegean Sea from Troas. They were certain the Lord called them to preach the gospel there (16:10).

After sailing from Troas, they went northwest to the island of Samothracia and then to Neapolis, known today as the picturesque Greek port of Kavala. Luke, the author of Acts, had a meticulous eye for detail. Neapolis was their first point of contact with Europe. The apostles went from there to Philippi, which was the chief city of that part of Macedonia and a colony of Rome. They dwelt there for several days (16:12). Despite its prominence, it did not appear to have a Jewish synagogue, which meant the number of male Jews was insufficient to have a quorum. The church that was birthed from this apostolic visit was known for its generosity and was the subject of the **Epistle to the Philippians**, which teaches us how to have joy in all circumstances.

On the sabbath day, instead of going to a synagogue, Paul and Silas went to the riverside. Prayer was made there. The apostles were going to practise outdoor evangelism since there was no apparent synagogue. They sat down by the riverbank and spoke to the women who were there (16:13). A businesswoman named Lydia was by the riverside. She was from Thyatira and sold purple dye. Lydia was a God-worshipper (either a God-fearer or in between a proselyte and a God-fearer). God opened her heart so that she listened attentively to the gospel message from Paul (16:14). She not only was 'open', she believed and received the gospel.

Sixteen: The Gate of Europe

Lydia and her household were baptised in the name of the Lord. She then gave Paul and Silas an invitation they could not refuse. *'If ye have judged me to be faithful to the Lord, come into my house, and abide there'* (16:15). For them to say 'No' was tantamount to implying that Lydia was not faithful to the Lord. So she persuaded them and they came into her house as honoured guests.

> LESSON FOR LIFE: Spirit-filled ministry is like the sailboat: hoist your sail on the mast, catch the wind of the Spirit and you will go places in God.

Trouble in Philippi (16:16–40)

The devil was losing ground to the church and its fearless apostles. When that happens, expect a fight. The trouble that was about to erupt was a sure sign that the apostles were on the right track and doing the right thing. As they went to prayer, they encountered a young woman with the spirit of divination. Her soothsaying was the source of much income for her masters (16:16).

The woman followed the apostles and said, *'These men are the servants of the most high God, which shew unto us the way of salvation'* (16:17). There was nothing wrong or false with her words; they were true enough. The problem was the spirit behind those words; it was vexatious, persistent and devilish. These utterances continued for many days. The patience of the apostles was running out. Paul was 'grieved' by the spirit behind this proclamation. Finally, he had had enough. He turned and spoke to the spirit – not the woman but the spirit in her – and commanded it come out of her in the name of Jesus Christ (16:18). Within the hour, she was set free.

The masters of the young woman were distraught. Now that she no longer had the spirit of divination, she could not be a source of great income for them. As a reaction, they seized the apostles and took them to the marketplace (16:19) where the rulers were located. The men complained to the magistrate about the apostles (16:20). They were called 'Jews' who troubled the city. To add to their complaint, the masters said that the apostles taught strange customs that were not lawful to receive or observe because the Philippians were Romans (16:21), not Jews.

This complaint accomplished its purpose. The multitude in Philippi rose up against the apostles. The magistrates tore their clothes as a sign of outrage and commanded the apostles to be beaten (16:22). This was before they were even given a chance to defend themselves (an un-Roman thing to do). After receiving many stripes, the apostles were cast into prison (16:23) and the jailer was commanded to keep them securely. The jailer took his commission seriously. He thrust the apostles into the innermost prison and put their feet in the stocks (16:24). Humanly speaking, there was no way they could set themselves free.

> LESSON FOR LIFE: Trouble is an equal opportunity harasser: it afflicts the rebellious and righteous. Yet God will redeem the trouble of the righteous and turn it for their good.

In our culture of victimhood, we take offences seriously, no matter how slight or imagined. Playing the victim card has become common – for some, even a game – where you can receive attention, celebration, compensation and entitlement. However, in the end, victimhood is futile, self-defeating, puts your life on hold and stunts your spiritual growth.

Though horribly and unjustly treated, Paul and Silas demonstrated a better way. After leading the household of Lydia to faith and planting a church in the city, they were satanically attacked and genuinely mistreated. Few would blame them for 'licking their wounds' and plotting revenge. Yet, that's not how they responded. At midnight, when many would be sleeping, the apostles were praying and praising. Though located in the innermost prison, their voices were loud enough for the other prisoners to hear them (16:25). Prayer, praise, thanksgiving and worship are all part of the language of faith. Send your praises

Sixteen: The Gate of Europe

upwards and the blessings of God will come downward thanks to the Holy Spirit.

Was the earthquake a result of prayer and praise? Yes, it was. The earthquake came suddenly, shook the foundations of the prison, all doors were opened and everyone's chains were loosed (16:26). Prayer and praise bring liberty.

It wasn't just the earth that was shaken; so was the keeper of the prison. The earthquake woke him up from a dead sleep. He saw that the prison doors were open and surmised that there was a great escape of prisoners (16:27). If this were the case, he believed there would be retribution from the Roman officials. Better to pull his sword and commit suicide than face imperial capital punishment, which could include crucifixion. Paul, who saw what was about to happen, cried out in a loud voice to the prison keeper, 'Don't do yourself any harm; all the prisoners are still here' (16:28). The prison keeper called for the light, came into Paul's cell (16:29) and fell at his feet. After bringing out the apostles, he asked the million-dollar question: '*Sirs, what must I do to be saved* (16:30)?' Can any question be more important than this?

The response to the jailer's question could not be simpler: '*Believe on the Lord Jesus Christ, and thou shalt be saved, and thy house (16:31).*' Just like what happened in Lydia's case, if you believe, you can also lead your household to faith. God has a wide fishing net. The apostles spoke the word of the Lord to the jailer and his household. Though there is the promise of household salvation in verse 31, it can only come to pass when they hear the word of the Lord.

> LESSON FOR LIFE: Sow praises in the heavens and God will rain down blessings on earth.

God used the unjust imprisonment of Paul and Silas to bring salvation to the household of the Philippian jailer. After sharing the word of the Lord with them, the apostles had their wounds washed (16:33). Then they immediately baptised the jailer and his household; as we observed, there was little waiting between repentance and water baptism in the **Book of Acts**. After the baptism, they went to the jailer's home, where they had a meal. He rejoiced and believed God with all his household (16:34). Thus, the jailer of Philippi had gone from being a custodian to a grateful, generous host of the apostles, just like Lydia.

In the morning, the Philippian magistrates sent the sergeants and told them to free the apostles (16:35). The keeper of the prison told this saying to Paul. *'The magistrates have sent to let you go: now therefore depart, and go in peace'* (16:36). Paul was rightly indignant at the underhanded dealings of the Philippian officials. He and Silas had been brutally beaten in public, even though they were never tried nor convicted. This is even more unacceptable because they were Roman citizens and had been denied their most basic human rights. They were also cast into prison, though they lacked a fair trial. All of this had been done in public. Now magistrates wanted to release them quietly? No, declared Paul, if they want him and Silas to leave Philippi, they need to come to the jail personally and bring them out (16:37).

The sergeants told Paul's words to the magistrates. When they heard they were Romans, they feared greatly (16:38). This was a breach of Roman protocol which guaranteed certain rights to its citizens. The officials came to the apostles, brought them out of the prison precincts and begged them to leave the city (16:39). Unlike the jailer or Lydia, the shaken Philippian officials were in no mood to be hospitable. It seemed unfair that the apostles, having done nothing wrong, were still asked to depart the city and leave the infant church behind. Yet the rest of the continent of Europe needed the gospel, of which Philippi was Paul's first port of call.

Before voluntarily leaving the city, the apostles visited Lydia and the brethren. They 'comforted them' and then left (16:40). This again raised an interesting question: how could these young churches, planted during Paul's missionary journeys, survive once the apostles departed? Their pastors and leaders had no formal training and had none of the

Sixteen: The Gate of Europe

resources available to church workers today. The answer is the Holy Spirit: the same Person who birthed the church and inspired the Scriptures was able to be their comforter, teacher and guide in all situations. As Jesus says in **John 14:26**, *'But the Comforter, which is the Holy Ghost, whom the Father will send in my name, he shall teach you all things, and bring all things to your remembrance, whatsoever I have said unto you.'*

The grace, joy and tenacity kept the apostles travelling the gospel road in Europe, specifically Greece. Next stop: Thessalonica.

> LESSON FOR LIFE: When God is all you have, you will discover that God is all you need.

Welcome Holy Spirit

---

[51] G2967 - kōlyō - Strong's Greek Lexicon (kjv). Blue Letter Bible. Accessed 9 Apr, 2024. https://www.blueletterbible.org/lexicon/g2967/kjv/tr/0-1/

CHAPTER SEVENTEEN

The Road to Athens

Who: Paul, Silas, Timothy, Luke

What: Missionary journey through Greece

When: Second missionary journey, stage two

Where: Thessalonica, Berea and Athens

Why: Macedonian call

How: By the power of the Holy Spirit

> *Then Paul stood in the midst of Mars' hill, and said, Ye men of Athens, I perceive that in all things ye are too superstitious. For as I passed by, and beheld your devotions, I found an altar with this inscription, TO THE UNKNOWN GOD. Whom therefore ye ignorantly worship, him declare I unto you.*
> — *Acts 17:22–23*

Ministry in Thessalonica (17:1–9)

Having left Philippi, the apostles Paul and Silas travelled through two cities named Amphipolis and Apollonia until they arrived in Thessalonica. Unlike Philippi, Thessalonica had a Jewish synagogue (17:1). Since there was no local church, the synagogue was the place to meet. Besides, this was Paul's custom all his life, being in the synagogue on the sabbath day. So, for three sabbath days in a row, Paul went to the synagogue at Thessalonica and had a discussion, even a debate, out of the Scriptures (17:2). The topic? That Messiah would suffer, die and then

Welcome Holy Spirit

rise from the dead. Furthermore, Jesus of Nazareth, the One Whom Paul preached about, was the long-awaited Messiah of Israel (17:3).

These strategic visits netted stunning results. Some of those present believed and aligned themselves with Paul and Silas. Perhaps their biggest win was a great multitude of devout Gentiles, and many of the 'chief women' (17:4) believed in the gospel.

Yet where there was a spiritual triumph, there came worldly trouble. Those Jews in the synagogue who did not believe saw the success of the apostles and were motivated by envy. They aligned or recruited unsavoury, vile people, gathered a crowd and set the entire city in an uproar. Then they attacked the house of Jason and sought to bring the men out to the people (17:5). The men were not present so Jason, a local man from Thessalonica, and some of the brethren were taken to the rulers of the city. They screamed this accusation: *'These (the apostles) that have turned the world upside down are come hither [here] also'* (17:6). This was meant to be a grievous accusation, but it ended up being a lofty accolade. The gospel can disrupt the (dis)order of this fallen world.

Jason was blamed for receiving the apostles (17:7), who taught doctrine contrary to the decrees of Caesar. The most grievous of these was that there was another king – a rival to the emperor – called Jesus. Those who heard these things, including the rulers and the people, were greatly disturbed (17:8). The harassment this contention spawned would follow the apostles even to the next city. After securing Jason and the others, the men were let go (17:9). Things were getting too hot to handle, so the local brethren sent Paul and Silas to the next city, Berea, by night (17:10). Their first destination upon arrival was the Jewish synagogue.

Persecution is no picnic yet often it serves as a purifying fire. Out of the flames came two magnificent New Testament epistles: **1 and 2 Thessalonians.**

> LESSON FOR LIFE: The gospel and Word of God are like a two-edged sword: well-received by the righteous and vehemently rejected by the wicked.

Seventeen: The Road to Athens

The Bereans were 'more noble' than the people of Thessalonica. They received the word of God with all openness of heart and mind. Also, they practised discernment by searching the scriptures daily to see if the apostles' teaching was accurate (17:11), which it was. As a result, many believed, including the honourable Greek women and the men (17:12). It appeared that the Gentile receptivity to the gospel was much more than the Jews. When the unruly, unbelieving Jews of Thessalonica heard that the word of God was preached in Berea by Paul, they came to town and stirred up the people (17:13). The distance they travelled was seventy-three kilometres (forty-five miles). Upon arrival, they became a riotous crowd.

For the third time in Europe, the apostles were forced to leave the city and the young church behind. The difference was that this time, only Paul needed to leave town while Silas and Timothy stayed in Berea (17:14). Paul was sent by sea, not by land. When he arrived in Athens, he immediately gave the command for Silas and Timothy to join him as soon as possible (17:15). They dutifully departed Berea and were on their way.

> LESSON FOR LIFE: The church would be a better shape if we all had the 'Berean mindset' of open heart, ready mind and searching the scriptures daily.

In the Heart of Greece (17:16–34)

Paul and Silas had completed successful ministry in Philippi, Thessalonica and Berea. Though he had ferocious opposition from unbelievers in each of these cities, the fact is that viable churches had been planted and would continue to thrive. Now, he went ahead of his team to Athens and while waiting for them, his spirit was stirred up because he saw so much idolatry (17:16). The city was steeped in heathenism more than philosophy, and this atmosphere was grievous to the apostle. Little did Paul realise that his spontaneous visit to Athens planted the seed for the eventual supplanting of the ancient Greco-Roman gods and goddesses by the Christian Church.

Paul was in full debate mode. First, he debated *'in the synagogue with the Jews, and with the devout persons'*. In the marketplace, he would talk with anyone willing to meet with him (17:17).

The elite eventually showed up on the scene: philosophers of the Epicureans and Stoics encountered him. Epicureans were linked to stimulating, sensual enjoyment, especially with fine food and drink. Stoics belonged to a philosophical school that did not show pain in the face of hardship; people should be calm and unmoved by emotions and passion, and accept their fate in life without complaint. Both these groups encountered Paul in the marketplace, where he spoke to them of Jesus and the resurrection from the dead (17:18). Some dismissed him as a 'babbler.' Others were highly curious when they heard Paul offering a 'new' but strange (to them) god. No doubt this topic attracted a lot of attention, and he drew an impressive crowd.

The people brought him to the Areopagus so that he could speak of this 'new doctrine' that had come to their attention (17:19). The Areopagus (the name is Greek; the Latin name is 'Mars Hill') was a hill in Athens west of the Acropolis. A highly empowered council had met there in antiquity but eventually, it was now only used in judicial decisions, including for capital crimes. The people brought Paul here so that he could speak of this 'new doctrine' that had come to their attention. The Athenians said that the apostle brought 'strange things' to their ears and they wanted more information (17:20). At least they were open-minded enough.

Before focusing on Paul's message, Luke makes an interesting comment about the Athenians and foreigners in Athens. They like to sit around and hear and discuss the latest ideas (17:21). The Bible encompasses two world views: the Hebraic mindset of ancient Israel, which is practical and action-orientated, and the Hellenistic mindset of ancient Greece, which is abstract, philosophical and cerebral. We need

Seventeen: The Road to Athens

both and our Bible reflects this. Paul understood both worldviews, being born and raised in the Diaspora but trained in Jerusalem and a 'Hebrew of Hebrews' (Philippians 3:5). That's why he was an ideal apostle to the Gentiles.

> LESSON FOR LIFE: As Paul learned to make himself at home in any environment with any kind of people, the Holy Spirit can internationalise anyone to be all things to all men so that some may be saved (1 Corinthians 9:22).

Paul's moment had come. Standing in the middle of the Areopagus, he addressed the 'men of Athens' and referred to their grievous idolatry as a starting point for his message. Referring to the multitude of idols, he said it was obvious that they were a 'religious' or 'superstitious' people (17:22). This can mean that they were mythical, illusory, irrational or traditionally religious people. Using a well-known monument as a point of reference, Paul then used it as a springboard for his sermon. The reason he said the Athenians were religious or superstitious was because he *'beheld their devotions'* (17;23). He also noted the presence of the altar *'To the Unknown God'* (17:23). Then he made a bold statement: the one you ignorantly worship I want to declare to you (17:23). The unknown God, who was not unknown to Paul, was about to be made known to the Athenians.

Paul offered a basic theology lesson by describing the nature of God. He is called Creator, the one who made the world and all things which are in it. He is the Lord of heaven and earth and, as such, does not dwell in temples made with human hands (17:24). God is not served by human hands as if He needed anything (17:25). On the contrary, it is God who gives life, breath and everything else, visible and invisible. From 'one blood', meaning there was a first family (first was Adam and Eve, then Noah and his wife), God made all the nations that dwell on planet Earth. Listen to this statement: God had *'determined the times before appointed'* (17:26) when and where we would live. The implication is that this was planned by God before we were born, perhaps even before creation. In any case, God has been wonderfully involved in our lives; He is closer than our next breath.

Why did God plan for you and me to live where we live in the 21st Century? The reason is found here in verse 27: that we should seek the Lord. If we will wholeheartedly search, we will find Him. This should not be hard because He is not far from any of us (17:27). *'For in him we live, and move, and have our being'* (17:28). This applies to all people. Some of the Greek 'poets' or 'philosophers' say we are also His offspring (17:28). Paul's basic theology lesson was not just good for the Athenians but also is very helpful for us today.

Paul employed the phrase given by the Greek poets and philosophers that we are 'God's offspring.' He used this idea to tell us not to view God as someone who can be reproduced in works of men's hands: *'gold, or silver, or stone, graven by art and man's device'* (17:29). Any attempt to describe God through handicraft will fall far short of His true glory, will be erroneous and will often be a distraction from worshipping God in spirit and in truth (John 4:24).

God had overlooked heathenism, idolatry and ignorance in the past. However, now that Christ has died and risen and the remission of sins is available in His Name, we have to have a fresh approach. Paul says *'but now'*, meaning this present era, God is commanding *'all men every where to repent'* (17:30). This means Jews and Gentiles, in Israel and among the nations, male and female, slave and free, have the opportunity and responsibility to commence a new and living connection with the living God and this begins with repentance. Repentance is the prerequisite for salvation and revival. It helps us to have a fresh start.

The reason to repent is because there is an appointed day of judgment in the future. God will judge the world with righteousness. He will do this with the centrepiece of a Man whom God has ordained. The assurance and guarantee that this day and this Man will come is because He has risen from the dead (17:31).

Seventeen: The Road to Athens

When the resurrection from the dead was mentioned, it caused a great commotion among the listeners. Some people were derisive and mocking. Others, however, wanted more information and said, *'We will hear thee again of this matter'* (17:32). The verse simply states Paul departed from among them (17:33). In this one message on Mars Hill, Paul did have some fruit to his account. While there is no mention of supernatural signs and wonders (Athenians prefer to philosophise) nor mention of a viable church beginning at that time, Dionysius the Areopagite and Damaris became believers and others with them (17:34). In addition, we don't have an Epistle to the Athenians. What we know for sure is that Paul visited the city of Athens and, being filled with the Spirit, some people came to faith, including prominent ones. In the land of intellectual giants like Socrates, Plato and Aristotle, the light of God had come.

The sojourn in Europe has just begun. More adventures – and troubles – awaited the apostles in Corinth.

CHAPTER EIGHTEEN
Revival in Corinth

Who: Paul and the Apostles

What: Effective ministry in carnal Corinth

When: End of the second, beginning of the third missionary journey

Where: Corinth

Why: The Spirit led them to fulfil the Great Commission

How: By the anointing and power of the Holy Spirit

> *Then spake the Lord to Paul in the night by a vision, Be not afraid, but speak, and hold not thy peace: For I am with thee, and no man shall set on thee to hurt thee: for I have much people in this city.*
> — *Acts 18:9–10*

Ministry in Corinth (18:1–11)

After his unplanned meeting in Athens, it was time for Paul to move on. He made the journey westward from Athens to Corinth (18:1). This city is eighty-three kilometres (fifty-two miles) west of the Greek capital. A viable church was about to be planted here and became the object of two magnificent New Testament epistles, **1** and **2 Corinthians**.

Corinth was the capital of Achaia in Greece, the richest yet most depraved, wild and worldly city in the country. Strategically located at the isthmus (narrow neck of land) that connects the Peloponnesian Peninsula in the south with the rest of Greece to the north, its location afforded it two harbours: Lechaeum which leads to Italy and Cenchrea which points towards Asia Minor.

Until the Corinth Canal was built in 1893, ships either had to be transported by land from one harbour to another or sail the three hundred and twenty-kilometre (two hundred miles) sea journey around the peninsula, which at times could be dangerous due to bad weather.

Corinth's location made it a crossroads for trade and travel. Along with its commercial importance, Corinth had a plethora of philosophies, false religions and a corrupt culture. At the top of the six hundred-metre hill called Acrocorinthus was a temple of Aphrodite, the 'goddess of love'. To supplement her theme was one thousand slave girls who doubled up as temple prostitutes called *hieroduli*. So sordid was the reputation of Corinth that one of the Greek words for 'fornication', *korinthiazomai*, meant to 'play or act like a Corinthian' and was synonymous with revelling, debauchery and all sorts of immorality.[52]

This was the milieu Paul found himself in when he arrived in the city. He would be greatly aided by some new friends that he found there. For in Corinth was a special couple who served as valued partners of Paul in the ministry. Aquila, born in Pontus in Asia Minor, had recently come from (the church in) Rome, along with his wife Priscilla. Claudius Caesar had commanded all Jews to leave the city of Rome (18:2) and that included Jews who believed in Jesus, too. Their dislocation led them to Corinth, where they were destined to meet Paul (18:2).[53] Paul, Priscilla and Aquila dwelt together since they had the same occupation: tent-making (18:3).

As was his predictable custom, on the sabbath day, Paul went to the local synagogue and sought to convince Jews and Greeks about the gospel (18:4). Finally, Silas and Timothy arrived from Macedonia to Corinth (apparently, they were not with him in Athens). Once they were in the city, Paul was 'pressed in the spirit' (18:5), which probably means that he was greatly burdened for the local Corinthians. He made a

Eighteen: Revival in Corinth

greater effort to devote all his time to preaching the gospel and proving that Jesus is the Messiah.

As was also the custom, after the preaching of the gospel in the synagogue, some of the Jews said 'Yes' and others 'No.' In the case of Corinth, the opposition not only rejected the gospel, but they also blasphemed (18:6). So Paul did a dramatic action. He took his garment and shook it in their presence, which is tantamount to saying he was washing his hands of them. They were given the words of life and the gospel of salvation; their rejection of it meant they would have no one else to blame but themselves. Their warning was served. Now Paul was 'free', because he had discharged his duty to preach the gospel but he was not responsible for their rejection thereof. Thus, their blood was on their own heads. Then he made the major announcement: *'From henceforth I will go unto the Gentiles'* (18:6). And he did – but that was not the end of the matter concerning his Jewish people.

> LESSON FOR LIFE: The great darkness of Corinth meant that the light of the gospel, when it came, shone brighter.

After his declaration of going to the Gentiles, you would think that Paul would go far away from the synagogue. Instead, he went into the house of a God-fearer named Justus, which was right next door to the synagogue (18:7). So, he really did not go far at all and that is a testament to his entire ministry, where Israel's condition and salvation were never far from Paul's thoughts. But there would be a definite change of ministry emphasis, from Paul's nation to the nations of the world. Corinth, as a strategic city, would help the apostles make this important transition. When you consider that the newly born Christian faith found its most fertile soil among the Gentiles, it truly is a marvel.

Considering the spiritual darkness in Corinth, what followed next was no less than bona fide Holy Spirit revival. Crispus, the chief ruler of the synagogue, and his family became believers in Messiah. Many Corinthians believed and were baptised (18:8). The Corinthian revival resembled a move of God similar to what Barnabas and Paul had experienced in Antioch. That's why it appears Paul had no time for tent-making because there was so much work servicing the young church in Corinth. As we learn from the two epistles that bear this city's name, there would be teething problems like factionalism, compromise, flirting with worldliness and the use and misuse of spiritual gifts while holding onto fleshly things.

Paul received an incredible word from the Lord. Like the Macedonian call, it came as a night vision. He was told to not be afraid, but to speak up and not to hold his peace (18:9). We do not get the impression that Paul was shy about anything, let alone speaking about the Lord. Let us remember, however, the rough treatment Paul had had in Philippi, Thessalonica and Berea; such experiences could make people more hesitant (though he spoke up in Athens). Yet here we have the Lord Himself telling Paul to speak up and not to hold back on anything. In essence, Paul was exhorted from heaven to do what he normally did very well – speaking boldly in the Name of the Lord.

What was the basis of Paul's fearless speech? The presence of the Lord, *'For I am with thee'* (18:10). It reminds us of **Psalm 23:4**, that even though we *'walk through the valley of the shadow of death'*, we will *'fear no evil'*, for the Lord is with us.

The promise of God's presence can make any coward courageous. Facing the schoolyard bully is a daunting prospect for a young boy, but when his big brother comes and stands by his side, he has nothing to worry about. Now he can play in the schoolyard with confidence because Big Brother is there.

So it is with the presence of God. Jesus told Paul that He was with him, and no one would hurt him. Why? Apart from His presence, Jesus also had many people in this city (18:10). So the Lord and His people are the reason we need not fear anything. After this visitation, Paul committed himself to staying in Corinth for eighteen months. He taught many people the Word of God (18:11).

Eighteen: Revival in Corinth

Trouble in Corinth (18:12–17)

Paul's ministry in Corinth was as successful as anywhere else. Yet, as always, it stirred up fierce opposition, as usual, driven by envy. While Gallio was deputy of the region of Achaia, the unbelieving Jews *'made insurrection with one accord against Paul, and brought him to the judgment seat'* (18:12). This is why the Lord spoke to him in 18:9–10 to speak up and not be afraid – no one would harm him. He knew what lay ahead and fortified Paul's faith. The promises of protection were true (and still are), but it didn't mean that human opposition wouldn't attempt to harm him, which was exactly what happened here.

His Jewish opponents accused the apostle in front of Gallio that Paul was teaching people to worship God contrary to the Law of Moses (18:13). Two issues: Gallio was a civil deputy and a Gentile; what would he know or care about Jewish law? Also, they were merely stating their opinion regarding Paul's being a law-breaker, even though it can be argued that Paul lived in perfect harmony with the Law, as did Jesus the Messiah, Whom Paul served.

Paul was never lost for words, and he was about to speak when Gallio began to address his Jewish adversaries. If Paul had broken the civil law or practised lewdness, then Gallio would have dealt with this complaint (18:14). Since the controversy was about words, names and the law of Moses, that was an internal Jewish matter. Gallio would not judge in this case (18:15). That would be like asking the Supreme or High Court to settle a theological dispute – it just won't happen. To seal the decision, Gallio drove the accusing party out of the judgment seat (18:16).

Like it or not, the case was dismissed! The (Gentile) crowd felt embarrassed, humiliated and outraged. They grabbed Sosthenes, a man with a Greek name but who was the chief ruler of the synagogue. They beat him up right there in the courtroom (18:17). Yet Gallio paid no attention at all. That was *their* problem. They had made the mess and they would have to clean it up themselves.

Welcome Holy Spirit

Though, in one sense, Corinth was like Paul's other places of ministry – arrival, revival and opposition – yet, unlike Philippi, Thessalonica, and Berea, where Jewish opposition drove Paul out of town, this time, thanks to the earlier words of Jesus (18:9-10), the wind was taken out of their sails. They retreated to the synagogue and Paul was free to stay and continue his ministry for a season in Corinth.

> LESSON FOR LIFE: When trouble hits, remember that God is with you and for you. His presence will shrink the problem.

Paul Returns to Antioch (18:18–23)

Paul spent eighteen months in successful ministry at Corinth. A growing viable church was founded, and he was kept busy. Yet, he also must have raised up local leadership, because he felt ready to move on. He sailed to Syria (which may have included Antioch, Caesarea and Jerusalem). His valuable partners in ministry, Priscilla and Aquila, were with him. Paul stopped at the Corinthian port of Cenchrea, now called Kechries, about fifteen kilometres (nine miles) east of the city, from where you could sail to Asia. Here he made a vow and shaved his head (18:18). In the Bible, Jews shaved their hair and beards in times of distress, repentance or mourning (Job 1:20; Jeremiah 48:37) or when they wanted to cleanse themselves ceremonially (Leviticus 14:9; Numbers 8:7). Paul was ready to visit Jerusalem before returning to Antioch.

Paul spent a brief time in Ephesus, where he left Aquila and Priscilla. He entered the synagogue and debated with the Jews there (18:19). In this case, they were so interested in what he had to say that they asked Paul to stay in the city longer, but he declined (18:20). He was a man on the move.

Why did he refuse? Why was he in a hurry to leave? Paul, in his own words, said, *'I must, by all means, keep this feast that cometh in Jerusalem: but I will return again unto you, if God will'* (18:21). Paul, the Hebrew of Hebrews, but more importantly an apostle of Christ to the Gentiles, had

Eighteen: Revival in Corinth

to get to Jerusalem *'by all means'* to *'keep this feast'*. He does not specify which feast he had in mind or why it had to be observed there. The apostle expressed his willingness to return to Ephesus if God willed it. God was willing because Paul returned to Ephesus on his third missionary journey and spent two years there (Acts 19:10).

He sailed from Ephesus to Caesarea, the grand port and Romanised city, from where he ascended to Jerusalem. Though the holy city was not named explicitly, he had 'gone up' and saluted the church (this has got to be the Jerusalem church, not the one in Caesarea, since there is no ascent there. It is at sea level).

From Jerusalem, he *'went down'* to Antioch (18:22). Going to Jerusalem is always an ascent, geographically and spiritually, and leaving the holy city is always a descent. The return to Antioch marked the completion of Paul's second missionary journey. Though Luke, author of Acts, is replete with details, here he uses an economy of words. After spending time in Antioch, Paul departed and returned to Asia Minor. He visited the regions of Galatia and Phrygia for the express purpose of building up the disciples (18:23) in faith and practice. The apostle was heading towards Ephesus. Without fanfare, the third missionary journey had begun.

Introducing Apollos (18:24–28)

In a milieu that admired great knowledge and oratory, Apollos fit the bill. He was a Jewish man who came from the grand Hellenistic and Roman city of Alexandria, Egypt. He was very knowledgeable of the Scriptures and eloquent, too (18:24). He arrived in Ephesus, almost like a forerunner to Paul's pending two-year ministry. Apollos would break up the fallow ground, making it ready for planting seed.

He was instructed in the way of the Lord and very fervent in spirit – he was 'revived'. His erudition and speaking skills, fuelled by passion, made him like the fireworks on America's Fourth of July. Whatever he preached and taught, he did with diligence, especially of the things of

Welcome Holy Spirit

the Lord. All good. Yet, he had a limitation: Apollos only knew the baptism of John (18:25). So, was he already of believer in Jesus? Or was he a pre-believer? The text does not say and, frankly, we would be only guessing.

Apollos spoke boldly in the synagogue in the presence of Priscilla and Aquila. They took him aside and showed him *'the way of God more perfectly'* (18:26). It appears that dear Apollos was a gifted man who only knew God 'in part'. Thanks to this extraordinary couple, the missing pieces of the puzzle were found and snapped into place. And thanks to Apollos that, despite his great knowledge, he was still teachable.

Since Apollos planned to go to Greece (presumably Corinth), he was highly commended by the believers in Ephesus. The Corinthians were told to receive him wholeheartedly. They apparently did and he was a great help to those who believed in the gospel of grace (18:27). Apollos watered the good seed that Paul had sown (1 Corinthians 3:6) and the harvest continued to bear fruit.

Armed with the full gospel and the power of the Spirit, Apollos powerfully and publicly persuaded that Jesus of Nazareth is the Messiah (18:28). Apollos will be mentioned seven times in **1 Corinthians** and also in **Titus 3:13**. He was a valued partner in ministry and a great help in Corinth, though some wanted to get to his faction (1 Corinthians 3:4).

God's delays are not denials. Ephesus, the place Paul wanted to visit but was forbidden by the Holy Spirit (16:6–7), was about to open its doors to the apostle. He was about to minister at Ephesus – at last.

LESSON FOR LIFE: If you want to grow in God and be mightily used of Him, never stop being open and teachable, just like Apollos (Acts 18:26).

Eighteen: Revival in Corinth

[52] https://earlychurchhistory.org/daily-life/ancient-corinth-a-symbol-of-sin/ Accessed 11 April 2024.

CHAPTER NINETEEN

Ephesus At Last

Who: Paul

What: Ministry in Ephesus

When: During the third missionary journey

Where: Ephesus

Why: Paul was able to minister in a city once off-limits to him

How: Led by the Holy Spirit and waited for His timing

> *And this continued by the space of two years; so that all they which dwelt in Asia heard the word of the Lord Jesus, both Jews and Greeks.*
> — *Acts 19:10*

Ephesian Pentecost (19:1–7)

Though the church at Corinth had its issues, as outlined in the two epistles that bear its name, Paul's ministry there was very effective. We could call it a ministry success story. Now he was heading towards the city – a major one – that he had longed to reach but couldn't ... until now. It was the centre of Diana (Artemis) worship, a fertility goddess who was often depicted by sensuous idols. Paul was on his way to Ephesus, where he would leave an even greater footprint. The ancient world, including the cult of Diana, would be shaken to the core because of the gospel work there.

Welcome Holy Spirit

In **Acts 18**, Paul said he was willing to return to Ephesus if God willed (18:21). God was willing. Apollos was left in Corinth to strengthen the church. Paul arrived at Ephesus and found 'disciples' there (19:1). It is unclear whether they were Christians or pre-Christians since John the Baptist and others also had disciples.

Paul asked an important question: did you receive the Holy Spirit since you believed (19:2)? (Some modern translations say 'when' you believed.) First, the Holy Spirit is instrumental in our conversion, and He immerses (baptises) us into the Body of Christ (1 Corinthians 12:13). In other words, we become part of the universal church when we repent and are born again. However, the implication in this question is of a deeper Biblical experience: have you been baptised/filled with the Holy Spirit since you came to faith? Not all will agree with this assessment, but it is a constant in Acts and throughout the New Testament. Jesus says John baptised with water, but His disciples will be baptised in the Holy Spirit (1:5).

The Ephesian disciples said they did not even know there was a Holy Spirit. Paul asked them which baptism they received. Reply? They were baptised with 'John's baptism', meaning John the Baptist (19:3). Paul explained that John's baptism was the baptism of repentance, pointing people to believe in the coming One, Jesus Christ (19:4). John was the forerunner of Christ, pointing the way to His appearance.

The Ephesians disciples – there were twelve of them (19:7) – wasted no time in submitting to Christian baptism in the Name of the Lord Jesus (19:5). In **Matthew 28:19**, Jesus alludes to the triunity of the Godhead by commanding baptism in the Name (singular) of the Father, Son and Holy Spirit. It appears that either formulation at the time of water baptism – Jesus' Name or the Triune God – was acceptable to the apostles.

A surprise 'bonus' manifested just after the water baptism. When Paul laid his hands on the Ephesians, the Holy Spirit came upon them. They spoke in tongues and prophesied (19:6). This is what happened on the Day of Pentecost (Acts 2), at Cornelius' house (Acts 10) and now in

Nineteen: Ephesus at Last

Ephesus. Speaking in tongues became the sign of the Spirit baptism for the apostles and the sign they expected from others. The lack of tongues does not mean a person is devoid of the Holy Spirit, because He is instrumental in our salvation (1 Corinthians 12:3; 13), but it is a consistent and desirable sign for those who want to be empowered and emboldened by God.

> LESSON FOR LIFE: Christian growth is not determined by how long you believe but by how hungry you are for God's Word and how thirsty you are for the Holy Spirit.

Ministry in Ephesus (19:8–20)

Immediately the scene changes. As was his custom when arriving in a new city, Paul started his ministry in Ephesus by going to the Jewish synagogue. He did this for three months, *'disputing and persuading the things concerning the kingdom of God'* (19:8). This is a good length of time but apparently not all would be convinced. Certain ones simply refused to believe. They were 'hardened', which is another word for 'blindness'. Furthermore, they spoke evil of the gospel before the multitude. Paul then left the hard-hearted behind and separated the disciples. Now, instead of debating in the synagogue, he shifted the debate venue to the school of Tyrannus (19:9).

Paul continued his ministry in Ephesus for two years. The result was that all Jews and Gentiles who dwelt in the province of Asia, where Ephesus is located, heard the word of the Lord Jesus Christ (19:10). Paul's faithfulness and consistency reaped wide coverage for the gospel. Remember that Paul was not allowed to come to this place in **Acts 16** because the time was not right. Yet, now he finally made it to Ephesus and Asia, he was able to spend a considerable amount of time and reap a great harvest.

Welcome Holy Spirit

As normal, Paul demonstrated signs and wonders along with the preaching of the gospel (Mark 16:17; John 14:12). In Ephesus, it says that God brought *'special miracles'* through the hands of Paul (19:11). The desire for healing and miracles was so great that it did not even require Paul's physical presence. Handkerchiefs and aprons (scarves) that came from Paul's body (hands) were used. These same devices would be put on the sick and the diseases departed or when put on the demon-possessed, the evil spirits went out of them (19:12). No marketing campaign can match the attention-grabbing qualities that a powerful, irrefutable demonstration of the supernatural can bring. It is part of the believers' heritage when they welcome the Holy Spirit.

Paul's anointing for healings, miracles and deliverances caught the attention of certain itinerant Jewish exorcists. They decided they wanted to cast out evil spirits the way Paul did. It is a classic case of 'monkey see, monkey do'. Since Paul was so effective in deliverance ministry by using the Name of Jesus, they thought they could do the same. So, they used the simple command: *'We adjure you by Jesus whom Paul preacheth'* (19:13). The seven sons of Sceva, a Jew and chief of priests, quoted this declaration of deliverance (19:14).

The evil spirit had other ideas. It spoke through the demonised man and said, *'Jesus I know; Paul I know, but who are ye?'* (19:15). Even if people in the flesh are clueless about Christ's true identity, the demon world is not. Remember the devils knew and confessed exactly who Jesus was – the Son of God (Matthew 8:29).

The demonised man, after asking the question, leapt on the seven sons of Sceva, overcame them and beat up all of them. They fled from the house wounded, naked and humiliated (19:16). It is not enough to use the name of Jesus; you have to know Him and be authorised by Him before you can see powerful results. Remember, blasphemers misuse Jesus' name and it does not bring forth any divine manifestations. This incident became well known through Ephesus to the Jews and Gentiles. Great fear (of God) came on all of them. And the name of Jesus? This

Nineteen: Ephesus at Last

event helped to magnify it (19:17), so God received the glory through it all.

Those who did come to faith came forward, confessed and showed their works (19:18). This presumably meant that they displayed what they had done in their previous dark past. Those who believed had previously practised sorcery; they brought their books and had one great bonfire. The value of these books and items was fifty thousand pieces of silver (19:19). All that we read in the last verses led to the following outcome: the Word of God powerfully grew and prevailed in all God intended (19:20).

> LESSON FOR LIFE: The ministry in Ephesus showed that neither Satan nor demon power could prevent the word of God from going forth.

Trouble in Ephesus (19:21–41)

After the botched exorcism by the seven sons of Sceva, the focus returned to Paul and his ongoing travels. Passing through Macedonia and Achaia, he wanted to go first to Jerusalem and then to Rome (19:21). He *'purposed in the spirit'*. And, yes, he would end up first in Jerusalem and then Rome, but the journey would be longer and more unexpected than anyone could anticipate. Paul dispatched Timothy and Erastus, who had ministered to him, to Macedonia. However, Paul remained in Asia *'for a season'* (19:22). His continued presence would become problematic, as in other places, for no other reason than the stunning success of the gospel ministry caused the 'gods' to be angry.

During the time of Paul's sojourn in Ephesus, there was no small stir about the growing church. The reasons were economic and spiritual: the Goddess Diana (Artemis) industry was losing money and would, in due time, go out of business (19:23). This was despite the fact that her temple was one of the seven wonders of the world and a major pilgrimage site.

Demetrius was a silversmith for the temple of Diana and made a fortune in the process (19:24). He was very threatened by the impact the gospel had on this cult and his trade. As a result, he was motivated to take action however unethical, misguided and violent it would be.

Demetrius called his fellow craftsmen together and gave them a 'call to arms'. In his speech, he emphasised that *'by this craft we have our wealth'* (19:25). For the carnal man, money is everything. Then he targeted Paul in his speech, highlighting that the apostle had vast influence in Ephesus and the province of Asia. He was persuading people to forsake idolatry; if the object was made by man's hands, it could not possibly be a god (19:26). Since there were many statues and figurines of Diana of the Ephesians, this put their livelihood in jeopardy.

To drive home the point and to provoke action, Demetrius warned his fellow craftsmen that they were in danger of losing their businesses. And there was more bad news. The temple of the great goddess Diana would be despised despite its status as one of the great wonders of the world. Her magnificence would be destroyed, even though all of Asia and the world worshipped her (19:27). After hearing these things, the multitude cried out, *'Great is Diana of the Ephesians'* (19:28).

With help from the devil, Demetrius' stirring speech accomplished what he wanted. He pressed the 'hot button', and a full-blown riot was about to erupt. The entire city was full of confusion. The mob lashed out and grabbed Gaius and Aristarchus, Paul's companions from Macedonia, and they headed to the theatre (19:29). This structure is still in existence today when you visit Ephesus, and they claim that it holds twenty-five thousand. It is always a moving experience standing in a place that is mentioned in the Bible.

Paul – not one to be left behind – was determined to go to the people and state his case, presumably in the theatre, but the other disciples kept him from doing so (19:30). Paul's influential friends, known as *'the chief of Asia'*, sent him a message and said to stay away from the theatre (19:31). Paul amazingly complied. As much as the great apostle gave all appearances of being unstoppable, the fact is that he could be a man of submission, too.

Nineteen: Ephesus at Last

If Paul and the believers were clear in what they needed to do, the mob was not. Some were shouting one thing and others something else. The confusion meant that there were various noises, and a few people did not even understand what they were doing or why (19:32). This can be a dangerous thing when you have a mob stirred up to a mindless frenzy, courtesy of an unscrupulous Demetrius.

Alexander was called upon by the Jews and drawn from the multitude. He beckoned with his hands and wanted to offer a defence to the people (19:33). As soon as the crowd heard that Alexander was a Jew, they did not want to listen to him (19:34). They then united into one voice and chanted for two hours, *'Great is Diana of the Ephesians'*.

The anonymous town clerk of Ephesus became the hero of this narrative (we hear little about Paul or the church in this incident). This man demonstrated exceptional wisdom and courage, which are essential for leadership that makes a positive difference amid an emergency. He sought to appease the angry, riotous crowd by speaking words of reassurance to the men of Ephesus. The town clerk reminded them that the world recognised the city of the Ephesians as worshippers of Diana, whose image fell down from Jupiter (19:35), the father of the Greco-Roman gods. The clerk exhorted them that since Diana was universally recognised and admired, they should calm down, listen and not act foolishly (19:36). In the process of causing a stir, the mob had grabbed certain innocent men. The town clerk says this was wrong, because they had not robbed temples nor blasphemed the gods (19:37). In essence, they were not guilty of sacrilege; therefore, why were they seized? This was not the Roman way.

The hero clerk concluded that if Demetrius, the ringleader, and the craftsmen who worked with him, had an accusation against any person, then do it in the right way. The law courts were open, and the deputies were ready to serve. Let them deal with the situation in a lawful manner (19:38) and not take matters into their own hands, which would be making a bad situation even worse. Any questions, problems, complaints or concerns, let them be handled properly through a lawful assembly (19:39).

Then the clerk issued a final warning: the Ephesian town clerk highlighted the dangers the multitude faced. They could be called into question for today's unrest. The Romans wanted peace; Pax Romana (peace of Rome) had little tolerance for those who wanted to disturb the public. If there was disorder – and especially when there was no good reason for it – there could be serious consequences (19:40). This was another incentive for the crowd to quieten down.

The town clerk's words must have had a sobering and calming effect. The crowd had become quiet and remained so. When he saw that they were no longer agitated, he then dismissed the assembly (19:41). The great tumult of Ephesus had come to a peaceful conclusion.

With peace having returned to Ephesus, Paul was positioning himself for the next phase of ministry. It would include a long farewell, which we are about to hear.

CHAPTER TWENTY

The Long Farewell

Who: Paul

What: Farewell speech to the Ephesian elders

When: The third missionary journey

Where: Troy and Miletus

Why: Paul was going to Jerusalem

How: Paul decided and was bound in spirit.

> *And now, brethren, I commend you to God, and to the word of his grace, which is able to build you up, and to give you an inheritance among all them which are sanctified.*
> — *Acts 20:32*

Time to Leave Ephesus (20:1–16)

Normally, after a great trial, it is advisable not to 'cut and run' but to hold steady and discern what God's will is. In Paul's case, after the uproar in Ephesus at the theatre had subsided, he called the disciples together. It was time to say goodbye and to prepare for the next leg of his apostolic ministry. He embraced them all and left them behind as he returned to Europe and the region of Macedonia (20:1).

Paul toured Macedonia, which is in the north, extensively and gave much exhortation to the believers. Once this was fulfilled, he went south into Greece itself (20:2).

Welcome Holy Spirit

Paul spent three months in Greece. He was about to sail to Syria. In Hebrew, Syria is known as Aram and was meant to be ruled out of Damascus. During the New Testament, the region known as Syria included parts of Palestine and Asia Minor, perhaps much of the eastern seaboard of the Mediterranean from Antioch to Gaza, otherwise known as the Levant. When Paul discovered that certain (hostile) Jews wanted to ambush him, he went a different route and returned via Macedonia (20:3).

Paul apparently did not travel alone. His companions in Asia included Sopater of Berea, Aristarchus and Secundus of Thessalonica, Gaius of Derbe, and Timothy, and Tychicus and Trophimus of the Roman province of Asia (20:4). Some of these people we will hear of again in Acts and the New Testament. Paul's companions went ahead of him from Macedonia into Asia Minor (20:5). They waited for him at Troas, in the north-west corner of the country.

It was time to set sail. *'And we sailed away from Philippi'* implies that Luke was with Paul at the time. As we learned, Philippi is in Macedonia, and Troas, though not far away, is located in another continent. It took them five days to reach Troas and they stayed there seven days (20:6). This was during the time of unleavened bread, namely, the Passover period.

> LESSON FOR LIFE: The rich and meticulous details provided by in the Book of Acts give added credibility to its historicity.

'And upon the first day of the week, when the disciples came together to break bread ...' (20:7) – note that the disciples came together 'upon the first day of the week'. While the Bible does not give much detail, it appears that Sunday was a chosen day for Christian fellowship. John received the **Book of Revelation** when he was in the Spirit on the Lord's Day (Revelation 1:10), which is normally considered to be Sunday. As the Saturday sabbath was a memorial of creation, Sunday is a memorial for the 'new creation' which was made possible by the resurrection of Jesus

Twenty: The Long Farewell

Christ from the dead. On this particular Sunday, Paul intended to leave Troas the next day so he shared with them at length until midnight (20:7).

The multitude were gathered in the upper chamber and many lights (oil lamps) were lit (20:8), perhaps smoking which depleted the air quality. Normally, the bright lights would be an incentive to stay awake. Eutychus was introduced as a young man (age unknown) who fell into a deep sleep, despite all the many bright lights and people in the room. He sat on the windowsill. Since Paul *'was long preaching'*, Eutychus simply could not keep his eyes open. Fighting sleep can be a titanic battle – and he lost. Deep sleep came upon him, and he fell from the third loft and presumably died (20:9). This is enough to ruin any sermon!

Someone had to take quick action, and that someone was Paul. He went down, fell on the body of Eutychus and embraced him. Then the apostle made the following declaration: don't be troubled anymore. The life of Eutychus was in him (20:10). Life within brings action from without; the life of Christ in Paul (Galatians 2:20) brought life to Eutychus.

Even with the fact that Eutychus was raised to life, the people at Troas were understandably shaken. After what had happened, what were they to think? So, Paul went into damage control mode: he acted as if nothing had happened. He returned to the upstairs room, ate a meal and continued his long talk until the break of the day. Remember, he was not sure if he would see these people again, so he wanted to impart as much as he could while he was yet with them. Needless to say, they were greatly comforted (20:12) by God's mercy, compassion and power towards Eutychus and them. As for Eutychus, he was brought back to the people as one who was alive, despite his fall and supposedly fatal injury. The role of the Holy Spirit in this miracle was unmistakable. After all this, Paul left Troas to continue his journey (20:11).

The next section of the narrative is part of Paul's long journey on the third missionary trip from Corinth to Judea via the Aegean islands. The travelling team, which, by implication included Luke, the author of Acts, went ahead and sailed to Assos. They intended to pick up Paul on the way. The apostle had intended to walk instead of sail (20:13) and had prepared accordingly. Assos was a departure port in the district of Mysia, Proconsular Asia, on the north shore of the Gulf of Adramyttium. Paul walked thirty-two kilometres (twenty miles) from Troas to there; the sea journey was forty-eight kilometres (thirty miles). Lesbos was around eleven kilometres (seven miles) away.

The next verses speak of place names found in the Aegean Sea, close to the coast of Asia Minor. The companions of Paul met him at Assos and brought him onto the ship. They sailed from there to a place called Mitylene (20:14). It was the chief city of the island of Lesbos. Paul stayed here for a night. Then they sailed by Chios, an island only eight kilometres (five miles) from the mainland, and anchored for one night.

From there, they sailed to the large island of Samos, forty-two kilometres by thirty-two (twenty-seven by twenty miles) in dimension and around sixty-seven kilometres (forty-two miles) from the city of Smyrna. Afterwards, they tarried at Trogyllium (20:15), which was on the mainland of Asia Minor.

Paul's Long, Sad Farewell (20:17–38)

After this, they arrived at Miletus, also on the mainland, where they held a special meeting with the elders of the Ephesian church. Though Paul was fond of the church at Ephesus, he did not want to stop there or sojourn in the Roman province of Asia. As a determined man, he was in a hurry to get to Jerusalem for the feast of Pentecost (20:16). Paul invited the elders of the Ephesian church to come to meet with him at Miletus, a distance of forty-eight kilometres (thirty miles) from Ephesus (20:17).

The elders showed up and were treated to a very moving speech. The apostle began by saying that from day one, they had known what kind of man he had been with them at all times, ever since his arrival in Roman Asia (20:18). He had served the Lord with all humility of mind

Twenty: The Long Farewell

and heart, shedding many tears and enduring all kinds of temptations from the schemes of those Jews who furiously refused to believe the gospel (20:19). Despite the opposition, Paul had soldiered on in Ephesus. He had shared everything he had and held back nothing, with the goal of giving the Ephesians only that which was profitable for them, both in public and from house to house (20:20).

'... *testifying both to the Jews, and also to the Greeks, repentance toward God, and faith toward our Lord Jesus Christ*' (20:21): this is a choice verse that summarises Paul's message throughout all his missionary journeys. His testimony to Jews and Gentiles was the pathway to salvation. It has nothing to do with religious works or good intentions. It starts with repentance towards God – a sense of remorse, changing one's actions, attitude and words, and going in a new direction by the fear of the LORD. After repentance comes faith towards our Lord Jesus Christ and His gospel. The grace of God saves us (Ephesians 2:8; Titus 2:11) and faith taps into that grace and pipes it into our lives. Repentance and faith are listed as foundational doctrines of the Christian faith (Hebrews 6:1).

Then came a sharp turn from foundational doctrine to Paul's own life. He claimed that he was going '*bound in the spirit*' (20:22)[54] to Jerusalem. He seemed to imply that it was the Holy Spirit who was leading him there, though the reality is not as simple. It appeared that the apostle to the Gentiles was most determined to go to the city of Jerusalem with Herod's temple, no matter what. From the time of his arrest in chapter twenty-one until the end of **Acts 28**, there is only one mention of the Holy Spirit and that is in the very last chapter. Paul said he did not know what awaited him in Jerusalem (20:22). Of interest, from Miletus until he arrived in Jerusalem, he would be prophetically forewarned in detail about what lay ahead. In fact, the Holy Spirit told him that in every city, afflictions and imprisonment awaited him (20:23).

Yet this bold fearless apostle was not bothered by the suffering that lay ahead. All he cared about was finishing his ministry with joy (20:24).

Welcome Holy Spirit

He received this ministry from the Lord Jesus to testify to the gospel of the grace of God.

Then came the difficult part. Paul told the Ephesian elders to whom he had preached the kingdom of God that they would see his face no more (20:25). You can almost hear the gasps of grief as he uttered these words. That being the case, he made a declaration: since I won't see you again, please note that I am innocent of the blood of all men (20:26). This was because Paul did not step back from declaring all the counsel of God (20:27). Having faithfully delivered God's message to the nations, the rest was up to his hearers to heed the Word and put it into practice or, by implication, face the consequences.

> LESSON FOR LIFE: Even the most Spirit-filled, Spirit-led people can still default to being self-led. Wait on God and make sure it is He Who is ordaining your next move.

Paul went from personal to prophetic: He warned the Ephesians elders of the challenging times to come. First, he told them to 'take heed' to themselves and the flock of God. The Bible gives us warnings to watch out against deception, delusion and wolves in sheep's clothing. We are to practise self-control and Godly living, thus 'taking heed' to ourselves. We are also to be watchful for the people God has committed to our care. It is God the Holy Spirit who made us overseers of the flock of God, whom Christ has purchased with his own blood (20:28). We are to feed them with the good Word of God.

Then came the Spirit-inspired apostolic and prophetic warning about enemies outside and inside the church. The first lot of enemies were external. As soon as Paul, an apostolic father figure and protector, departed, the 'grievous wolves' would come into the church and attack the flock. These wolves would be in the form of false apostles, christs, teachers, prophets and brethren (20:29). They especially liked churches such as Ephesus which had larger numbers. No one would be spared the attack.

Twenty: The Long Farewell

If you think that is bad enough, listen to this: a second group of enemies who attack would be from the local church itself. From their own members, individuals would arise and speak devilish things. Their goal was to create factionalism and draw disciples unto themselves (20:30). It's the age-old classic quest for power. In every sense of the word, by their perverse words and their schism, they show themselves to be heretics. These are people who should be shunned and avoided. In these warnings, Paul showed immense pastoral care for the Ephesian elders and congregation.

For us today, our safety comes by being watchful or, as Jesus said, *'Watch and pray'* that you enter not into temptation (Matthew 26:41). Paul tells us in **1 Thessalonians 5:6** to *'watch and be sober'*. Failure to watch means a person is spiritually sleeping or drunk, which will render them vulnerable to the 'wolves'. In addition to watching, we need to remember that over three years, Paul warned them night and day, with tears (20:31), about the dangers roundabout. The warning Paul gave to Ephesus applies to us today.

After reissuing these heavy-duty warnings, Paul ended his message with a note of hope. He commended the Ephesian elders and church to God. He could not personally watch over them anymore, but God could and would. They were also committed to God and the word of His grace. This 'word of grace' can edify or build up the saints where they will also receive an inheritance, along with all those who are sanctified in Christ (20:32).

> LESSON FOR LIFE: Heed the Holy Spirit's 'early warning service' and it will save you from a lot of grief.

As Paul concluded the visit at Miletus, he reminded them of the kind of man he was. He did not covet anyone's silver, gold or clothing (20:33), having done his best to provide for his own needs and those of his companions. He did not want himself and the team to be a financial burden to the church. The Ephesian elders were witnesses to these facts

Welcome Holy Spirit

(20:34). Of course, churches today should have an attitude of double honour to ministers, especially those who labour in the word and doctrine (1 Timothy 5:17). Take good care of those who ministered to you in the priceless things of God; you will be greatly rewarded for doing so.

Paul said his example was good for everyone. His labour helped to support the weak. In addition, Paul said they were an affirmation of Jesus' words: *'It is more blessed to give than to receive'* (20:35). While such a quote is not found in the gospel narratives, there is no doubt that it is consistent with the teaching and lifestyle of Christ. He was the ultimate giver and was honoured accordingly.

After he had spoken these moving words, Paul knelt and prayed with the elders (20:36). It was a highly emotional farewell with weeping, hugging and kissing (20:37). The major reason for this outpouring of affection and passion was his words that they would see his face again (20:38). The finality of it was overwhelming. After it was all over, they escorted him to the ship where he would head towards Jerusalem.

Though Paul did not expect a peaceful time in the Holy City, little did he, or any mere mortal, foresee the volcanic eruption his visit would spawn. The details await us in the following chapter.

> LESSON FOR LIFE: Goodbyes are never easy but if handled the right way, they can inspire people to rise up and fill the gap.

---

[54] The Greek word for Spirit is *pneuma*, used three hundred and eighty-five times in the New Testament and translated as 'wind', 'breath' and 'spirit'. It can refer to the Holy Spirit and also the human spirit (1 Thessalonians 5:23). G4151 - pneuma - Strong's Greek Lexicon (kjv). Blue Letter Bible. Accessed 31 Jan, 2024. https://www.blueletterbible.org/lexicon/g4151/kjv/tr/0-1/

CHAPTER TWENTY-ONE

Appointment in Jerusalem

Who: Paul

What: Returns to Jerusalem and causes a riot

When: End of the third missionary journey

Where: From Miletus to the Temple Mount in Jerusalem

Why: Paul was determined to return to Jerusalem, no matter what

How: Paul was bound in spirit (20:22).

> *Now when we had discovered Cyprus, we left it on the left hand, and sailed into Syria, and landed at Tyre: for there the ship was to unlade her burden. And finding disciples, we tarried there seven days: who said to Paul through the Spirit, that he should not go up to Jerusalem.*
> *— Acts 21:3–4.*

Journey to Jerusalem (21:1–16)

Paul concluded his third missionary journey. His goal now was to get to Jerusalem by the Day of Pentecost; in fact, he had an 'appointment in Jerusalem' at the House of the Lord. Yet, this man who braved so much opposition throughout his ministry was going to have a 'Jerusalem appointment' that would be the greatest trial he had ever faced. The first trial was in Jerusalem and the second on the high seas. In both cases, his life was in serious jeopardy and the odds were against him. From this chapter until the end of the **Book of Acts**, Paul will be held in captivity.

Welcome Holy Spirit

After saying farewell to the elders of Ephesus, they boarded a ship and sailed on the Aegean Sea. The first place they came to was Cos, a small island north-west of Rhodes. It is the reputed birthplace of Hippocrates the physician, from whom we get the Hippocratic oath. The next day, they sailed to the large island of Rhodes, seventy-four kilometres (forty-seven miles) long and twenty-nine kilometres (eighteen miles) broad. It housed one of the seven wonders of the world, the Colossus of Rhodes, which was a brazen statue of Apollo with legs so high that ships could sail between them. After having stood for sixty-six years, it was cast down by an earthquake in 224 BC. Then they sailed onto Patara on the south-west coast of Lycia (21:1).

At Patara, they found a ship sailing to Phoenicia and boarded it (21:2). Now on the new ship, the apostolic team sailed past Cyprus which was on the *left*, meaning they sailed to the south of the island nation. The goal was to reach the Levant, the eastern seaboard of the Mediterranean. This was largely Roman Syria, which included Phoenicia and Israel. Phoenicia is modern Lebanon, the great ancient maritime entity that dominated the Mediterranean. As we learned, this was part of the region referred to in antiquity as *Syria*.

They landed in the famous city of Tyre, for there they unloaded the ship (21:3). There are notable prophecies about Tyre, and the 'prince of Tyre' is an allusion to Lucifer/Satan in **Ezekiel 28**.

In Tyre, it was discovered that there were disciples. So the apostles stayed there one week. During that time, these disciples said to Paul *'through the Spirit'* that he should not go up to Jerusalem (21:4). Taking the verse at face value, Paul was warned that there was trouble ahead if he proceeded. This word by the Spirit, coming from people who probably did not know Paul before, provides extra insight.

After the seven days in Tyre, they went to the port to set sail southward. The disciples came with their families until they led them to the port. They kneeled on the shore and prayed and then departed. The apostles took the ship and the locals returned home (21:5–6).

Twenty-One: Appointment in Jerusalem

Sailing southward, the apostles ended up in Ptolemais, whose name is derived from the Ptolemaic dynasty of Hellenistic Egypt. It was known in the Old Testament and today as Accho, and also had the English name 'Acre' when the medieval Crusaders had a strong presence here. Accho belonged to the tribe of Asher, but they could not drive out the Canaanites (Judges 1:31); thus, it remained outside of Israelite rule for much of the Biblical period. The apostles greeted the brethren there but stayed only one day (21:7) and planned to proceed to Caesarea.

> LESSON FOR LIFE: Thanks to the work of the Holy Spirit and the church, in just a few short years there appeared to have been a strong Christian presence throughout much of the ancient Near East.

'We that were of Paul's company' (21:8) proceeded from Ptolemais and arrived at Caesarea. Their destination was the home of Philip the evangelist, one of the seven (6:5), where they lodged (21:8). An interesting note is the emphasis on Philip's four virgin daughters. It says that they prophesied (21:9). In **1 Corinthians 11:5**, Paul implies the possibility that women can prophesy in the church. Huldah was an accredited prophetess in the Old Testament (2 Kings 22:14; 2 Chronicles 34:22). When you live a life in the Holy Spirit, you are empowered to do whatever He leads you to do, no matter who you are.

Though Paul was in a hurry to get to Jerusalem for Pentecost, it says that the apostles stayed in Caesarea for *'many days'* (21:10). Perhaps they arrived early and had extra time or maybe Paul had second thoughts about going to Jerusalem thanks to the prophecy of the disciples of Tyre. The text does not say. We remember this highly pagan coastal city as the place of Gentile Pentecost (Chapter 10). It served as headquarters for the Roman procurator. Agabus, a recognised prophet from Judea, came down to Caesarea for a visit (21:10). He was going to tell Paul things he would prefer not to hear.

This man did an interesting prophetic act. He took Paul's belt and tied his own hands and feet. Then he prophesied in the Name of the

Welcome Holy Spirit

Holy Spirit that the Jews at Jerusalem would bind up the owner of this belt and deliver him to the Gentiles (21:11). The gist was correct: the Jews would attack the owner of the belt who would end up in the charge of the Gentiles; the detail is that he was attacked and beaten by the Jews and in a sense rescued by the Gentiles from certain death; it was the Gentiles who bound him (21:33). Again, however, like in Tyre, this was a prophetic warning, his second in a row. The testimony of two credible witnesses was considered valid.[55]

Paul's travelling companions and local hosts in Caesarea were understandably alarmed by this message. It was not the first time they heard of a warning about serious trouble waiting for Paul in Jerusalem. They pleaded with the apostle, with tears, not to go up to the Holy City (21:12). But it was an exercise in futility.

One poignant moment led to another. Paul responded to them by asking why they were weeping and breaking his heart (21:13). He then proclaimed that he was ready to be taken into captivity and, if necessary, die in Jerusalem for the Name of the Lord Jesus. Paul would not be dissuaded from visiting the Holy City. When it became obvious that Paul was going to Jerusalem, no matter what, the people desisted from further pleading. They gave a simple statement: The will of the Lord be done (21:14). Ultimately, that is your best recourse in any circumstance; this phrase is wonderfully embedded in the Lord's Prayer (Matthew 6:10; Luke 11:2).

> LESSON FOR LIFE: Once you recognise that there is nothing more you can do about a situation, commit it all to God and declare that it is His will that should be done. It brings great relief and peace.

Once the time came, Paul and his companions packed their bags and went 'up' to Jerusalem (21:15). From a pious person's point of view, going to Jerusalem is always an ascent, even a promotion. In addition to Paul's normal companions, some of the brethren from Caesarea also

Twenty-One: Appointment in Jerusalem

made the ascent to Jerusalem including Mnason, an 'old disciple' from Cyprus, who served as host to the apostles (21:16).

Meeting with the Jerusalem Elders (21:17–25)

Once they reached Jerusalem, the leadership of the local church received them gladly (21:17). Yet the smiles were short-lived because it was time to discuss the looming issue. The day after their arrival, Paul and his companions had an appointment with James the Just and the Jerusalem elders (21:18). James was the 'bishop' of the mother church and, as we recall, had an important role in the Council at Jerusalem in **Acts 15:13**.

After the greetings, Paul gave an account of his multiple missionary journeys and of the churches planted among the Gentiles (21:19). When they heard the report, they glorified God. Then the Jerusalem elders got down to the business at hand. They declared that 'many thousands of Jews ... believe' (21:20). It appears the Jerusalem church had been busy with evangelism, too. These believing Jews were *'all zealous of the law'* (21:20). It seemed that it was okay for a Jew to believe in Jesus while being 'zealous' for the law of Moses; the main issue was not to see it as a means of salvation or impose it on the Gentiles. Of course, the upcoming destruction of the Jerusalem temple in 70 AD would make it impossible to fulfil some of the laws; for example, animal sacrifices and burnt offerings.

The Jerusalem elders continued their message that the gospel-believing, Torah-observant Jews, were told that Paul was teaching Jews in the Diaspora to forsake Moses, not to have children circumcised and not to observe the customs (21:21). There is no record of Paul doing any such thing. However, he did teach that circumcision does not save, the condemnation from the law is gone and that ceremonies are not necessary but optional and okay. It was feared that Paul's presence could trigger a violent reaction, like before (Acts 9:29–30).

Paul was indisputably a great man of God, among the top five influential people who ever lived. The church owes him much, including

Welcome Holy Spirit

half of our New Testament. Yet his uninvited presence in Jerusalem at that time was more of a burden than a blessing. The two warnings he received en route to Jerusalem, plus the report that had just been given by the mother church's elders, pointed to a potential time bomb. And when it detonated, it would dwarf anything he experienced on his missionary journeys. The reason is Jerusalem, the city of the great king, also killed the prophets, crucified the Saviour and was about to detonate by the mere presence of Paul before he could utter one word in public. The worst was yet to come.

What should they do about this grave prospect (21:22)? The multitude would hear that Paul had arrived, and they would gather together. A great tumult was a real possibility. The grass was dry and there were sparks everywhere. So, what could they do to avoid trouble? Now that they knew the problem, could they come up with a solution? A 'good idea' was hatched.

The Jerusalem elders gave the following advice and wanted Paul to do what they said. Four men have made a vow (21:23), possibly like the Nazarite vow. Paul was instructed to take the four men and be purified with them. He was to pay their expenses (for example, for lambs, rams, oil and flour). After that, they would shave their heads (including Paul's, presumably). After these actions, Paul would look as kosher as any other observant Jew, and it would neutralise the perception that Paul was 'anti-Moses, anti-Law'. It was meant to convey the message that the apostle walked in an orderly manner and kept the law (21:24). Though it was a 'good idea', unfortunately, it did not work at all. The spirit of trouble proved to be too potent to be appeased by external religious works.

As a note of conciliation, knowing Paul's anointing for Gentile ministry, the Jerusalem elders reminded him about the outcome of the Council at Jerusalem where he was personally present. A letter had been sent by his hand that the Gentiles were not bound to keep the law of Moses. All they had to remember was to abstain from things offered to idols, blood, strangled and fornication (21:25).

Twenty-One: Appointment in Jerusalem

Trouble at the Temple (21:26–40)

Though strong-minded, Paul had shown himself to be a man under authority. He complied with the wishes of the Jerusalem elders. He took the men, purified himself with them and entered the temple to signify the accomplishment of the days of purification. After that, an offering would be made for each one of them (21:26). So far, so good.

This exercise in public relations seemed to work and all was going according to plan … until the end of the week. The Jewish pilgrims from Asia Minor could not believe their eyes: there was Paul, in the temple itself. The man they feared and reviled so much back home was within their reach. What you are about to see is PDS or 'Paul Derangement Syndrome'. All balance, sense, calmness and truthfulness went out the window. The Jews of Asia seized Paul (21:27) and cried out for help from the *'Men of Israel'*. Their accusation against Paul? He was accused of teaching against the law of Moses, the temple and all things associated with it. He allegedly 'polluted' the holy place by bringing Gentiles inside (21:28).

The mob violated the Ninth Commandment which says, *'Thou shalt not bear false witness against thy neighbour'* (Exodus 20:16). They falsely accused him of bringing Greeks (Gentiles) into the temple. The excuse was that they saw Trophimus the Ephesian with Paul in the streets in Jerusalem, and then assumed that he snuck him into the sacred precincts (21:29).

The famous 1st century AD Jewish historian, Flavius Josephus,[56] said there was a wall within the temple compound. Signage at the wall, written in Greek and Latin, said that any Gentile who went beyond the wall would be responsible for their own death, which would inevitably follow. Would Paul, who showed such a spirit of compliance to authority, dare to violate this prohibition? Most unlikely. But as Winston Churchill once said, 'A lie gets halfway around the world before the truth has a chance to get its pants on.'[57]

Welcome Holy Spirit

It does not take much to motivate an agitated religious crowd to mob violence. All the city of Jerusalem was in an uproar and the people ran together to get in on the action. Paul, already seized, was dragged out of the temple precincts, and the doors were shut (21:30). This simple statement says a lot. Paul would never again enter into the sacred compound, known as the place of sacrifice. He would never walk freely in Jerusalem again, either. Furthermore, we hear no more about Herod's temple after this except for its prophesied destruction in 70 AD. Also, Paul's enemies shut the door to the temple because it was better to kill him outside than within the sacred precincts. From this point, the temple is no longer part of the New Testament narrative: *'the doors were shut.'*

The hysterical PDS mob sought to kill Paul, and they almost succeeded. But before they could do it, news came to the ears of the chief captain of the band that all of Jerusalem was in full-blown riot mode (21:31). Those in charge were commissioned by Caesar to keep the peace, Pax Romana, at all costs – or else.

The chief captain's name was Claudius Lysias (Acts 23:26). He was located in the Antonia Fortress, just north of the temple mount. Originally built by John Hyrcanus during the Hasmonean period, it was called Baris. Decades later, Herod the Great beautified this castle and named it after his friend, Mark Anthony. It was here that Jesus had met Pontius Pilate.

A Jerusalem riot was Rome's worst nightmare and the tumult needed to cease – fast. The captain wasted no time; he had to stop this runaway bushfire. He immediately took centurions and soldiers who ran to the scene. Once the mob saw these Roman soldiers, they stopped beating Paul (21:32). His life was saved at the last minute.

This is the beginning of Paul's long captivity. It started with a bang. If Paul had any idea how much he would suffer and, by extension, his travelling companions and the Jerusalem church itself, would it have changed his mind? What happened and would continue to happen to Paul did not just affect him but many others.

Twenty-One: Appointment in Jerusalem

> LESSON FOR LIFE: We always need to tread wisely by considering how the impact of our actions can touch those we love.

Ironically, being in the custody of the Roman authorities was a refuge, a Cave of Adullam (1 Samuel 22:1–2) experience. Had he remained with the mob, he surely would have been killed. Human nature often brings forth the worst in people when they arouse so much animosity. The chief captain, who took Paul from the hands of the rioters, commanded that he be bound with two chains. Then he demanded to know who he was and what he had done (21:33) that sparked such a furious riot.

When someone hears something that causes a strong, violent reaction, loss of control or even a meltdown, we say they are 'triggered'. Before Paul could even defend himself, his enemies began to cry various and contradictory things – unhinged, emotional and at times incoherent. They were triggered. Since the captain couldn't make sense of their accusations, he commanded that Paul be taken into the Antonia Fortress (21:34). Paul had to be carried by the soldiers up the stairs because the people were so violent (21:35). The multitude came following after Paul, chanting, *'Away with him'* (21:36). This could be a death chant (John 19:15; Acts 23:18).

As Paul was being led to the fortress, he asked the captain if he could speak to them. The captain responded by asking if Paul knew Greek (21:37), which of course he did. Claudius Lysias was possibly weak in Latin but could converse with the apostle in Greek. From here, he started to question him further.

The captain asked if Paul was the Egyptian who led four thousand men into the wilderness who were all murderers (21:38), perhaps terrorists. Josephus speaks about him.[58] He was an anonymous rabble-rouser who stirred up a crowd, provoked a strong Roman military action and then escaped from capture while several hundred of his followers were killed. The term 'murderer' is Σικαριων, *Sicarii*, who were

Welcome Holy Spirit

assassins. They had a crooked knife under their garments which they slipped between the victim's ribs, especially in a crowded street.

Paul of course denied that he was 'the Egyptian' or any type of malefactor. He said he was a Jew from the city of Tarsus in Cilicia in Asia Minor, which was not some remote wide spot in the road. Since he was a Jew, he asked for permission to speak to his fellow Jews (21:39). Paul was granted permission by the captain. He stood on the stairs, beckoned with his hand for silence and when he began to speak in the Hebrew tongue (21:40), the rioters down to listen. What amazing compliance from a group who was trying to murder Paul; but then again, he had the anointing of the Holy Spirit, and this gave an authority that eluded the religious establishment (Matthew 7:39). We will learn much from the speech he was about to give.

> LESSON FOR LIFE: In light of the trauma Paul had just endured, his willingness to speak to his enemies was boldness by the Holy Spirit.

---

[55] Two or three witnesses is a testimony established: Deuteronomy 17:6; 19:15; Matthew 18:16; 2 Corinthians 13:1; 1 Timothy 5:19; Hebrews 10:28)

[56] Flavius Josephus, *The Jewish War*, lib. v. cap. 5, sec. 2.

[57] https://www.azquotes.com/quote/56289 Accessed 13 April 2024.

[58] *Antiquities*, lib. xx. cap. 8, sec. 6; *The Jewish War*, lib. ii. cap. 13, sec. 5

CHAPTER TWENTY-TWO
Paul's Defense in Jerusalem

Who: Paul and the Crowd

What: His defence

When: After his arrest

Where: The Antonia Fortress, Jerusalem

Why: To understand and placate the hysteria and rioting

How: From the Roman barracks

> *Men, brethren, and fathers, hear ye my defence which I make now unto you.*
> — *Acts 22:1*

Paul's Defense Before the People (22:1–21)

The Jewish people are often considered as one big family, related by blood, heritage, and divine covenants. The same mindset can exist among Christians, where it is not uncommon to refer to a fellow Christian as 'brother' or 'sister'. That is probably the reason Paul addressed his fellow Jews as 'men, brethren, and fathers' (22:1). He asked them to listen to his defence (*apologia* in Greek, from where we get the word 'apologetics'). When his opponents heard him speak in Hebrew, they became all the more quiet and listened attentively. It is possible that they had thought Paul was a Gentile teaching against Jewish things. Now, by hearing the Hebrew language, they came to see him as 'one of them' (22:2). Language can be a great unifier that transcends ethnic, social or religious differences (the same applies to mutual interests in food, sport and hobbies).

Speaking in Hebrew, Paul told the people he was a Jew from Tarsus in Cilicia, Asia Minor. Yet, he also knew Jerusalem well because he was brought up here. He dropped the name of his esteemed and well-known mentor Rabbi Gamaliel, who spoke in **Acts 5**. He was taught according to the perfect manner of the law of the fathers, testifying that he was as zealous for God then as his listeners were now (22:3). He was not a seditionist or heretic.

He referred to the early church as 'the way' and says he had persecuted them unto death, binding and imprisoning men and women (22:4). It was probably the stoning of Stephen, where young Saul of Tarsus had stood by the cloaks of the executioners, that had motivated him to destroy the church.

Paul continued to lay out his Jewish credentials before the crowd. He was known by the high priest who had approved of his work. This was in addition to the elders, from whom he received paperwork endorsing his persecution of the church. With these papers, he had gone to Damascus to bring Jewish believers bound for judgment and punishment in Jerusalem (22:5).

At noon, as they had drawn close to Damascus, heaven's light had suddenly shone round about him (22:6). (The story of Paul's experience on the Damascus Road will be told three times in the **Book of Acts**, in chapters 9, 22 and 26). The light from heaven had caused Paul to fall to the ground. He had then heard heaven's voice saying, *'Saul, Saul, why are you persecuting Me?'* (22:7 NKJV). Obviously startled by this supernatural epiphany, Paul had inquired who it was who spoke to him. The reply: *'I am Jesus of Nazareth whom you are persecuting'* (22:8). Remember that Saul/Paul was not on his own; he had had travelling companions with him on the Damascus Road. They had seen the same bright light that he had and were very afraid. Yet they had not heard the voice that Paul had heard (22:9). The message had been reserved for him alone.

Twenty-Two: Paul's Defense in Jerusalem

> LESSON FOR LIFE: When a person persecutes a member of the Body of Christ, they are simultaneously doing so to Jesus, Who is the Head of the Body.

Here is another sign that strong-minded Paul could also be submissive. At the time he saw the light and repented, he had asked a very important question: *'What shall I do, Lord?'* (22:10). If Jesus is Lord of your life, this should be the most important question you ask Him. Discipleship means, among other things, knowing God's will and doing it. Paul's repentance meant that instead of persecuting Jesus and His Church, he was now submitted and committed to both. Jesus told Paul to arise and go into Damascus – which was his plan, anyway. In Damascus, he would be told of all the things which he must do.

Paul had continued onward to Damascus. Yet he had done so in a state of repentance, humility and faith, not arrogance nor murderous hatred. Since he had been blinded by the great shining and bright light representing God's glory, he had had to be led by the hand into the city (22:11).

Changing the spotlight momentarily, the focus was now on Ananias, introduced as a devout man regarding the Law of Moses. He had a good reputation among those Jews who dwelt in Damascus (22:12). Ananias had come to Paul, called him by name, stood and said, *'Brother Saul, receive your sight'* (22:13). Within one hour, Paul could see again and looked Ananias in the eye.

Ananias affirmed that the 'God of our fathers' had chosen Paul for a holy calling. He would know his will, see the Just One and hear His voice (22:14). Paul was ordained, among other things, to bear witness to all men, Jew and Gentile, of all that he had seen and heard (22:15). So, instead of opposing Jesus, Paul would now become His greatest advocate and tireless apostle. Ananias then asked him, 'What are you waiting for (22:16)? Get up, be baptised, and wash away your sins as you call on the Name of the Lord.' The Scripture says that whoever calls on the Name of the Lord shall be saved (Romans 10:13).

Paul spoke of his first visit to Jerusalem after he had repented and came to faith in the Messiah. He had been at the temple and had fallen into a trance while praying (22:17). He had heard the voice of Jesus again. The Lord told him to quickly get out of Jerusalem. Why? Because those who dwelt there would reject Paul's testimony about Christ (22:18). Since Jesus told Paul to get out of Jerusalem years earlier because it would not receive his testimony, where in Acts did the Lord 'change His mind' and tell the apostle it was okay to go back?

Paul then dialogued with the Lord, since he believed he could convince the Jews in Jerusalem about Christ, due to his former notorious lifestyle. He was the one who had imprisoned believers and beaten them in every synagogue (22:19). When Stephen the martyr was slain, Paul had stood by the cloaks and consented to his death (22:20). He reasoned that his high profile and the complete turnaround would be persuasive to the Jews. We all offer our 'but Lord' excuses: I am not ready, I am not able, please find someone else. Yet, let's remember that God knows best. Jesus was firm. He commanded Paul to leave Jerusalem immediately and go far away unto the Gentiles (22:21).

Paul and the Roman Commander (22:22–30)

Paul's opponents listened silently and patiently to his story until he got to that very part – *'unto the Gentiles'*. These Jewish zealots hated the Gentiles and hated Paul for even mentioning them. They began to scream and shout hysterically, saying, *'Away with such a fellow from the earth: for it is not fit that he should live* (22:22).' Apparently, in their opinion, neither were the Gentiles. They cried out, took off their clothes and even threw dust in the air (22:23). Like a child throwing a tantrum, they would not be content until the powers that be took strong action.

There is something in human nature that wants to castigate a man when he is kicked to the ground; the fact that his enemies were so

Twenty-Two: Paul's Defense in Jerusalem

virulent implied there must be something seriously wrong with him! So, the Romans, not understanding Hebrew or why the crowd had gone wild, decided to scourge Paul to elicit a confession about why he was so vilified (22:24). They figured he knew why the crowd had gone so ballistic. Just as they had tied him up and were ready to apply the whip, Paul asked the key question: isn't it against the law to scourge a Roman citizen, especially one who is un-condemned (22:25)? Good question, and one that saved his skin.

The centurion, who was only doing his duty, knew well enough to be careful. He ran to tell the chief captain that Paul claimed to be a citizen (22:26). Roman citizenship had privileges. No time was wasted. The chief captain came and questioned Paul: 'Are you really a Roman citizen?' The apostle replied 'Yes' (22:27). The chief captain then said that he had paid a princely sum to become a Roman. Obviously, he was not born one and could have been one of the many ethnicities that encompassed the Roman Empire. He could have even been a local Near Eastern Semite. It has been speculated that the 'Roman troops' that destroyed Jerusalem in 70 AD were, at least in part, local Near Easterners rather than Italians.

Yet Paul's circumstances were different. He was not 'naturalised' as a Roman; he was born into the flock or 'freeborn' (22:28). Such versatility – being a Jewish, Greek-speaking, Roman citizen – made Paul able to relate to all kinds of people, Jew and Gentile (1 Corinthians 9:22). The chief captain decided to drop the 'examination by scourging' and was very nervous about the possible outcome for even suggesting it. After all, he had just bound an untried, un-condemned Roman citizen (22:29).

The next day the chief captain knew that he would hear about the Jewish accusations against Paul. So, he loosed him from his bonds. At the same time, he commanded the chief priests and the council to appear, and Paul would stand before them (22:30). Then he could learn what all the fuss was about.

CHAPTER TWENTY-THREE

From Jerusalem to Caesarea

Who: Paul and his enemies

What: Testifies and is moved from Jerusalem

When: After his defence in Jerusalem

Where: Jerusalem and Caesarea

Why: For his protection and to exercise Roman due process of law

How: The Holy Spirit used the might of Rome

> *But when Paul perceived that the one part were Sadducees, and the other Pharisees, he cried out in the council, Men and brethren, I am a Pharisee, the son of a Pharisee: of the hope and resurrection of the dead I am called in question.*
> — *Acts 23:6*

He was warned at least twice not to go to Jerusalem, for trouble, even death, awaited him. Yet Paul, apostle to the Gentiles, went to antiquity's most Jewish city, complete with God's temple, for reasons that are not recorded in Acts and possibly not made known off the record.

After the riot, Paul had a chance to speak to the crowd, who listened patiently until he mentioned the word 'Gentiles.' The tumult began again. The Romans now took charge but since the issue at hand was religious, Paul would stand before the Jewish council with the chief priests, presumably the Sanhedrin. Like his Master, he would face inquisition by the elders of his people. What we will discover is that

Jerusalem, the city that kills the prophets and stones God's messengers, would settle for nothing less than Paul's death. For this reason, he would be spirited out of the city and sent to Caesarea.

The reason is that Paul had an appointment in Rome.

Paul Before the Sanhedrin (23:1–11)

When it was time to speak, he addressed them as *'men and brethren'* and vindicated himself as one living with a good conscience before God until now (23:1). No hypocrisy or deception was part of his confession.

No sooner had he finished that statement that the high priest commanded that Paul be smitten on the mouth (23:2). Paul had not even had a chance to lay out his case or offer a rebuttal of the accusations. The same thing had happened to Jesus. It was a mark of highest contempt and symbolically meant to shame and silence the apostle. Why the anger? Because Paul dared to say that he, an apostle of Jesus Christ and propagator of His gospel, would dare to have a 'good conscience'. Of interest is that the Romans did nothing to stop or censure this action; they would not interfere in a family squabble.

While Jesus had been restrained in His response to this nasty slap, Paul was not. He lashed out at the high priest as a whited-walled hypocrite. He continued by saying the priest pretended to judge Paul according to the law and then commanded him to be smitten, contrary to the law (23:3). Paul's foes had a simple comeback: are you attacking God's high priest (23:4)?

Remarkably, Paul stepped back and quietly confessed that he did not know his attacker was the high priest. Perhaps because Paul had been absent from Jerusalem for so long, he had not kept up with the Jewish hierarchy. Then, quoting the law (Exodus 22:28), Paul made the statement that he should not speak evil of the ruler of his people (23:5). The implication was that had Paul known this man was the high priest, he would have had a more subdued response, like Jesus.

Twenty-Three: From Jerusalem to Caesarea

After this vexatious situation, Paul demonstrated his clever side. He perceived that two sects of Judaism were represented in the hearing: Pharisees and Sadducees. Paul would play them off against each other. He declared in the present tense: '*I am a Pharisee, the son of a Pharisee: of the hope and resurrection of the dead I am called in question* (23:6).' Neither he nor the other apostles considered themselves as 'ex-Jews' and in Paul's case, he was still a Pharisee, not a retired one. This was even though he served a Messiah who was rejected by the Jewish establishment. It has been said that John Wesley (1703–1791), founder of the Methodist church, considered himself an Anglican to his dying breath. Paul was in the same category.

> LESSON FOR LIFE: Whether a wise move or not, Paul's ill-fated visit to Jerusalem gave him another opportunity to share the gospel with his Jewish people.

Paul's plan to 'divide and conquer' his inquisitors worked. There came dissension between the Pharisees and Sadducees and the council was divided (23:7). Sadducees were the ones who did not believe in the resurrection, in angels or spirits. However, the Pharisees believed in all these things (23:8). Amazingly, the Pharisees now decided to defend Paul as 'one of their own'. They declared that they found no evil in him (23:9). If a supernatural being had spoken to him, then they better not fight against God; the same advice given by the revered rabbi, Gamaliel (Acts 5:38-39). The disputing among them was so great that the atmosphere in the room was highly charged. The Roman chief captain feared that Paul, now the rope in the Pharisee-Sadducee tug of war, would be torn into pieces. So, the soldiers were commanded that Paul be forcibly taken from the council (23:10) and brought to the fortress for safekeeping.

Another day, another drama, trauma and tumult for Paul in Jerusalem. He had been on a knife's edge since the Temple Mount riot. When things could not have been lower, the Lord Himself visited him the following night. He said, 'Cheer up, Paul. You have testified of me in

Jerusalem. I will make sure you get to Rome to do likewise' (23:11). It is a promise Paul would hold onto tightly as the months and years went by.

We can debate whether Paul made the right decision on going to Jerusalem – a move that caused pain and anguish for him and the mother church – but the occasion was used by God for testifying of Christ to people in power. Paul needed this reassuring word from Jesus because he would endure several years of confinement in Caesarea, several hearings and then a lengthy sea journey to Rome that should have ended in a deadly disaster. Yet, for the grace and promise of God, which Paul no doubt held onto, he did make it to Rome.

Conspiracy to Murder Paul (23:12–22)

But it almost didn't happen. Now, at the dawn of a new day, a conspiracy to murder was being hatched by certain religious Jews. They came together and made a vow that they would not eat or drink until they had killed Paul (23:12). Failure to perform the vow would result in a curse. More than forty men were part of this conspiracy (23:13).

It is amazing how much animosity Paul received, but then again, the Scripture teaches that the flesh (religion and carnal human effort) persecutes the Spirit (Galatians 4:29), meaning those who are born again and baptised in the Holy Spirit. It was no different in the life of Jesus. His greatest opponents were not the card-carrying sinners nor the Roman occupiers but the religious establishment elite.

The forty-plus conspirators took their plans to the chief priests and elders to gain their blessing on their vows. They proclaimed that they were under a curse to abstain from food and drink until they had killed Paul (23:14). They could have been the zealots or Sicarii who were terrorist-like, slipping daggers in between Roman or rival ribs. Having lost custody of Paul, the conspirators and the council were going to trick the Romans into surrendering him. How? By saying they needed to make further inquiries of Paul. When he was brought back to them, the

Twenty-Three: From Jerusalem to Caesarea

conspirators would slay him (23:15). Though the text does not directly say, the chief priests and elders must have approved the plot.

By the providence of God, Paul's nephew, his sister's son, happened to be there when he heard of the conspiracy. His instinct was to immediately go and tell his uncle (23:16). Paul, a quick mover, called the centurion and asked him to take his nephew to visit the chief captain because he had a message (23:17). The centurion took Paul's nephew to the chief captain and said 'Paul the prisoner' wanted him to bring this young man. He had an urgent message (23:18); indeed, it was a matter of life and death.

The chief captain took the young man aside and asked him privately what his secret message was (23:19). Paul's nephew told him that the Jews conspired to request, indeed demand, that Paul be brought to the council tomorrow as though to inquire of him more perfectly (23:20). It was a ruse, and the captain was urged to not agree with their demand. The young man explained that there were more than forty men who had bound themselves with an oath that they would neither eat nor drink until they had murdered Paul (23:21).

The eyes of the conspirators were looking to the chief captain to make their plot come to pass. He took the message and then sent Paul's nephew away. Before his departure, he warned him not to speak to anyone that he had shown these things (23:22). A sense of real Roman justice was about to manifest (not the Pilate version of justice that crucified the Man he knew was completely innocent but wanted to pacify the angry mob).

Paul Sent to Safety at Caesarea (23:23–35)

The chief captain wasted no time. He ordered two hundred soldiers, seventy horsemen and two hundred spearmen to safely take Paul to Caesarea in the third hour of the night (23:23). This grand escort of four hundred and seventy men was all done for Paul's sake to save his life. Paul was provided with a horse so he could be safely sent to Felix the governor (23:24). His headquarters were at Caesarea, as were Pontius Pilate's before him. We do not know what happened to the forty-plus zealots now that their plot had been foiled. Did they break their fast, eat and get a curse, or did they starve to death? Unlikely. They probably found a legal loophole.

Having put in a hard day's work, the chief captain of Jerusalem's Roman contingent had one more task to do. He needed to explain to the governor in Caesarea whom he was sending his way, and why. So, Claudius Lysias wrote a letter to Felix to explain why he now had a new guest. He addressed him as 'the most excellent governor' (23:25–26). Lysias described how Paul had been taken by the Jews and would have been killed. However, *came I with an army, and rescued him*' (23:27). It took an 'army' to save Paul. The captain added that he understood his prisoner was a Roman citizen, thus deserving of imperial protection and a fair trial.

The letter continued. In order to find out why the Jews were so violently against Paul, he had been brought to their council (23:28). When the dust had settled, Lysias found that the dispute had to do with Jewish law. But from a Roman point of view, Paul had done nothing deserving of death or imprisonment (23:29).

But there was more. When Lysias discovered that there was a conspiracy to kill Paul, he immediately arranged to send him to Felix. There, his Jewish accusers could come to the governor and say in his presence publicly what they had against Paul, who was now under Roman patronage and protection. The imprisoned apostle would also be allowed to speak in his defence. And with the final farewell, Lysias had discharged his duty (23:30) and could move on.

The big battalion of soldiers took Paul in the night to Antipatris. At that point, safely out of Jerusalem and the Judean mountains and now on the coastal plain, the soldiers parted from the horsemen. They returned to the 'castle', probably the Antonia Fortress (23:31–32). The next morning, they arrived in Caesarea. Both Paul and the letter from Lysias

Twenty-Three: From Jerusalem to Caesarea

were delivered to Felix (23:33). When Felix read its message, he immediately asked Paul from what province he was from. He answered, Cilicia, the region in Asia Minor where the city of Tarsus was located (23:34).

After hearing that Paul was from Cilicia, he said he would wait for his accusers to show up before hearing him. There are two sides to every story, and it was important that both be present so that one could piece together the 'true story'. Paul was kept in Herod's judgment hall (23:35), built by Herod the Great, in proximity to the governor.

What happened when Paul's accusers arrived? We'll find out in the next chapter.

LESSON FOR LIFE: God can use all kinds of people, including those who don't know Him, to rescue His holy ones from danger.

CHAPTER TWENTY-FOUR
Paul's Defense Before Felix

Who: Paul, Felix, Tertullus and other adversaries

What: Paul's defence before Felix

When: After Paul's arrival in Caesarea

Where: Caesarea

Why: He had been accused of a capital crime

How: By the Jewish leaders

> *... touching the resurrection of the dead I am called in question by you this day.*
> — *Acts 24:21*

The Case Against Paul (24:1–9)

As an apostle of Christ, Paul travelled much. During his three missionary journeys, he found fruitfulness and success wherever he went, even with the furious opposition he encountered in many places. However, the current journey was by far the longest and hardest of all. No public ministry, no churches planted, no pastors raised up – just physical abuse, long fruitless hearings, and continued confinement. Since his arrest in Chapter Twenty-One, Paul was in custody and would remain so for the rest of the Book of Acts. He would get to address the governor, Felix, but had to wait five days for his accusers to arrive from Jerusalem. This included Ananias the high priest himself, along with the orator and spokesman, Tertullus, and the elders (24:1). They 'descended' from Jerusalem and the mountains to go 'down' to the coastal plain. They also 'descended', morally and spiritually, by falsely accusing the man of God and great apostle. Their mission was to lay before the governor their case against Paul.

'Golden-mouthed' Tertullus addressed Felix with flattery: Affirming the people of Israel enjoyed great quietness, meaning the Pax Romana or Roman peace. His 'providence' was the source of very worthy deeds done to the Jewish nation. All these benefits they accepted from the governor, Felix, with great thankfulness (24:2–3). Did Tertullus really believe these words of his? Was he and the Jewish elders truly thankful for Felix's administration? And was Felix really that wonderful? Highly unlikely on all counts.

After these flowery words, the orator got right down to business. He did not want to be further tedious with Felix, with continued flattery – he wanted him to listen to their grievance in just a few words (24:4). Tertullus went from high praise for Felix to serious accusation against Paul. You would not recognise Paul by the description given. Tertullus called Paul a 'pestilent' fellow. This word means 'annoying', 'troublesome', 'harmful', 'dangerous to public morality and life' and even 'deadly'. In the perversity of this fallen world, a man who was commissioned by Almighty God Himself to bring words of life and peace was now accused by his enemies of being a source of darkness and death.

Of course, nothing could be further from the truth. Paul was accused of sedition with Jews around the world, meaning he incited people to rebel against the authority of the religious rulers. He was also called a 'ringleader' of the sect of the Nazarenes (24:5), the only accusation that was not a total lie.

The false witness did not stop there. Without producing a shred of evidence, Tertullus continued the narrative. Paul was in the process of profaning the holy temple when he was 'caught in the act' and apprehended. The Jews then were going to judge him according to the

Twenty-Four: Paul's Defense Before Felix

Law (24:6). Of course, the truth was that Paul was conducting himself with complete propriety at the temple precincts, but his accusers had violently seized him and planned to beat Paul to death without due process of law. Had he gone to trial, he would have been immediately condemned and executed.

The testimony of Tertullus continued. He falsely claimed that Lysias the chief captain came and interrupted the administration of Jewish law by 'violently' seizing Paul from the Jews (24:7). The truth was Lysias saved Paul from the lynch mob. The Romans had made it clear that the Jewish accusers of Paul must appear and make their case in an open and accountable forum at Caesarea since a fair and safe hearing was clearly not possible in Jerusalem. At the very minimum, Paul had no need to fear a slap on the face for defending himself. So now it was up to Felix to examine these things for himself (24:8). All the Jerusalem contingent present at the hearing, including Ananias the high priest, gave assent that the things reported of Paul were so (24:9). They not only conspired to kill Paul; they also conspired to kill the truth as well.

> LESSON FOR LIFE: No matter how pious-looking you may be, forsake the truth and you forsake and are forsaken of God.

Paul's Defense before Felix (24:10–23)

After being beckoned by Felix the governor to speak, Paul began his defence. He said that he would cheerfully answer for himself before Felix because he had been a judge in Israel for many years (24:10).

First, Paul emphasised that the events that led to his audience with Felix had begun no more than twelve days earlier when he arrived in Jerusalem to worship (24:11). These were eventful and tumultuous days. It takes time to foment sedition, so how could he do this in a mere few days? Their charges were baseless. Far from being pestilent and seditious in the temple precincts, to profane the holy place, Paul described what truly happened. He at no time disputed with people at the temple. He did not incite to violence or commit sacrilege at any time. This was true on the mount, in the synagogue and also in the streets of the city (24:12). Paul courageously and rightly stated that his accusers were unable to prove any of the accusations they had made of him to this day (24:13).

Changing direction, Paul focused on his Messianic faith. His accusers said the way of the Nazarenes was heresy, yet Paul affirmed that their beliefs were Scriptural and orthodox. The apostle affirmed that, like his enemies, he continued to worship the God of his fathers, Abraham, Isaac and Jacob. His view of Scripture was high and he believed *'all things'* written in the Law and in the prophets (24:14). Nothing unorthodox or heretical at all.

Then, Paul went to the core of his belief system. He had hope in God, which, paradoxically, his accusers share, that there will be a resurrection of the dead. This includes the righteous and unrighteous (24:15).

> *And many of them that sleep in the dust of the earth shall awake, some to everlasting life, and some to shame and everlasting contempt.*
> — **Daniel 12:2**

> *Most assuredly, I say to you, the hour is coming, and now is, when the dead will hear the voice of the Son of God; and those who hear will live … Do not marvel at this; for the hour is coming in which all who are in the graves will hear His voice and come forth —those who have done good, to the resurrection of life, and those who have done evil, to the resurrection of condemnation.*
> — **John 5:25, 28–29** (NKJV)

The resurrection of the dead is the core doctrine of Biblical Christianity; the entire chapter of **1 Corinthians 15** is dedicated to this subject. If there is no general resurrection from the dead, then Christ did not rise either. If Christ did not rise, our faith is vain, we are yet in our sins and they that are 'dead in Christ' have perished eternally (1 Corinthians 15:13–18).

Twenty-Four: Paul's Defense Before Felix

These are dire consequences but, thank God, Jesus did rise from the dead and all we who believe the gospel rise with Him.

Paul came to the closing lap. Because of his call and belief system, he worked harder to have a clear conscience before God and man (24:16). He did nothing to deliberately offend anyone or live a life inconsistent with his profession of faith. He said that his only offence was belief in the resurrection of the dead, something that his accusers believed too.

So, what was Paul doing in Jerusalem? He said that his purpose in returning to the holy city was not to cause trouble. He wanted to bring alms for the poor and offerings towards God. This private personal visit to the holy city was after many years of absence (24:17).

What about the Jews of Asia, the ones who started the riot in the first place? Paul said he caught their notice after seven days at the temple. When they found him, he was purified in the precincts and was neither with a multitude, nor was he amid an insurrection (24:18). He was basically 'doing the law' and minding his own business. The Jews of Asia should have done the right thing and put in a formal complaint, not start a riot. They should have been at this very tribunal in Caesarea if they had a legitimate grievance against Paul (24:19), which, of course, they did not.

In addition to the Jews of Asia, what about the Jerusalem Jews standing before Felix today? Let them affirm what provable crime the Jewish high council found Paul guilty of (24:20). Again, Paul hammered the point that the only 'crime' he committed was affirming the doctrine of the Pharisees: that there is a resurrection from the dead (24:21). This, and only this, was the reason he had landed in such irrational circumstances.

After hearing the charges and defence, Felix now had a better understanding of the infant Christian faith. He decided to defer judgment on the matter until the chief captain, Lysias, came to Caesarea. Then, he would know the full details of this troubling case (24:22). Felix deferring the case meant that Paul remained in custody, though it is very clear that he was innocent of any crimes deserving imprisonment or death.

> LESSON FOR LIFE: Most of the time, wisdom decrees that you do not waste time answering your critics, since it will distract you from your call; but occasionally an answer is required. Paul's case was one of those times.

Though Paul was denied his freedom, he was still given special concessions. He was not to be chained or bound; he could be 'free range' in the confined precincts. Also, his friends were allowed to have visitation rights and minister to him (24:23). These were nice things, but they didn't compensate for the injustice of a deferred hearing, decision, and release.

Paul, Un-convicted, Held in Captivity (24:24–27)

Felix was married to a Jewish woman named Drusilla. After certain days, Paul was summoned by Felix to share his faith in Christ (24:24). The anointed apostle was more than happy to give Bible lessons to the Roman governor. He spoke about weighty doctrines like righteousness, self-control and divine judgement in the future. At this point, Felix became nervous and abruptly terminated the discourse. He told Paul to go back to his place and when the time was right, he would call for him again (24:25).

We soon discover that 'noble Felix' (v. 3) was not noble at all. The governor was looking for a bribe from Paul so that he could be set free (24:26). The apostle of God was not a corrupt man and could not be corrupted, either. Felix invited Paul regularly and spoke with him; he heard more gospel but received no money. Perhaps Felix did feel some attraction to the word of God, since it should have been obvious earlier on that no money would be offered. We have no record of Felix coming

Twenty-Four: Paul's Defense Before Felix

to faith, and his frequent visits with Paul meant he would have no excuse when in the future he stands before the throne of judgment.

Two years transpired and Paul, under Felix's administration, was still in custody. No trial, no release and no justice. Felix wanted to please the Jewish leadership by keeping Paul in prison (24:27), again demonstrating his corruption. Then Felix was replaced by Porcius Festus. The new man in town would take a different and better pathway than his predecessor.

Jesus spoke to Paul that he would go to Rome and testify of Him there (23:11), just as he testified in Jerusalem. Yet Paul was not a free man. How would he get there? The answer is found in the next chapter and the title tells you how.

CHAPTER TWENTY-FIVE

'I Appeal to Caesar'

Who: Festus, Paul and Agrippa

What: Paul's defence before Festus

When: After his Jerusalem enemies made accusations

Where: Caesarea and Jerusalem

Why: Accusations and a murder conspiracy

How: Through his knowledge of Roman citizenship and its benefits

> *Then said Paul, I stand at Caesar's judgment seat, where I ought to be judged: to the Jews have I done no wrong, as thou very well knowest. For if I be an offender, or have committed any thing worthy of death, I refuse not to die: but if there be none of these things whereof these accuse me, no man may deliver me unto them. I appeal unto Caesar.*
> — *Acts 25:10–11*

Paul Appeals to Caesar (25:1–12)

Paul was left in captivity and limbo in Caesarea. The breaking of the stalemate was made possible by the appointment of a new Roman governor. His name was Festus and he replaced the corruptible and contemptible Felix. He no sooner was in the new seat of power in Caesarea than, after three days, he paid a visit to the Jewish priestly class in Jerusalem (25:1). It was these people with whom he would have to work during his managerial tenure. Seeing that they had the ear of the

Welcome Holy Spirit

new governor, the high priest and chief priest lodged a complaint against Paul and asked Festus to acquiesce to their demands (25:2).

At this point, Paul had been imprisoned in Caesarea for over two years by Felix, though he was not convicted of any crime. He was a political prisoner. Yet though the apostle was 'out of sight,' he was not 'out of mind' with the religious establishment. In this part of the world, people have long strong memories: they do not forget and, hence, they do not forgive.

The priests wanted a favour from Festus: send Paul the prisoner up from Caesarea to Jerusalem so he could stand trial. Their motive was not justice but murder (25:3) – they wanted to fulfil the oath that the forty-plus men made two years earlier (23:12, 24). If Festus was purely political, he would have immediately granted their request. If he could get on their right side, it would make his job easier by their good report to Rome.

However, Festus was not just a 'man of action,' he had a sense of propriety. He believed it was appropriate and procedural for Paul to remain in Caesarea. He would be going there soon (25:4) and then he could assess the situation better. Perhaps he was aware of the earlier murder plot, but it also could be that the Lord prevented Festus from transferring Paul to Jerusalem, knowing certain death awaited him. After all, Paul was appointed by God to go to Rome and the road to Rome did not lead to Jerusalem.

Festus then issued an invitation: if any of Paul's accusers were able, they should go to Caesarea and make their accusations there. This would be in front of a proper Roman hearing (25:5) to ascertain if he was truly an evildoer or not. Festus sojourned in Jerusalem for ten days. He then returned to Caesarea, and on the very next day after his arrival, he commanded that Paul be brought before him (25:6). Festus wasted no time.

> LESSON FOR LIFE: God's sovereignty and power are so great that He can use people of position to do His will, even if they do not know Him personally.

Twenty-Five: 'I Appeal to Caesar'

The man of God now stood before the man of Rome. His Jewish accusers came down from Jerusalem and, as expected, made many grievous complaints, but they could neither agree nor prove anything. The same thing had happened at the trial of Jesus where the accusers were motivated by envy, which makes people irrational and deceitful.

The apostle was allowed to respond and made a three-fold defence of his conduct. He said he had not violated 'the law of the Jews,' nor had he defiled the temple in Jerusalem, nor in things Roman (of Caesar). In ecclesiastical and civil affairs, Paul was blameless (25:8).

Earlier, Festus refused to transfer Paul back to Jerusalem to stand trial, as demanded by the religious hierarchy. This was a providential move. It was safer to face his accusers in Caesarea rather than in Jerusalem where his enemies reigned supreme. Now Festus wanted to 'play politics' by getting Paul to agree to stand trial before him in Jerusalem (25:9). His motive, like Felix's, was 'to shew the Jews a pleasure' (24:27).

If Paul wanted to save his life and make it safely to Rome, as Jesus promised, then Jerusalem was the last place he should go. So, he said that he was standing before Caesar's judgment seat, which is where he should be judged. He has not violated the Jews' law, their holy place, or all things Roman. Then he boldly told Festus that he knew these things 'very well' (25:10). Courageously, Paul said that he did not refuse to die if he had committed a capital crime. However, he had not, so no one had the right to deliver him over to the very people who had falsely accused him and called for his blood. Instead of going backward to Jerusalem, he wanted to go forward to Rome. Then, he pulled out his secret weapon: *'I appeal to Caesar'* (25:11). This was his right as a Roman citizen; furthermore, it would get him a free one-way ticket to the Imperial City. Festus affirmed that since Paul had appealed to Caesar, to Caesar he would go (25:12). This would get the governor off the hook regarding Paul's Jerusalem accusers.

> LESSON FOR LIFE: God's plan to get Paul to Rome to testify of Christ came to pass, even though He used unusual methods to get him there.

Welcome Holy Spirit

Paul Before Agrippa and Bernice (25:13–27)

Paul was heading to Rome at Caesar's expense, but not just yet. There was some paperwork to fill out. One of the key questions: why was Festus sending Paul to Rome? What crime had he committed? How do you answer such a question when the accused had not violated Roman law? Festus would need some help and it came in royal form. The great-grandson of Herod the Great, and son of Herod Agrippa I, the king named Agrippa II, had come with his wife, Bernice, to Caesarea. Their purpose was to welcome Festus to the office of governor (25:13).

After the royal couple had been in Caesarea many days, Festus informed them about a certain man left imprisoned by Felix, namely Paul (25:14). He spoke about his meeting with the chief priests and elders of the Jews and how they wanted Paul to have a judgment against him (25:15). Then Festus reminded the king about the 'Roman' way. It was not *the manner of the Romans* to send a person for execution before he faced his accusers and had a chance to defend himself regarding the crime of which he was accused (25:16).

Roman-style justice was just, but so was the Mosaic Law. No one was to be executed unless the crime was affirmed by two or three witnesses.[59] The witnesses had to be credible and their testimony agreed. Yet in the Sanhedrin trials of Jesus and Paul, their accusers were false witnesses and no two testimonies agreed. So, while the accusers paid lip service to Moses, they failed to follow his precepts.

Festus continued his story to Agrippa. When the Jews had come down from Jerusalem to Caesarea to accuse Paul, he had sat on the judgment seat and brought Paul to the hearing without any delay (25:17). Festus expressed surprise, even shock, that the accusations were not what he expected (25:18). The way Paul's accusers spoke, you would have thought he was a grand thief, a mass murderer, a merciless rapist, a person of ill-repute and thoroughly immoral. Yet, when the emotive accusations came pouring forth, Paul's alleged crimes did not even come

Twenty-Five: 'I Appeal to Caesar'

close to these things. Why then all the hysteria and venom on the part of Paul's enemies? Again, their motivation was riddled with envy.

> LESSON FOR LIFE: In a dispute, always be principled and procedural. Require irrefutable evidence and justice is more likely to occur.

So why the commotion? What were the issues? The issues revolved around the Jewish religion, which Festus calls *'their own superstition'* (25:19). The other issue was about a man called Jesus. From a Roman point of view, he was dead (25:19), having been crucified on the cross under the administration of Pontius Pilate. From the 'gospel and truth' vantage point, Jesus is very much alive. Were these accusations against Paul 'much ado about nothing?' The answer was 'Yes', but it did not stop Paul from remaining in prison. The worldly rationale was that if a person is the source of great anger and consternation to many people, there must be something wrong with him, even if they could not figure out what.

As mentioned earlier, Festus offered Paul the option of being tried in Jerusalem and gave his excuse as to why he was willing to go there *'because I doubted of such manner of questions'* (25:20). He lacked the confidence to judge on issues of Jewish law; adjudicating in Jerusalem would make more sense, he reasoned. However, there was no good reason for Paul not to be tried in Caesarea, which was relatively close to Jerusalem. He could always bring Jerusalem-based experts of the Law to his court. Plus, there was a good case to argue that Paul couldn't get a fair trial in Jerusalem. When Paul said he wanted to meet Caesar Augustus, Festus affirmed that to Caesar he would go. In the meantime, Paul would be confined until Festus was ready and able to send him to Rome (25:21).

Festus' story aroused the interest of King Agrippa II. He expressed an interest in meeting Paul the prisoner. This seemed unusual since the aristocracy normally did not want to mix with accused criminals, though it was obvious Paul was not a typical criminal at all. Nevertheless,

Welcome Holy Spirit

Agrippa II was curious to hear from Paul, and this would give the apostle a platform to proclaim the gospel yet again. After the king announced his interest, Festus responded that he would hear Paul on the morrow (25:22). The next day, in conformity with protocol, Agrippa and Bernice entered the hearing room with great pomp; along with them were the chief captains and principal men of Caesarea. Once this distinguished group were assembled and seated, it was time for Paul to be brought forth by the command of Festus (25:23). His appearance at the hearing would leave an impression that will be etched into eternity.

> LESSON FOR LIFE: Though a prisoner, the anointing on Paul's life meant he would never lack the opportunity to speak of gospel grace.

Festus announced to King Agrippa II and all those present in the chamber that Paul had been condemned by the Jerusalem leadership as unworthy to live (25:24); in other words, in their eyes, he had committed a capital offence. Yet the governor's examination had found nothing in Paul or his activities that was worthy of death, at least from a Roman civil viewpoint. So, when the apostle appealed to Caesar Augustus, Festus was determined to send him to Rome (25:25).

Yet there was a problem. Festus admitted he was at a loss to find a reason to send him to Augustus. How do you explain to a pagan emperor about the trials of a Jewish holy man? So, Festus told King Agrippa that he needed his assistance in formulating a rationale for Paul's despatch to Rome (25:26). He reasoned that Agrippa, being a local king in Israel, would understand Jewish things far better than him. This was technically correct, but the Herodian dynasty was not known for being kosher Jews. Conclusion: Festus said it was unreasonable to send a man to trial, especially in Rome, when not even able to articulate adequately the accusations made against him (25:27).

Both Felix and Festus knew the man was innocent and should have been released immediately. Whether it was corruption or fear of displeasing the Sanhedrin, they kept Paul in custody. Despite all this, the

Twenty-Five: 'I Appeal to Caesar'

hand of the Lord was upon this situation. This apparent injustice led to the fulfilment of the express will of Jesus, Who said that Paul would testify of Him both in Jerusalem and also in Rome (Acts 23:11). His appeal to Caesar was a one-way ticket to the Imperial City. But before he could go to Rome, Paul needed to meet his local king, Agrippa (Matthew 10:18). This will happen in the next chapter.

---

[59] Deuteronomy 17:6; 19:15; Matthew 18:16; 2 Corinthians 13:1; 1 Timothy 5:19; Hebrews 10:28.

CHAPTER TWENTY-SIX
Paul With King Agrippa II

Who: Paul, Agrippa, and Festus

What: Paul's defence before Agrippa

When: After meeting Festus the Governor

Where: Caesarea

Why: *'Things of which I am accused by the Jews'*

How: Agrippa's Throne

> *And ye shall be brought before governors and kings for my sake, for a testimony against them and the Gentiles.*
> —**Matthew 10:18**

> *Then Agrippa said to Paul, 'You almost persuade me to become a Christian.'*
> —*Acts 26:28 (NKJV)*

Paul Stands Before Agrippa (26:1–18)

Paul had one more meeting with key people before being dispatched to Rome. While it might be tedious to have meeting after meeting, with little resolution, every meeting was an opportunity to share the gospel. This meeting before King Herod Agrippa II, Bernice and Festus would be no exception. Jesus said that His followers would be brought before *'governors and kings'* and here that word was coming to pass. In another sense, the meeting with Agrippa II was a dress rehearsal for the big

Welcome Holy Spirit

meeting before Caesar in Rome. Agrippa invited Paul to speak for himself. The apostle stretched forth his hand and began his defence (26:1).

Paul began his message by expressing happiness because he got to answer for himself before the king about all issues whereof he has been accused (26:2). Not only did he get to defend himself in true Roman fashion, but he would no doubt turn the narrative to focus on the good news of Christ. He called Agrippa an 'expert' in all the customs and questions of the Jewish people. This means he should, in theory, have understood where Paul was coming from, certainly more than the Roman governor. The apostle then asked the king to listen to him patiently (26:3). This meant 'to get comfortable' because his speech would be lengthy.

Paul began by saying that the Jews of Jerusalem knew the type of life he had lived since his youth (26:4). He was born in Tarsus in Asia Minor but grew up in Jerusalem among his fellow countrymen. He studied under the respected rabbi, Gamaliel.

His accusers should have known from the beginning that Paul was a member of a Jewish religious sect, namely a Pharisee (26:5). As we learned earlier, there were several Jewish sects in the first century AD: Sadducees, Essenes, Zealots, Herodians and Pharisees. The latter had two things in common with the young church: their teachings were the closest to that of Jesus and both survived the Roman onslaught of 70 AD, which resulted in the demise of Jewish autonomous rule for nearly two millennia.

Getting to the crux of the matter, Paul made an incredible claim: the only reason he was on trial was because of the hope of the promise made by God *'unto our ancestors'* (26:6). That hope was the resurrection of the dead.

LESSON FOR LIFE: Paul's remarkable boldness in the face of adversity can be rightly credited to the fullness and power of the Holy Spirit.

Twenty-Six: Paul With King Agrippa II

Paul made a valid claim: he had been accused by the Jerusalem leadership of a capital crime because he had affirmed the death, resurrection and Messiahship of Jesus. The main reason to see Jesus as the Messiah/Son of God was because of His resurrection from the dead (Romans 1:4). Because He had risen, this was the guarantee that one day everyone else would rise, too. Paul said the 'twelve tribes', serving God day and night, had the same hope (26:7). It is because of this very hope that he was now being accused by the leaders of his people.

Paul asked a rhetorical question of Agrippa II and the others: why should it be considered an incredible thing that God raises the dead (26:8)? This statement raised issues of the character of God. The Almighty promised a resurrection. He always tells the truth and keeps His promises. God can raise the dead and this is guaranteed by His power and Word. Agrippa would have been familiar with this, for Jewish belief affirmed God's veracity and omnipotence.

Paul confessed that he was once committed to the destruction of the faith he now promoted (26:9). He had once dedicated himself to acting against the interests of the name of Jesus of Nazareth. Paul's war against the early church was done in Jerusalem, and this was well-known. He had received the authority to imprison believers. If they were sentenced to death, like Stephen in **Acts 7**, he had approved of their execution (26:10). Now, the apostle was experiencing the same treatment that he gave to other believers.

Paul continued his narrative as the persecutor (this is the third time in the **Book of Acts** that Paul's salvation story was told). He had punished people often in every synagogue and forced them to blaspheme. Yet this was not enough: he had travelled outside of Israel to continue his devilish activities – all in God's service, or so he thought. He mentioned going to Damascus with authority from the chief priests in Jerusalem (26:11–12).

As Paul and his party had drawn closer to the Syrian capital, something unexpected had happened: a powerful light from heaven, brighter than the sun, had shone around the men (26:13). The man whose labour and attitude had been hidden by darkness was confronted with the 'light of the world', Jesus Christ (John 8:12). When darkness had collided with God's light, something had had to give: Paul and his party fell to the ground.

> LESSON FOR LIFE: The promises of God are so great, and yet our earthly lives are so short, that He will raise us from the dead in order to fulfil every detail.

While on the ground, the voice had spoken to him in Hebrew and asked, 'Saul, Saul, why are you persecuting me (26:14)? It is hard for you to kick against the goads.' In other words, resistance was useless. Paul, dumbfounded, had asked who it was that spoke. He identified Himself as Jesus, the One whom Paul had been persecuting (26:15).

After identifying Himself, Jesus had given Paul some simple, clear instructions. Rise, stand on your feet. There is a purpose for My appearing to you. I am making you a minister. You will be a witness of all you have seen and also of those things which I appear to you (26:16). The word 'witness' in Greek is μάρτυς, (*mar'-toos*), a martyr, someone who bears witness with word, action and indeed their entire life. Jesus promised to deliver Paul from his people and Gentiles, to whom he was being sent (26:17). Nothing could happen to him outside of God's will.

Ultimately this was Paul's mission: Jesus would use him to open the eyes of the people, turn them from darkness to light, and from the power of Satan to God. This is a great transformation. Those who receive the Word of God will have forgiveness of sins and a heavenly inheritance among those who are sanctified by faith in Jesus (26:18). It is a great inheritance that comes from a great salvation.

Paul Testifies to the World (26:19–23)

'Whereupon, O king Agrippa, I was not disobedient unto the heavenly vision' (26:19) – this has to be one of Paul's most famous statements, one that

Twenty-Six: Paul With King Agrippa II

summarises his ministry well. Vision is the roadmap that lights a fire in the soul. Without it, the people perish (Proverbs 29:18). Paul's heavenly vision began when he encountered Jesus on the Damascus road. It continued to guide him for the rest of his life. The vision decreed that Paul would be a chosen servant of Christ and a witness to the Gentiles, kings and the children of Israel (Acts 9:15). In addition, he would also see how much he would suffer for Christ's name (9:16). His suffering would be used to purify him and spread the gospel even more.

Paul's encounter with Christ on the Damascus road had led to his repentance. Now, as an apostle, he encouraged people in Damascus, Jerusalem and Judaea, and the Gentiles to repent, turn to God, and do the works that correspond with repentance (26:20). John the Baptist, who conducted the 'baptism of repentance', also required 'fruits of repentance' (Matthew 3:8; Luke 3:8). Again, we affirm that repentance, salvation and revival go hand in hand.

> LESSON FOR LIFE: The power of Paul's testimony is this: if God can change a bully from a sinner to a saint, He can change anyone.

Getting to the heart of the matter, Paul said it was for this reason – his obedience to the heavenly vision and calling people to repentance – that the militant Jews had caught him in the temple and tried to kill him (26:21). Despite such devilish and deadly opposition, Paul had continued his labour for the gospel to that day (26:22). By God's help, Paul had continued his witnessing ministry to small and great, saying nothing different from what was proclaimed by Moses and the prophets. Considering that Paul stood before some of the most important people in the nation – the governor and the king – he was fulfilling the divine mandate while defending himself. So, what did Moses and the prophets say? That Christ would suffer, be the first to rise from the dead – and never die again – and He would be a light to the Jewish people and the Gentiles (26:23).

By now it should be clear that what was meant to be a hearing for the defendant had turned into a gospel-sharing session. Eventually, there

Welcome Holy Spirit

was bound to be a reaction – a strong one. Festus interrupted Paul's speech and said he was *'beside himself'*, accusing him of being insane. Much learning had made him crazy (26:24), said the governor. What was the governor's motivation? Conviction? Curiosity? Whatever the reason, it did not deter Paul from speaking out. Without missing a beat, Paul respectfully affirmed that he was not crazy but spoke words of reason and truth (26:25).

> LESSON FOR LIFE: Like Paul, God has a heavenly vision for us all and, like Paul, we need to make it our number one priority.

Having addressed Festus the governor and affirming that he was not crazy, Paul turned his focus on King Agrippa II. The apostle said that Agrippa was very familiar with the things in which he spoke. Nothing was hidden from him because the birth and growth of the Christian church was *'not done in a corner'* (26:26). This means it was not done in some obscure place, but began, front and centre, in the city of Jerusalem during a major pilgrimage feast. Like concentric circles emanating from the impact of a rock on the pond, so the gospel spread openly throughout the ancient world.

Paul's Gospel Appeal (26:27–32)

Paul the prisoner was most audacious. Though he was the one on trial, he turned his attention to his judges and asked them the pertinent questions. In Agrippa's case, he inquired if he believed in the prophets. As a king of the Jews, Agrippa should have known something about this topic. Then Paul added, 'I know that you believe' (26:27).

Agrippa gave an intriguing statement to Paul's question. Instead of saying, 'Yes, I believe in the prophets', he said that Paul had *almost* persuaded him to be a Christian. We have already learned that the name 'Christian(s)' is only used three times in the New Testament. It was used first in Antioch to describe the followers of Jesus. Though perhaps coined

Twenty-Six: Paul With King Agrippa II

in derision, the name has since become one of great honour that is recognised worldwide for the followers of Christ.

Agrippa was an 'almost' Christian: he identified with much of what Paul said but was not ready to repent, believe and receive the gospel. In the annals of eternity, being an 'almost Christian' will not be good enough. Quick on the mark, Paul responded to Agrippa that he wished to God that the king, and all who heard him, would be just like the apostle – saved, redeemed, delivered, sanctified – except for the chains that he wore (26:29)

After this statement, there was no altar call, tears of repentance nor commitment to the gospel. Instead, the governor, king, Bernice and those who were with them rose abruptly and prepared to leave the room (26:30), even before Paul had finished his speech. The meeting was over. In a time of consultation, the key parties came to the same conclusion: this man has done nothing worthy of death or imprisonment (26:31). Agrippa came to an important conclusion: Paul was an innocent man. By rights, he should have been released from captivity immediately; there was no justification to keep him in chains any longer.

> LESSON FOR LIFE: The gift of the gospel, when lived to the full, makes room for you and brings you before significant people like Caesar (Proverbs 18:16).

However, he could not be released because he had appealed to Caesar. What appeared to be an anomaly – justice delayed, justice denied – had been ordained by God so that Paul could keep his appointment with Caesar in Rome. He would testify to him like he did to everyone else; his royal status did not matter, but the gospel did. After all, Jesus said Paul would witness about Him before kings and, on a separate occasion, he would testify in Rome. This word was about to come to pass.

Welcome Holy Spirit

After a needlessly lengthy sojourn in Caesarea, the wheels were now turning for the next phase of Paul's journey: Rome. The voyage, as we will see in the next chapter, will take unexpected and dangerous twists and turns. Something significant awaited him in the Imperial City; this helps explain how the forces of hell harnessed the force of nature to try and prevent his arrival.

CHAPTER TWENTY-SEVEN

The Stormy Voyage to Rome

Who: Paul, sailors and prisoners

What: Sea journey to Rome and the storm

When: After leaving Caesarea by sea

Where: Mediterranean Sea

Why: Paul's appointment with Caesar

How: Bad advice countered by God's grace.

> *For there stood by me this night the angel of God, whose I am, and whom I serve, Saying, Fear not, Paul; thou must be brought before Caesar: and, lo, God hath given thee all them that sail with thee. Wherefore, sirs, be of good cheer: for I believe God, that it shall be even as it was told me.*
> *— Acts 27:23–25*

Paul's ill-fated trip to Jerusalem led him to much trial and tribulation. After being stranded in custody at Caesarea for over two years, the new governor, Festus, expedited his case.

It was determined that he should go to Rome because he had appealed to Caesar. The trip to Jerusalem would be dwarfed by an even more ill-fated voyage to Rome. It would have ended in catastrophe except for one thing: the Lord personally assured Paul, before and during the voyage, that he would make it to Rome.

Welcome Holy Spirit

Paul's positive, faith-filled response (27:25) made all the difference between a death by drowning and an audience with Caesar. And as a bonus, the Lord spared the lives of everyone else on board. The time of his departure was at hand.

Paul Sets Sail for Rome (27:1–12)

'And when it was determined that we should sail into Italy ...' (27:1). By all appearances, Luke, the (human) author of Acts, was part of the journey and described it in great detail. When it was time to set sail, Paul and others were delivered to Julius, a centurion of the Augustus band. At Caesarea, they entered a ship of Adramyttium (27:2). After they departed, the ship sailed to the ports up the Levantine coast with Aristarchus, a Macedonian from Thessalonica. On the morrow, the ship landed in the Phoenician city of Sidon. Julius treated his most important prisoner with great kindness. He graciously permitted Paul to meet with his friends and to be refreshed by them (27:3). Prisoners might have visiting rights, but this gesture appeared to be exceptional. From Sidon, the ship departed from the Levantine coast and headed towards the island of Cyprus. It sailed close to its southern shore since the wind was against them (27:4). The normally idyllic Mediterranean Sea could be very turbulent at certain times of the year, and they probably set sail in that period. Staying close to land was one way to stay safe.

Sailing on the open sea but close to the southern coast of Asia Minor – specifically the regions of Cilicia and Pamphylia – the ship came to Myra, a city of Lycia (27:5). Here they changed ships, though no reason was given. Perhaps it was a bigger ship that could handle the turbulence better, though this is only conjecture (27:6). In any case, they were on an Alexandrian ship heading for Italy. But the sailing was anything but smooth. It sailed slowly for many days because the wind would not allow them to proceed as normal. They sailed past Cnidus, Salmone and the southern part of Crete (27:7).

Sailing with great difficulty, they arrived at Fair Havens near Lasea, a city of Crete. It was decision time: where should they anchor the ship

Twenty-Seven: The Stormy Voyage to Rome

during the winter months? Since it had taken too long to get to Crete, they had lost valuable time. To continue the voyage was too risky because the 'Fast' had passed. The 'Fast' meant Yom Kippur, the Jewish day of atonement, which is the one communal fast of the year. This happens in the autumn so after the Jewish high holy days, a voyage on the Mediterranean in late autumn and winter can be dangerous (27:8–9). But where could they go? Paul, led by the Holy Spirit, boldly offered some sound advice.

Paul, though a prisoner, still retained his authority and anointing. He commanded a presence that people recognised instinctively, with respect. Plus, he was a very smart man, both in the natural and the spiritual; this added to the gravity of his words. So, it was without hesitation that he boldly told the captain that it was too risky to continue the journey. If they proceeded, there would be much damage to the ship, lading and the lives of the passengers (27:10). Paul was prophetic, but he also spoke as an experienced traveller. He knew a thing or two about shipwrecks since he had experienced three of them in his own life (2 Corinthians 11:25). Sailing in this season was dangerous.

> LESSON FOR LIFE: Flexibility is a must when you travel, so be informed, learn to allow yourself enough time and discern the right circumstances.

Paul was outvoted by the master, who was the pilot of the ship, and the ship's owner. They wanted to proceed with the journey, probably for commercial reasons. The centurion chose to listen to these two men instead of heeding the wisdom of Paul (27:11). They would pay dearly for this outcome.

The decision was made, and they must sail on, even if it was to another bay in Crete. This turned out to be a near-fatal move. Their current location, Fair Havens, was not suitable to spend the winter in, geographically or socially, because it was a small town. Their goal was to sail for another city of Crete, Phenice (Phoenix), only sixty-four kilometres (forty miles) away, which faced south-west and north-west, providing a better haven for them in which to spend the winter (27:12). They never got there.

The Furious Storm at Sea (27:13–38)

Appearances can be deceiving. There was a 'soft wind' and the captain decided it was okay to sail from one side of Crete to another, especially if they stayed close to the shore (27:13). It sounded like a reasonable proposition; however, it ended in disaster. There are 'good ideas' and 'God ideas', and you can count on the latter to deliver the desired result.

Not long after setting sail, the ship had the misfortune of encountering a Euroclydon, a northeaster, which could be like a cyclone. This wind blew them completely out to the open sea, where they were at the mercy of the elements. They could not withstand the wind or control the ship, so they let it go (27:14–15). Where they ended up was anyone's guess – the Mediterranean Sea was not small. They sailed by an island called Clauda and had much work to do to keep the ship afloat: this work included being taken up, using helps and undergirding the ship, but fearing they would run aground into the quicksand, they lifted up the sail and let the ship continue out to sea (27:16–17). Trying to anchor was just too dangerous.

The wind was so bad they felt like they were on a roller-coaster. They were *'exceedingly tossed with a tempest'* (27:18) and so the next day, they decided to lighten the ship by throwing the cargo into the sea. On the third day, they cast out the tackle with their own hands; perhaps Paul and the prisoners were involved in this process. Luke, the masterful historian, painted an accurate picture of terror and hopelessness during this Euroclydon. There was no sun, stars or moon in the sky for many days – that's how furious the storm was. The tempest itself was the roughest imaginable. At this point, all hope of being saved was now lost (27:20). To lack hope is a terrible condition because, in essence, it means that you have no future. It can lead to disappointment, depression and

Twenty-Seven: The Stormy Voyage to Rome

despair. Yet Paul had a word from Jesus that he would make it to Rome, and this was a good time to hang on to it.

No one had eaten for days because of the storm; perhaps they were seasick. Not the bashful type, Paul the prisoner showed leadership by speaking to the decision-makers of the ship. He reminded them they should have listened to him, and not set sail from Crete. Now they faced extreme harm and loss (27:22). That was the bad news but, fortunately, there was some miraculous good news. Despite this most dire circumstance, there was a reason to hope. Paul predicted that though the ship would be lost, no one would die because of this storm (27:22). This is an amazing statement of faith considering the dire circumstances they faced.

> LESSON FOR LIFE: Remember that faith, grace and peace, are freely available to you during all of life's storms.

What was the basis of Paul's confident confession? That very evening, an angel of the Lord came and stood by him. This angel belonged to God, Paul belonged to God and it is God Whom he served (27:23). There is no higher authority than this. The angel confirmed the word given to him earlier by Jesus Himself. Paul was told not to be afraid. He would keep his appointment with Caesar, which meant he was a candidate for a miraculous deliverance from the raging sea. And God was gracious; He would preserve the lives of everyone who was sailing with Paul (27:24). Everyone would be saved provided that they stayed on the ship until the very end, even if it crashed onto the shore – which it did.

Conclusion: *'Wherefore, sirs, be of good cheer: for I believe God, that it shall be even as it was told me'* (27:25). Upbeat Paul told his companions to cheer up; he had a sure word from God, Who could be trusted to keep His promise. They were going to survive, after all. This was not just wishful thinking; it was based on what God said.

Though everyone would be saved from drowning, they were going to run aground on a certain island (27:26). We call it a shipwreck. This meant the ship would not be saved, only the passengers (which is more important, anyway). That 'certain island' was Malta,[60] south of Italy. By now it was the fourteenth night of the storm. The sailors perceived that they were now close to land (27:27). How did they know? They took sounds and discovered the depth was twenty fathoms and then later fifteen fathoms (27:28). The time of reckoning was at hand.

> LESSON FOR LIFE: Whether in calm or storm, keep trusting God and He will direct your path (Proverbs 3:5–6).

The sailors were alarmed at these readings. It meant they were going to run aground and hit the rocks (27:29). So, they cast four anchors out of the stern and 'prayed' (wished) that the daylight would come sooner rather than later. Then came a self-serving plot: the sailors wanted to escape from the ship by letting down the lifeboat into the sea, pretending they would cast anchors in the foreshore (27:30). Paul found out about this and spoke sternly to the centurion and his soldiers. He solemnly warned them that the sailors must stay on the ship or there would be needless loss of life (27:31). This time, the ship's leadership listened to Paul; his authority, based on the Spirit's anointing, prevailed after all. They cut the rope and let the boat fall into the sea (27:32).

Paul went from being prophetic to pastoral. When the daylight arrived, he urged the men to break their forced fast which had lasted two weeks (27:33). Being in a ferocious storm was not conducive to hunger and eating. The apostle urged them to have some food because it was for their health. Then, as a good shepherd, he injected a word of encouragement: they would make it through this ordeal and not one hair on their head would fall to the ground (27:34), an idiom that they would survive completely intact.

> *And when he had said these things, he took bread, and giving thanks to God in the presence of all he broke it and began to eat.*
> — *Acts 27:35*

Twenty-Seven: The Stormy Voyage to Rome

This verse (27:35) is remarkably similar to those where Jesus broke the bread and fed the multitudes from a few loaves and fishes (not to mention breaking bread at the Last Supper and Emmaus). Paul first gave the invitation, 'Come and dine'. Second, he held up the food, in this case, bread. Third, he thanked God in public for who He was and for the food He had provided. Fourth, he broke the bread, which is the same as dishing up the meal. Fifth, he began to eat (27:35). God cares for the entire person: body, soul and spirit. That's why taking care of ourselves shows respect for the 'temple of the Holy Spirit' which is our body (1 Corinthians 6:19). Once Paul demonstrated leadership by example, the men with him cheered up, regained their appetite and ate food, too (27:36). The number of people on the ship was two-hundred and seventy-six (27:37).

> LESSON FOR LIFE: Never forget that God is present in the midst of every storm and will guide and provide all the way to shore.

The Shipwreck (27:38–44)

After the 'last supper' on the ship, they needed to lighten the load, so they tossed the wheat into the sea (27:38). Failure to do so would have prevented the ship from getting closer to land. At daybreak, they did not recognise the land. However, they saw a creek and shore and believed this was as good as any place to run the ship ashore (27:39). They cast off the anchors and left them into the sea. Simultaneously, they lessened the ropes that were attached to the rudders. Finally, they hoisted the foresail to the wind and essentially sailed to the shore (27:40). The ship sailed until the place of the two seas met and then ran aground. The front part of the ship was stuck in the shore and would not move. The hind end was broken up by violent surf (27:41).

The ship made it close enough to shore so that people could safely escape to land. However, the danger was not over; this time, it was of human origin. The soldiers wanted to kill the prisoners in case they escaped. This would include Paul (27:42). Their motive was self-interest;

Welcome Holy Spirit

it was not uncommon for soldiers to face capital punishment if the prisoners under their watch escaped custody (12:18–19).

The centurion intervened so that Paul would be spared execution. This was the third time in Acts where Romans intervened to save Paul from death. And because Paul was saved, all the other prisoners were saved with him. Then the centurion commanded the soldiers who could swim to jump into the sea and get to land (27:43). For those men who could not swim, they would need to cling to floating debris and head towards the shore. In any case, they all escaped safely to the land (27:44). God's promise to deliver Paul and his sailing companions was fulfilled – of course.

Now that they had made it safely to land in Melita, what would happen next? And how did Paul get to Rome? These questions, and more, will be answered in the next and final chapter.

> LESSON FOR LIFE: Hold onto the promises of God despite circumstance and you will safely make it to your desired haven.

---

[60] In an email dated 23 July 2024, best-selling author Eric Metaxas, quoting from a December 1988 article in the German magazine *Die Zeit* entitled 'Paul Was Never in Malta.' The alternate site of the shipwreck is Kefalonia, the largest of the Ionian Islands in western Greece. Malta has a strong tradition behind it, complete with St. Paul's Bay. While it is beyond the scope of this book to affirm or deny the identity of the place of the shipwreck, this is the first time this author has heard of a challenge to identifying Malta as the place of the shipwreck.

CHAPTER TWENTY-EIGHT
Paul in Melita and Rome
(or In Caesar's Shadow)

Who: Paul the prisoner

What: Arrived and settled in Rome

When: After the shipwreck at Melita

Where: Melita, Italy and Rome

Why: Paul's appointment with Caesar

How: Roman system and the grace of God

> *And Paul dwelt two whole years in his own hired house, and received all that came in unto him, Preaching the kingdom of God, and teaching those things which concern the Lord Jesus Christ, with all confidence, no man forbidding him.*
> *— Acts 28:30–31*

Sojourn in Melita (28:1–10)

The men of Paul's ship, having escaped death, recognised the island as Melita, the old name for Malta (28:1). This island is eighty kilometres (fifty miles) south of Sicily, and it is thirty-two kilometres long, twenty kilometres wide and ninety-six kilometres in circumference. It has been occupied by the Phoenicians, Carthaginians, Greeks, Romans, Byzantines, Moors and others. After British rule that lasted for one hundred and fifty years, it gained its independence in 1964.

Welcome Holy Spirit

It was the beginning of winter, with rain and cold on every side. The locals showed great kindness to the stranded men, receiving them graciously and kindling a fire on their behalf (28:2). The natives were described as 'barbarous' but may not have been intended as an insult; it could simply mean that their language was hard to comprehend. Paul used this phrase in **1 Corinthians 14:11**.

After being in a perilous storm, a shattering shipwreck and now on a Mediterranean island in the cold season, Paul was understandably keen to help warm up himself and his fellow passengers. He assisted the natives in kindling the fire, thus showing the servant's heart which is to be expected from a minister of God. While he was putting the sticks on the fire, a viper came out of the heat and attached itself to Paul's hand.

Watching this frightening spectacle were the locals. Who is this man? Is he a murderer? He may have escaped death at sea, but the gods execute vengeance by land (28:4). They reasoned that the viper was on Paul's hand because he was a murderer who had escaped death at sea but the gods would not allow him to live. They expected Paul to drop dead at any moment.

With remarkable calm, Paul shook the viper into the fire and suffered no ill effect (28:5). Whenever we have an unwanted event, person or circumstance come into our lives, the best thing we can do is 'shake it off' and get on with life. Though Paul got on with his business, the natives of Melita were watching and waiting to see if Paul would swell up and collapse to the ground. After a great while, seeing that nothing bad was going to happen to him, they decided he was a god (28:6). Made in the image of God and anointed with divine power, Yes, but a god himself, No.

Favour seemed to be following Paul everywhere he went: escaping a shipwreck, encountering hospitable natives, deliverance from the viper and now taken into the house of Publius, the chief man of the island. The other two hundred and seventy-five men on the ship had their lives spared in the shipwreck because they were travelling with Paul, the

Twenty Eight: Paul in Melita and Rome

favoured man. Publius had Paul and his company stay with him for three days (28:7).

The father of Publius was sick. Though the text does not state the precise nature of the illness, it could have been something common like dysentery, fever or cholera. Paul fearlessly came into the sick room and prayed with the laying-on of hands. Publius' father was immediately healed (28:8).

> LESSON FOR LIFE: God's favour on your life will both open doors, reap provision and find an entree with people; but it can also arouse satanic opposition.

When the news spread that Publius' father had been divinely healed, others on the island who had diseases came to Paul and also received healing (28:9). Whether they came to faith in Jesus or a church was planted in Melita, the text does not say. This may have been the first apostolic visit to the Mediterranean island. Luke the physician said that the natives of Melita honoured the apostolic team with many honours. At the time of departure, they gave them *'such things as were necessary'* (28:10). Would to God more people showed this kind of comprehensive, 'extra mile' hospitality and generosity today!

On to Rome (28:11–17)

After three months, the apostles departed Melita on a ship from Alexandria that had spent the winter on the island. The signs of this ship, Castor and Pollux (28:11), were heathen. Their departure may have been in late January, which is still winter, but everything is more stable then and it is easier to sail. They landed at Syracuse, the capital of the island of Sicily. If Italy physically resembles a leg in a boot, Sicily is the football. The apostles spent three days there (28:12).

In travel, you have to be flexible and equipped, but things happen that can take you off course and schedule. Though prisoners, they fetched a compass and landed in Rhegium, a city and promontory in

Welcome Holy Spirit

Calabria (today known as Reggio). The city is at the very tip of the 'toe' of Italy. Its original name meant 'break off', because it appears that it was here that the city broke off from Sicily. After one day, when the soft south wind blew, they set sail for Puteoli (28:13), known today as Pozzuoli. Here at Puteoli, they discovered there were 'brethren' who gave them an invitation to sojourn with them, which they did for seven days (28:14). Favour allowed Paul to have such flexibility en route to Rome.

From Puteoli, more brethren heard of Paul and his travelling party and came to meet him at Appius Forum and the Three Taverns. When Paul saw the love and care of these believers, he 'thanked God' and 'took courage' (28:15). Here is another glimpse of the apostle's humanity: strong and courageous as he was, enduring trying circumstances can take its toll. The love of these believers, which mirrored the love of God, had a rejuvenating effect on the apostle. A sense of relief, gratitude and encouragement came from such an encounter.

Once they reached the Imperial City, the centurion delivered the prisoners of Paul's ship to the captain of the guard. However, thanks to the favour of God, Paul was given a special concession. He was not lumped with the crowd; he was allowed to dwell on his own with only a single soldier to watch over him (28:16).

> LESSON FOR LIFE: Despite many dangers, toils and snares, the word of Jesus that Paul would make it to Rome had finally come to pass.

Meeting the Jews of Rome (28:17–31)

After three days Paul invited the leadership of the Jewish community to come meet with him. When they arrived, he gave an impassioned appeal, beginning with 'Men and brethren', using the phrase he employed before. Then he sought to vindicate himself against the accusations of his fellow Jews in Jerusalem. He had not sinned against his people nor the customs of their ancestors. Despite his blameless state, he had been delivered in Jerusalem into Roman custody (28:17). Paul

Twenty Eight: Paul in Melita and Rome

rightly recounted how the Romans had examined him and found he had done nothing to deserve capital punishment, or even imprisonment (28:18). As such, they would have let him go free.

The apostle recounted that the Jews would not accept this clear verdict of innocence on his behalf and had spoken against his exoneration. For this reason, Paul had felt 'constrained' to appeal to Caesar (28:19). This was not meant to be an indictment against his nation, simply a self-defence mechanism.

After giving the background information of why he was in Rome – in chains – he said 'for this cause', Paul had called to speak with them. He wanted to explain to them why the only reason he was in captivity that day was not because of any crime or transgression, but due to the 'hope of Israel' (28:20). This 'hope' was a reference to the doctrine of the resurrection, that of Christ, the saints and the general dead. Paul wanted to use this visit as a launch pad for presenting the gospel to his people.

In response, the Jewish leadership in Rome said that they did not receive any correspondence from Judaea regarding Paul. Neither had any who had come to Rome from Jerusalem spoken about him in any way (28:21). This is a point of interest: Paul's enemies in Jerusalem had made a big fuss about him to the Romans there and also were willing to travel to Caesarea to lodge their case against him. Yet, after Paul departed for Rome, it is as if they had ceased their campaign, content that the man they despised was no longer in the country.

Paul's guests then expressed interest in learning more about the Christian faith, which they called a 'sect'. They had only heard denunciations and evil words about it. Rather than be put off by the criticism of the faith, it aroused their curiosity (28:22). What a God-given opportunity to share the gospel.

A day was set aside for the *teach-in*. There was a capacity crowd that came to Paul's dwelling. There he expounded and testified about the kingdom of God. Concerning the person and work of Jesus, Paul

Welcome Holy Spirit

powerfully built his case that Jesus is Lord and Christ, using the law of Moses and the prophets (28:23). He had plenty of material from which to expound because his teaching went from the morning to the evening. After a day of teaching, what were the results? They were mixed: some believed in the words of Paul and others did not (28:24). This was what happened in every place he went during his three missionary journeys.

Then Paul gave them a quote from the prophet Isaiah:

> *Well spake the Holy Ghost by Esaias the prophet unto our fathers, Saying, Go unto this people, and say, Hearing ye shall hear, and shall not understand; and seeing ye shall see, and not perceive: For the heart of this people is waxed gross, and their ears are dull of hearing, and their eyes have they closed; lest they should see with their eyes, and hear with their ears, and understand with their heart, and should be converted, and I should heal them.*
> — Isaiah 6:9–10, Acts 28:25–27

It was obvious that there would be no consensus in this group (28:25). They departed in disagreement, even contention, after Paul spoke the above word from **Isaiah 6**. This passage is so important that it is quoted six times in Scripture.[61] It was an indictment of hard-hearted, hypocritical or 'head only' religiosity that claimed to be close to God but was far from Him. Position, pedigree, education, finances and connections may impress the world but mean nothing to God.

The **Isaiah 6** passage says such people will hear and see the things of God but it will be in vain. Their heart is callous, their ears are dull and their eyes are closed. Otherwise, they may perceive with ears, eyes and heart, turn, repent and be healed by God. This is not an easy passage to explain, but we understand that from the entire counsel of Scripture, those who are willing to listen and obey will have the blessing of God. For those who refuse to listen and obey, the above condition will apply.

Paul then boldly proclaimed that while there would be some Jews who rejected the counsel of God through the gospel (Isaiah 6 is still in his

Twenty Eight: Paul in Melita and Rome

mind), this same message would go to the Gentiles and *'they will hear it'* (28:28). After giving his final summary statement, the Jews departed from Paul's house and had *'great reasoning'* among themselves (28:29). The apostle had given them a lot of food for thought, and it would take much time to process it all.

As the **Book of Acts** draws to a close, it appears that Paul continued to be under house arrest while in Rome. He was waiting to meet with Caesar, and this had already taken two years. This is the same period he was imprisoned in Caesarea. The ridiculous thing about it all is that the Romans knew and affirmed that this man was innocent, having done nothing to earn imprisonment or capital punishment. It appears that there was no provision for posting bail and being free while awaiting trial; therefore, because of his appeal to Caesar, Paul had to be kept in confinement while awaiting his audience. In the meantime, Paul did not lack for company. People came to see him, and he welcomed them all (28:30). They may have come because of his notoriety, his eloquent words or even because they heard he had a healing ministry.

To all his visitors, Paul spoke on the surety and nature of God's kingdom and about the person and work of the Lord Jesus Christ. He did so with all confidence, and no one could work or stop him (28:31). On this note, the **Book of Acts** comes to an end. We hear nothing about any meeting with Caesar, if and when he was set free, what he did afterwards, etc. For further information, we are dependent on the writings of the church fathers and tradition. (Scholars believe that he was released, went as far as to Spain and returned to Rome where he was arrested and executed under the Roman emperor, Nero).

As we complete our study of the **Book of Acts**, we learned about the supernatural birth and growth of the Christian Church. As a bonus, we received insights about being baptised, filled and a lifestyle in the Spirit. The Holy Spirit was very much the senior partner with the apostles in terms of the birth and growth of the church. He is referred to fifty-one times in Acts. Of interest, while most of these references are found in the first twenty-one chapters, it is in the last seven chapters where He is not

Welcome Holy Spirit

mentioned; meaning from **Acts 21:11** until **28:25**, the last chapter. These chapters correspond with Paul's visit to Jerusalem, the riot at the temple precincts, his arrest, and his various trials in Jerusalem and Caesarea and the sea journey to Rome. In short, the omission of any mention of the Holy Spirit parallels the lengthy period Paul was in captivity. Of course, the promise of God's presence still was with Paul (Hebrews 13:5), but we hear nothing more of the Holy Spirit until he met with the Jewish community of Rome in **Acts 28:23–29**. While there is much we cannot explain in this omission, one thing is for certain: it is always wise to be led by the Spirit and obedient to His direction.

Despite the above comments, we give credit where it is due. Paul's apostolic ministry and its effectiveness were beyond dispute. Because of the Holy Spirit, this man left of legacy of church planting, Scripture writing and civilisational influence that is second to none (except, of course, for Jesus Christ Himself). His joy, fearlessness and also being targeted for trouble by envious opponents were a result of his walk in the Spirit.

The latter-day **Acts 29** is being written today.

If you, like the apostles of old, will welcome the Holy Spirit in your life, home and heart, you can be part of this glorious chapter.

---

[61] Isaiah 6:9–10 is quoted six times: Jeremiah 5:21; Ezekiel 12:2; Matthew 13:14; Mark 4:12; Luke 8:10; Acts 28:26-27.

Appendices

Appendix One
A Book of Acts Prayer

As we come to the end of this book, the following is a prayer you can pray to begin your long-term journey to living a 'Book of Acts lifestyle'.

Heavenly Father,

I thank you for your wonderful Son, my Saviour, Jesus the Messiah, Who was delivered for our offences, and was raised again for our justification.[62] *Thank you for the Holy Spirit who opened my heart and introduced me to your Son and helped me confess that Jesus is Lord.*[63] *Thank you also for the Word of God, which spawned faith in my heart*[64] *and was engrafted into my soul for salvation.*[65] *All three – Jesus, the Spirit and the Word – are the three-fold source of divine truth.*[66] *They wonderfully come together in the* **Book of Acts**.

Thank you for the **Book of Acts**, *which tells the story of the birth and growth of the church. What an inspiration to see the supernatural interface with the natural, the spiritual with the physical, the Jew and the Gentile. What a thrill to know that, according to Acts, the supernatural can become natural and second nature and where inspiration partners with the practical.*

By your grace, enable me to hunger for your Word more than for food itself.[67]. *Open up my eyes* **'that I may behold wondrous things out of thy law'.**[68]

Help me to thirst and drink deeply of the rivers of living water of the Spirit.[69]

Enable me to be continuously **'filled with the Spirit.'**[70]

Teach me how to walk in the Spirit so I am obeying You and not the lusts of the carnal nature.[71]

Open up to me the wonderful world of spiritual gifts; may I not be ignorant of them.[72]

Stoke in me a fire to eagerly desire the best gifts.

The world needs the gospel and the church needs revival. As I digest the message of Acts, enable me to serve you in the world and the church, led and empowered by the Holy Spirit.

Thank you that Your story and the early church's story has now become my story. By Your grace, let me play my part in writing Acts 29, for Your glory, the extension of Your kingdom, and the benefit of the church,

In the Mighty Name of Jesus,

Amen.

Declaration of faith (confess aloud):

I declare that in partnership with the Holy Spirit and guided by God's Word, I will help write Acts 29 for the sake of the last days Church and the world, in Jesus' Name.

Appendix Two
An Appeal

You have just read about the **Book of Acts**, the story of the birth and growth of the church. The breathtaking narrative of audacious faith, fearlessness and forbearance in the face of trouble, is an inspiration to all who read and heed its message. Yet all of this could be entirely lost if one fails to receive the wonderful gift of the gospel. The gospel is the 'good news' of Jesus the Messiah, Son of God and Saviour. He took the penalty of our sin upon Himself by dying on the cross and then rose again from the dead for our *justification*. This wonderful Bible word has two powerful meanings: first, justified people are declared 'not guilty'; second, justified people are declared *righteous* before God.

How do we receive this great gospel of salvation, which is impossible to earn? We receive this indescribably wonderful gift by faith. Please consider:

God has a plan: God's kingdom and your part in it have been known from before the foundation of the world (Ephesians 2:10).

You have a problem: While everyone has issues and problems, this particular problem is the biggest and most deadly of all. It does not come from circumstances or the actions of others. This problem is called *sin*. Sin means to 'miss the mark' or 'transgress God's holy standards'. Scripture is clear that everyone has a sin problem (Psalm 14:3; 53:3; Romans 3:10, 12, 23).

Sin has a high price: Sin does not bring mere inconvenience or dissatisfaction. **Romans 6:23** is very clear that *'the wages of sin is death'*. Left without remedy, our sin leaves us in a state of spiritual death, then physical death, and eventually eternal death, which means permanent separation from the source of all life, which is God.

There is only one remedy: Religion, good ideas, intentions and works cannot take away sin. The only remedy is receiving God's free gift of redemption by believing the gospel. **Romans 10:9–10** says:

> [t]hat if thou shalt confess with thy mouth the Lord Jesus, and shalt believe in thine heart that God hath raised him from the dead, thou shalt be saved. For with the heart man believeth unto righteousness; and with the mouth confession is made unto salvation.

The application of the remedy: It takes two things: repentance and faith, as affirmed by the Apostle Paul:

> *Testifying both to the Jews, and also to the Greeks, repentance toward God, and faith toward our Lord Jesus Christ.*
> *— Acts 20:21*

Repentance: This means to 'change' our attitude and actions. It also means to 'turn'. Repentance implies that a person, heading in one direction, changes their mind and turns in another direction. As Bible teacher Joy Dawson says, 'Repentance means being sorry enough to quit'. Without repentance, there is no salvation or revival.

> *Therefore leaving the principles of the doctrine of Christ, let us go on unto perfection; not laying again the foundation of repentance from dead works, and of faith toward God.*
> *— Hebrews 6:1*

Faith: We receive Christ and the gospel by faith. Now is the day of salvation (2 Corinthians 6:2). Jesus stands at the door and knocks; if you will open the door, He will come in (Revelation 3:20). Open your heart wide and let the King of Glory come in (Psalm 24:7, 9). Receive Christ today by faith. Biblical faith means to:

- **Believe**: God says so; therefore, accept His Word at face value (Romans 10:9).
- **Receive**: Open your heart and let Him come in (John 1:12; Revelation 3:20).

- **Confess**: Faith is activated by confession. Confess Christ as Saviour and Lord (Romans 10:9).

  Behold, I stand at the door, and knock: if any man hear my voice, and open the door, I will come in to him, and will sup with him, and he with me.
  — **Revelation 3:20**

- **Commit**: Surrender all to God. Commitment is the only way to obtain the full benefits of this great salvation (Psalm 37:5).
- **Trust**: Related to faith, trust is a solid confidence in God's ability, willingness, truthfulness, faithfulness and reliability. We are called to trust God with all of our hearts, all of the time, even when on occasion, it does not make sense to the natural mind (Proverbs 3:5–6). God's ways and thoughts are higher and better than ours.
- **Obedience**: This is the bottom line, and without your obedience, every other aspect of faith fails. If Jesus is to be your Saviour and Lord, you must obey Him in all things, great or small. The renowned hymn says it so well: *'Trust and obey, for there's no other way to be happy in Jesus, than to trust and obey'* (1 Samuel 15:22; Acts 5:29).

You may be a good, respectable person who believes in Jesus. You may attend church and even read the Bible. See, however, if you can answer the following questions:

- Have you ever asked Jesus Christ into your life (Romans 10:9–10; Revelation 3:20)?

- Is He living in your heart now (1 John 3:24)?

- Do you have 'peace with God' (Romans 5:1)?

- Do you know that your sins are forgiven and cleansed (1 John 1:9)?

- Do you have the 'new birth' (John 3:3)?

- Do you have the assurance of salvation (Romans 10:9–10)?
- Are you 'heaven-bound' (Hebrews 12:22–24)?
- Is your name written in the Lamb's Book of Life (Luke 10:20; Hebrews 12:23)?

If you cannot confidently say 'Yes' to all of these questions above, please say 'Yes' to this one:

Are you ready to receive Jesus Christ, here and now, as your personal Lord and Saviour? Are you prepared to make the wisest and most courageous decision of your life?

If so, pray this simple prayer of repentance and faith, with sincerity and conviction, and you can then say yes to all.

A Prayer of Salvation

Heavenly Father, I am pleased to hear the gospel.

I acknowledge that Jesus is the Messiah, Son of God, and Saviour.

I confess that I am a sinner in need of salvation.

I repent of all sins of the hands, head and heart.

As an act of my will, I say yes to the everlasting gospel by inviting Jesus into my heart.

Come in, Lord Jesus, take full control, wash me from my sins in your shed blood and deliver me from my sinful nature.

Thank you for the forgiveness of sins, the new birth and the gift of eternal life. By your grace, help me to live a God-honouring life,

In the Name of Your Son, My Saviour, Jesus Christ.

Amen.

Welcome to the Family of God!

If you have prayed this prayer, please let us know. Our web address is tan.org.au or Teach All Nations, P.O. Box 493, Mount Waverley, VIC 3149, Australia. Find a Bible-believing, Bible-based church and get involved in their discipleship program.

May your personal encounter with Jesus of Nazareth, Son of David, Son of God, Saviour, bring you untold blessings in the days ahead. Let others know that you belong to Him. The first coming of Jesus changed the course of history; of that, there is no doubt. At His second coming, the world will not just be changed – it will be transformed.

Now that you have been born again, you will be able to appreciate the **Book of Acts** and the entire Bible and bask in the great blessings God is ready to bestow on you.

May you play your God-ordained role in Acts 29.

---

[62] Romans 4:25

[63] 1 Corinthians 12:3

[64] Romans 10:17

[65] James 1:21

[66] John 14:6; 16:13; 17:17

[67] Deuteronomy 8:3; Matthew 4:4; Luke 4:4

[68] Psalm 119:18

[69] Isaiah 55:1; John 7:37–39

[70] Acts 2:4; Ephesians 5:18

[71] Galatians 5:16

[72] 1 Corinthians 12:1; see also verse 31.

Appendix Three
Outline of the Book of Acts

Part One: Outreach in Jerusalem	**1:1–8:4**
I. The Church is Born	**1:1–2:47**
A. Introduction to Acts	1:1–2
B. Resurrected Christ gives great commission	1:3–8
C. Christ's ascension to heaven	1:9–11
D. Waiting for the Holy Spirit	1:12–14
E. Matthias appointed in Judas' place	..1:15–26
F. Baptism in the Holy Spirit	2:1–4
G. Filled with the Spirit	2:5–13
H. Peter's first post-Pentecost sermon	2:14–41
I. Activities of the early church	2:42–47
II. Growth of the church	**3:1–8:4**
A. Healing of the lame man by Peter	3:1-11
B. Peter's second post-Pentecost sermon	3:12–26
C. Peter and John in custody	4:1–4
D. Peter message to the Sanhedrin	4:5–12
E. Peter is forbidden to preach by Sanhedrin	4:13–22

F. Apostles pray for Holy Spirit boldness	4:23-31
G. Sharing and caring of the early church	4:32–37
H. Ananias and Sapphira lie and die	5:1–11
I. Miraculous ministry of the apostles	5:12–16
J. Persecution of the Apostles	5:17–42
1. Apostles released from prison	5:17–28
2. Apostles testify to the Council	5:29–32
3. Advice of wise Gamaliel	5:33–39
4. Beating of the Apostles	5:40–42
K. Appointment of deacons	6:1–8
L. Stephen testifies and is martyred	6:9–7:60
M. Saul of Tarsus bullies the church	8:1–3
Part Two: Outreach in Judaea and Samaria	**8:4–12:25**
I. Ministry of Philip the Evangelist	**8:5–40**
A. Philip ministers in Samaria	8:5–25
B. Philip ministers to the Ethiopian eunuch	8:26–40
II. Repentance of Saul	**9:1-31**
A. Saul repents but is blind	9:1-9
B. Saul healed and filled with the Holy Spirit	9:10–19
C. Saul testifies in Damascus	9:20–22
D. Saul testifies in Jerusalem	9:23–31

III. Ministry of Peter   9:32–11:1

   A. Healing of Aeneas at Lydda   9:32–35

   B. Raising of Dorcas from the dead in Joppa   9:36–43

   C. Peter witnesses to Cornelius at Caesarea (Gentiles saved and filled with the Holy Spirit)   10:1–11:18

IV. Outreach of the Early Church   11:19–12:25

   A. Outreach of the church at Antioch   11:19–30

   B. Herod Agrippa I persecutes the Church and dies   12:1–25

Part Three: Outreach to the end of the earth   13:1–28:31

I. First Missionary Journey   13:1-14:28

   A. Saul and Barnabas dispatched for mission   13:1–3

   B. Cyprus ministry   13:4–13

   C. Ministry at Antioch in Pisidia   13:14–50

   D. Ministry at Iconium   13:51–14:5

   E. Ministry at Lystra   14:6–20

   F. Return to Antioch   14:21–25

   G. Report of the First Missionary Journey   14:26–28

II. The Council at Jerusalem   **15:1-3**

   A. Must Gentile believers keep the Law?   15:1–5

   B. Peter speaks of salvation by grace   15:6–11

   C. Testimony of Paul and Barnabas   15:12

   D. James testifies that Gentiles are free from the Law   15:13–21

E. Jerusalem Council writes to Gentiles churches	15:22–29
F. Report given at Antioch	15:30-35

I. Second Missionary Journey — **15:36–18:22**

A. Paul and Barnabas quarrel over John Mark	15:36–41
B. Lystra, Derbe and the circumcision of Timothy	16:1–5
C. Troas and the Macedonian call	16:6–10
D. Ministry at Philippi:	16:11–40
E. Thessalonica: *'Turned the world upside down'*	17:1–9
F. Noble Berea: they searched the Scriptures daily	17:10–15
G. Athens: Paul's sermon on Mars' Hill	17:16–34
H. Corinth: ministry over eighteen months	18:1–17
I. Return to Antioch	18:18–22

IV. Third Missionary Journey — **18:23–21:16**

A. Galatia and Phrygia: confirming the believers	18:23
B. Ministry of Apollos	18:24–28
C. Ephesus: three years of ministry	19:1-41
D. Macedonia: three months of ministry	20:1–5
E. Troas: Eutychus raised to life	20:6–12
F. Miletus: Paul's farewell to the Ephesian elders	20:13–38
G. Tyre: Paul warned not to go to Jerusalem	21:1–6
H. Caesarea: Agabus' disturbing prophecy	21:7–16

V. The Long Journey to Rome   **21:17–28:31**

    A. Paul testifies in Jerusalem   21:17–23:33

    B. Paul testifies in Caesarea   23:34–26:32

    C. Voyage, shipwreck, sojourn in Melita   27:1-44

    D. Paul's Arrival and Testimony in Rome   28:1–31

Our Gift to You

Thank you for reading *Welcome Holy Spirit*.

To show our appreciation,

you are invited to **download** a copy of

our free study guide that goes with this book.

It is suitable for personal and group Bible study.

To obtain your copy of the study guide to **Welcome Holy Spirit**

Log onto: tan.org.au

www.ingramcontent.com/pod-product-compliance
Lightning Source LLC
Chambersburg PA
CBHW062031290426
44109CB00026B/2593